Visual Basic® .NET:
A Beginner's Guide

About the Author

Jeff Kent is an Assistant Professor of Computer Science at Los Angeles Valley College in Valley Glen, California. He teaches a number of programming languages, including Visual Basic, C++, Java and, when he's feeling masochistic, Assembler, but his favorite is Visual Basic. He also manages a network for a Los Angeles law firm whose employees are guinea pigs for his applications, and as an attorney gives advice to young attorneys whether they want it or not. He also has written several books on computer programming, including (with co-author David Jung) *Visual Basic Annotated Archives* and *Debugging Visual Basic* for McGraw-Hill/Osborne.

Jeff has had a varied career—or careers. He graduated from UCLA with a Bachelor of Science degree in economics, then obtained a Juris Doctor degree from Loyola (Los Angeles) School of Law, and went on to practice law. During this time, when personal computers still were a gleam in Bill Gates's eye, Jeff was also a professional chess master, earning a third place finish in the United States Under-21 Championship and, later, an international title.

Jeff does find time to spend with his wife, Devvie, which is not difficult since she also is a computer science professor at Valley College. He also acts as personal chauffeur for his teenage daughters Elise and Emily, and when not driving them, in his spare time enjoys watching international chess tournaments on the Internet. His goal is to resume running marathons, since he feels the ability to run fast and far is important for a programmer, particularly when being chased by irate application users.

Visual Basic® .NET:
A Beginner's Guide

Jeff Kent

McGraw-Hill/Osborne

New York   Chicago   San Francisco
Lisbon   London   Madrid   Mexico City   Milan
New Delhi   San Juan   Seoul   Singapore   Sydney   Toronto

McGraw-Hill/Osborne
2600 Tenth Street
Berkeley, California 94710
U.S.A.

To arrange bulk purchase discounts for sales promotions, premiums, or fund-raisers, please contact **McGraw-Hill**/Osborne at the above address. For information on translations or book distributors outside the U.S.A., please see the International Contact Information page immediately following the index of this book.

Visual Basic® .NET: A Beginner's Guide

1234567890 FGR FGR 0198765432

ISBN 0-07-213120-9

Publisher   Brandon A. Nordin
Vice President & Associate Publisher   Scott Rogers
Acquisitions Editor   Ann Sellers
Project Editor   Monika Faltiss
Acquisitions Coordinator   Timothy Madrid
Technical Editor   Chris Crane, Karl Kemerait
Copy Editor   Lunaea Weatherstone
Proofreader   Mike McGee
Indexer   Irv Hershman
Computer Designers   Elizabeth Jang, Lauren McCarthy
Illustrators   Michael Mueller, Lyssa Wald
Series Design   Gary Corrigan
Cover Series Design   Greg Scott
Cover Illustration   Kevin Curry

This book was composed with Corel VENTURA ™ Publisher.

I would like to dedicate this book to Chemmber, who showed me in so many ways how wonderful life can be.

-Jeff Kent

Contents at a Glance

Contents

PART 1

Introduction to Visual Basic .NET

PART 2
Programming Building Blocks: Variables, Data Types, and Operators

PART 3
Controlling the Flow of the Program

Acknowledgments

It seems obligatory in acknowledgements for authors to thank their publishers (especially if they want to write for them again), but I really mean it. This is my third book for McGraw-Hill/Osborne, and I hope there will be many more. It truly is a pleasure to work with professionals who are nice people as well as very good at what they do (even when what they do is keep accurate track of the deadlines I miss).

I first want to thank Wendy Rinaldi, without whom this book, and indeed this entire Beginner's Guide series, would not have happened. I'm not sure if Wendy remembers, but we started discussing this series, albeit under a different name, back in late 1999.

I also must thank my Acquisitions Editor, Ann Sellers. Ann took Wendy's place when Wendy was promoted. While I was happy for Wendy about her promotion, I wasn't so happy for myself as I was losing Wendy as my Acquisitions Editor. It turned out I had nothing to worry about. Ann has been unfailingly helpful, kind, and patient, even through all the frustrations and severe time constraints that are inevitable when writing a "day and date" book that has to be released simultaneously with the product about which the book was written.

I next want to thank Tim Madrid, whose title, Acquisitions Coordinator, means he has to keep authors on schedule, a job akin to herding cats. Tim was kind and patient when I explained that I missed another deadline because the latest beta of Visual Basic .NET hosed my hard drive, my back went out, or the KGB introduced a virus into my computer (though he didn't buy the KGB excuse).

Lunaea Weatherstone did the copyediting, and was kind about my obvious failure during my school days to pay attention to my grammar lessons. She improved what I wrote while still keeping it in my words (that way if something is wrong it is still my fault).

Monika Faltiss, my project editor, did a masterful job coordinating the editing. When she told me when this book would ship, I laughed hysterically until I realized she was serious. Without Monika, this book would not have been on time.

There are a lot of other talented people behind the scenes who also helped get this book out to press, and as with an Academy Award speech, I can't list them all. That doesn't mean I don't appreciate all their hard work, because I do.

I also would like to thank David Jung, with whom I have co-authored several books. Due to the demands of his job and the birth of his first child, David experienced a temporary bout of sanity and took time off from writing books, so we did not collaborate on this one. However, he continued to be of great help in many ways, including being my Visual Basic "answer man." I'm pleased to report that David has made a full recovery from sanity and is back to writing books, so hopefully we will be collaborating again in the future.

Finally, I would like to give thanks to my wife Devvie and my daughters Elise and Emily for tolerating me while I was mumbling incomprehensibly about Visual Basic .NET, grumbling audibly about bugs in Visual Basic .NET betas, ranting loudly about deadlines for this book, and otherwise seeming to be in another world. I also would like to thank them for not having me committed when I talk about writing my next book.

Introduction

I have a confession to make. Visual Basic is not my first programming language, or even my second. I knew C++ and Java before I ever learned Visual Basic.

I learned Visual Basic at about the time version 4 was introduced. I was surprised that Visual Basic lacked object-oriented programming (OOP) features integral to C++ and Java.

Version 4, by introducing classes to Visual Basic, represented Visual Basic's first, halting step toward becoming an object-oriented programming language. Versions 5 and 6 represented further progress in that direction, but even with Version 6 Visual Basic lacked many OOP features.

With .NET, Visual Basic has arrived as a full-fledged object-oriented programming language. This is good news to most, though not all. It is good news if you are a new programmer. You will be able to apply the OOP concepts you will learn from Visual Basic .NET to other programming languages you likely will later learn. It also is good news if, like me, you already have programmed in another OOP language such as C++ or Java but are new to Visual Basic. You will be able to apply to Visual Basic .NET the OOP concepts you already know. However, it is a mixed blessing if you are already a Visual Basic programmer and have not dabbled much before with OOP. You not only have much to learn, but some to unlearn. Visual Basic .NET is very, very different from the prior versions of Visual Basic.

.NET means more than OOP support. Despite detractors who ridiculed it as .NOT—or my dubbing it .NUT when bugs in the beta versions were driving me nutty (some say more nutty)—.NET changes programming comparable to how jet engines changed the previous propeller-only world of aviation.

While .NET introduces many programming innovations, I believe OOP support is the most important change as far as Visual Basic is concerned. While I enjoy computer games as much as the next person (I particularly enjoy the one that pits hideous space beasts against community college administrators; go space beasts!), most programs are written to solve real-world problems. They therefore concern people, places, and things in the real world, such as customers, inventory, bank accounts, and so on. As explained in Module 1, these real-world people, places, and things are objects. OOP enables you to model your code to accurately represent them.

Why Did I Write this Book?

Not as a road to riches, fame, or beautiful women. I may be misguided, but I'm not completely delusional.

Given the tremendous changes .NET has brought to Visual Basic, there is a clear need for introductory level books on Visual Basic .NET. While I'm sure there will be plenty of other books written, I wrote this book because I believe I bring a different and, I hope, valuable perspective.

As you may know from my author biography, I teach computer science at Los Angeles Valley College, a community college in the San Fernando Valley area of Los Angeles, where I grew up and have lived most of my life. I also write computer programs, but teaching programming has provided me with insights into how students learn that I could never obtain from writing programs. These insights are gained not just from answering student questions during lectures. I spend hours each week in our college's computer lab helping students with their programs, and more hours each week reviewing and grading their assignments. Patterns emerge regarding which teaching methods work and which don't, the order in which to introduce programming topics, the level of difficulty at which to introduce a new topic, and so on. I joke with my students that they are my beta testers in my never-ending attempt to become a better teacher, but there is much truth in that joke.

Additionally, as I mentioned above, I learned OOP languages before I learned Visual Basic, and have taught C++ and Java for some years. Thus, the insights I have gained through teaching are not limited to Visual Basic, but also extend to the OOP concepts new to Visual Basic with .NET.

Finally, my beta testers… err, students, seem to complain about the textbook no matter which book I adopt. Many ask me why I don't write a book they could use to learn Visual Basic. They may be saying this to flatter me (I'm not saying it doesn't work), or for the more sinister reason that they will be able to blame the teacher for a poor book as well as poor instruction. Nevertheless, having written other books, these questions planted in my mind the idea of writing a book that, in addition to being sold to the general public, also could be used as a textbook.

Who Should Read this Book

Anyone who will pay for it! Just kidding, though no buyers will be turned away.

It is hardly news that publishers and authors want the largest possible audience for their books. Therefore, this section of the introduction usually tells you this book is for you whoever you may be and whatever you do. However, no programming book is for everyone. For example, if you exclusively create game programs using C++, this book may not be for you (though I may be your next customer if you create another space beasts vs. community college administrators game).

While this book of course is not for everyone, it very well may be for you. More programmers use Visual Basic to create Windows applications than any other programming language, and .NET has brought a sea of change to Visual Basic. This book is for you if you are learning your first programming language. It also is for grizzled Visual Basic veterans learning OOP concepts, and equally grizzled programmers in other languages who may know OOP but are learning Visual Basic. In short, this book is for you if you want to become or already are a Visual Basic programmer and want to master the fundamentals of Visual Basic .NET.

What this Book Covers

This book consists of 12 modules, divided into five parts. The first part (Modules 1–3) introduces you to Visual Basic .NET, and enables you to get up and running with your first Visual Basic .NET application. The second part (Modules 4–6) covers the building blocks almost all programs use, variables, data types, and operators. The third part (Modules 7–9) shows you how to use these programming building blocks in controlling the flow of your program, using control structures, loops, and procedures. The fourth part (Modules 10–11) covers the graphical user interface of your application. The fifth and final part is on handling errors, or better yet, preventing them, using structured exception handling and debugging.

I strongly believe that the best way to learn programming is to write programs. The concepts covered by the modules are illustrated by projects, which are explained step-by-step so you can create the project yourself. Each project can also be downloaded from the Osborne website (http://www.osborne.com/). The code used in each project is explained clearly and thoroughly.

This first part of this book, "Introduction to Visual Basic .NET," starts with Module 1, which answers the question: "What Is Visual Basic .NET?" This module explains what a programming language is and does, and as Visual Basic .NET is an "object-oriented" and "event-driven" programming language, just what those terms mean. Since an understanding of objects is essential even to get started with Visual Basic .NET, this module also explains the properties, methods, and events of an object, and the relationship between an object and a class.

Module 2 has you "Create a Visual Basic .NET Program Without Writing Code." While you won't have to write any code, there is code nevertheless, created by Visual Basic .NET, and you need to understand it, so this module explains that code, line by line. Of course, before you can create your first Visual Basic .NET program, you have to obtain Visual Basic .NET and install it. Therefore, this module will help you identify the version of Visual Studio.NET that is best for you. It also explains how to install and customize Visual Studio.NET, as well as clarify the relationship between the .NET Framework and Visual Studio.NET.

Though you can create a Visual Basic .NET program without writing code, the resulting program doesn't do much except display a window. Module 3, "Event Procedures, Properties, and Controls," shows you how to add functionality to your program. This module explains the concepts of and differences between design time and runtime, and how to determine and change the value of properties at both times. You also learn how to use the Toolbox to add controls to a form, and how to use the Windows Forms Designer to locate, size, and align controls. You then learn how to create event procedures, which contain the code that executes when the user interacts with your program, and how to use the controls you added to the form to display information.

Now that you are up and running with Visual Basic .NET, the second part of this book covers the building blocks of your programs, variables, data types and operators, starting with Module 4, "Variables and Data Types." The purpose of most information is to store and retrieve information. That information comes in different forms, such as numbers, text, dates, and so on. Consequently, Visual Basic .NET offers a number of different data types, each of which is explained in this module. The information may be stored in properties of objects in your application, or in variables that you create. This module shows you how to declare and use variables, and explains the concepts of variable scope and lifetime. The module winds up with constants, information storage locations like variables, but whose values never change.

Since the purpose of a variable is to store a value, a declared variable without an assigned value is as pointless as a bank account without money. Module 5, "Assignment and Arithmetic Operators," explains how you use the assignment operator to store values in the variables you learned to create in the previous module. Since there is considerable overlap among data types (for example, several may represent a whole number), you may attempt, intentionally or unintentionally, to assign a value of one data type to a variable or property of a similar but not identical data type. This involves type conversion, and this module thoroughly explains the concepts involved, including widening and narrowing conversions, type conversion keywords, and the Option Strict statement. This module then shows you how to use arithmetic operators to harness the computer's ability to perform extremely fast and accurate calculations. This module concludes by showing you a change machine application, which implements assignment and arithmetic operators, as well as introducing the InputBox function.

As programs become more sophisticated, they often branch in two or more directions based on whether a condition is True or False. For example, a calculator program would need to determine whether the user chose addition, subtraction, multiplication, or division before performing the indicated arithmetic operation. Module 6, "Comparison and Logical Operators," shows you how to use comparison operators to determine the user's choice. Sometimes you need to make more than one comparison at a time. For example, to determine if someone is eligible to vote, you have to compare both their age to the minimum voting age *and* their country of citizenship to being a United States citizen. This module will show you how to use logical operators to combine comparisons.

Now that we have covered building blocks, it is time to use them in the third part of this book, which concerns controlling the flow of your program. Module 7, "Control Structures," shows you how to implement the comparison and logical operators you learned about in the preceding module using control structures, specifically an If statement or a Select Case statement, so that different blocks of code execute depending on whether an expression evaluates as True or False. Since the application user interacts with your code, including If and Select Case statements, through the GUI (graphical user interface) of your application, this module will show you how to use two controls that are used with If and Select Case statements, the CheckBox and RadioButton controls. This module provides two projects to illustrate how to use the CheckBox and RadioButton controls with control structures.

When you were a child, your parents may have told you not to repeat yourself. However, sometimes your code needs to repeat itself. For example, if an application user enters invalid data, your code may continue to ask the user whether they want to retry or quit until the user either enters valid data or quits. Module 8, "Loops and Arrays," shows you how to use loops to repeat the execution of code statements. This module then explains arrays, which enable you to use a single variable to store multiple related values. Loops and arrays go together, as you use loops to assign values to and read values from arrays.

"Procedures" are the topic of Module 9. A procedure is a block of one or more code statements. All Visual Basic .NET code is written within procedures. While Visual Basic .NET has many built-in procedures, you are not limited to them. You can and should write your own procedures. This module will explain the different types of procedures and how to write them. It also will explain how you call a procedure so the code within it will execute, how you can pass information to the procedures, and how the procedures return information to the code that called them. This module concludes by rewriting the arithmetic calculator project in Module 7, this time using procedures you create.

The fourth part of this book covers the user interface, starting with Module 10, "Helper Forms." Forms are the most common user interface element in Visual Basic applications, and indeed Visual Basic .NET's automated creation of a Windows application includes a form that serves as the main application window. This form may be sufficient for a simple application, but as your applications become more sophisticated, the main application form will become unable to perform all the tasks required by the application and need help from other forms. This module shows you how to create and use three helper forms that will be workhorses in your applications, message boxes, dialog boxes, and owned forms. This module has three projects to illustrate the use of each of these helper forms.

Application users give commands to an application, such as to open, save, or close a file, print a document, and so on, through the graphical user interface of the application. Module 11, "Menus and Toolbars," covers the three most common GUI elements through which application users give commands to an application: the menu, shortcut or context menus, and toolbars. Commands, such as cut, copy, and paste, often may be duplicated in a menu, a context menu, and a toolbar, providing the application user with the convenience of three different ways to perform the same command. However, you don't want to write the same code three times, so this module shows you how to connect corresponding items in menus, context menus, and toolbars so they each execute the same code. This module concludes with a project that does just that.

Not to conclude this book on a negative note, but errors happen. Handling errors—or better yet, preventing them—is the subject of Module 12, "Structured Exception Handling and Debugging." Using an illustrative project, this module shows you how to implement structured exception handling, which enables your application to handle errors, clearly preferable to your application crashing to an inglorious halt with an uninformative message about some fatal error. This module then shows you how to hunt down and eliminate errors using the debugger built into Visual Basic .NET, and explains debugging techniques.

Following the modules is the Appendix, "Answers to Mastery Checks." Each module contains questions at the end (called Mastery Checks) that check to make sure you've absorbed the basics, and the Appendix provides the answers to these questions.

How to Read this Book

I have organized this book to be read from beginning to end. While this may seem patently obvious, my students often express legitimate frustration about books (or teachers) that, in discussing a programming concept, mention other concepts that are covered several chapters later or, even worse, not at all.

Therefore, I have endeavored to present the material in a linear, logical progression. This not only avoids the frustration of material that is out of order, but also enables you in each succeeding module to build on the skills you learned in the preceding modules.

Special Features

Throughout each module are *Hints*, *Tips*, *Cautions*, and *Notes*, as well as *detailed code listings.* There are *1-Minute Drills* that check to make sure you're retaining what you've read (and help focus your attention on the more important points). There are *Ask the Expert* question-and-answer sections that give in-depth explanations about the current subject. Included with the book and on the Osborne website are *Projects* that take what you've learned and put it into working applications. At the end of each module is a *Mastery Check,* which gives you another opportunity for review. The answers to the Mastery Checks are contained in the Appendix.

The overall objective is to get you up to speed quickly, without a lot of dry theory or unnecessary detail. So let's get started. It's easy and fun to create Visual Basic .NET applications.

Contacting the Author

Hmmm… it depends why. Just kidding. While I always welcome gushing praise and shameless flattery, comments, suggestions, and yes, even criticism also can be valuable. The best way to contact me is via email; you can use jkent@ genghiskhent.com (the domain name is based on my students' fond nickname for me). Alternately, you can visit my website, http://www.genghiskhent.com/. Don't be thrown off by the entry page; I use this site primarily to support the online classes and online components of other classes that I teach at the college, but there will be a link to the section that supports this book.

I hope you enjoy this book as much as I enjoyed writing it.

Part 1

Introduction to Visual Basic .NET

Module 1

What Is Visual Basic .NET?

The Goals of this Module

- Know what a programming language is and does
- Understand the meaning of "event-driven" and "object-oriented" programming
- Differentiate between an object's properties, methods, and events
- Understand the relationship between an object and a class

Programmers often refer to Visual Basic as "RAD." To a teenager, "RAD" means "radical," something novel and fascinating. To programmers, "RAD" means rapid application development, which may no longer be novel, but definitely is important—not just to programmers, but also to business people who hire programmers. The more time required to develop a product, the greater its cost. A product's sales will be hurt if lengthy development time means the product is not available until several months after its competition. Increased costs and decreased revenue have never been a formula for success. As the rate of change accelerates in our Internet economy, the time available to develop an application correspondingly shrinks. Thus, programmers who can develop quality applications quickly are in great demand and are paid accordingly. By contrast, programmers who are unable to cope with the pace of change have plenty of time to enjoy the great outdoors as they stand at freeway offramps with cardboard signs advertising their availability to program in exchange for food.

Visual Basic is so popular among programmers because of the many ways it enables RAD. In the very next module, you will be using Visual Basic to rapidly create your first Windows program. In fact, beginning programmers often are seduced by how easy Visual Basic makes creating a Windows application. They just plunge in and start writing programs without really understanding the code they are writing or how the different parts of the program fit together. That is a mistake. You would not want someone building a house for you to start hammering nails without having a plan and understanding how the various components (foundation, framing, electrical, plumbing) fit together.

Prior versions of Visual Basic let you write simple programs almost without knowing what you were doing. That's not the case with .NET, which requires some familiarity with certain programming concepts and terminology before you begin. These basics are covered in this module.

I have found a "chicken or the egg" conundrum in teaching programming over the last several years to community college students. Students need to understand the underlying programming concepts to intelligently write programs, but until they actually start writing programs, the underlying theory seems abstract and vague and therefore difficult to understand. This module strikes a compromise, providing an overview to familiarize you with the concepts and terminology you will encounter when you start programming in Visual Basic .NET, but deferring an in-depth discussion of these concepts until they arise in the programming projects in the upcoming modules.

Visual Basic .NET Defined

1

Visual Basic .NET is an *object-oriented programming language* for writing *event-driven Windows applications*. That is a mouthful, so the following sections will explain the components of this definition:

- **Visual Basic .NET Is a Programming Language**   Just what exactly is a programming language?

- **Visual Basic .NET Is Used for Writing Windows Applications**   We use Windows applications every day and take them for granted, but did you ever stop to think what makes an application a *Windows* application?

- **Windows Applications Are Event-driven**   Windows applications not only look different from non-Windows applications, but they behave differently as well.

- **The Visual Basic .NET Programming Language Is Object-oriented**   Advertisements for programming positions often ask for applicants who understand object-oriented programming. Just what is an object, and why are objects used in programming?

- **It's Not Just Visual Basic, It's Visual Basic .NET**   What difference has .NET made in the Visual Basic programming language?

Visual Basic .NET Is a Programming Language

Although this book is written in English, there are many languages, and this book could convey the same information in Spanish, French, German, or Chinese. Languages, despite their differences, perform essentially the same function, which is to convey concepts to a human reader or listener, whose brain then (hopefully) processes the information conveyed.

Similarly, Visual Basic is but one of many programming languages. Other popular programming languages include C++ and Java, but there are many, many more. However, all programming languages perform essentially the same function: to give instructions to a computer, which then executes those instructions. The result of the computer executing these instructions is a program, also called an application. A program may be as simple as displaying "Hello World" on your screen, or as complex as the application used to write this book, Microsoft Word.

Continuing the analogy, this book would be understandable in English to a reader only if the words were spelled correctly and the sentences followed rules of grammar. Similarly, your computer can convert the Visual Basic code into instructions to the computer only if the code is in the proper syntax. Visual Basic, like other programming languages, has rules for the spelling of words and for the grammar of statements.

Fortunately, Visual Basic's spelling and grammar rules are relatively easy to understand and master. This is no accident. The "Basic" in Visual Basic refers to the BASIC programming language. BASIC is an acronym for Beginners All-Purpose Symbolic Instruction Code. BASIC, whose origins date back to 1964, was intended to be not only a simple language to learn, but also a means by which students could learn more powerful languages, which in those days included FORTRAN. During the 1970s, none other than Bill Gates saw the potential in BASIC and had Microsoft develop and expand the language, which Microsoft has continued to do to this day.

Visual Basic has retained the relative simplicity of its BASIC predecessor and remains one of the easier programming languages to learn, partly because the language is very intuitive. For example, if you want to close a window, you use the Close method, or if you want to determine its width, you refer to its Width property.

Ask the Expert

Question: Why is computer programming so important?

Answer: Computers have tremendous calculating power and can store huge amounts of information. However, computers fundamentally have far more brawn than brain. They cannot do anything without a human being—namely, the programmer—telling them what to do. Computer programming enables us to harness and use the computer's tremendous potential.

Question: Does the computer understand Visual Basic code?

Answer: No. The computer fundamentally understands machine language, which is far closer to a series of ones and zeros than to the English language like syntax of Visual Basic. The first computers were little more than wires and switches in which the path followed depended on which switches were in the on (1) or off (0) position.

Question: How does the computer run Visual Basic code if it does not understand it?

Answer: A compiler and other components of Visual Studio.NET translate your Visual Basic code into machine language.

Question: Why not just write code in machine language instead of Visual Basic?

Answer: You could, and some people do write code in machine language. However, it is much easier to write code in Visual Basic than in machine language. First, one instruction in Visual Basic requires many instructions in machine language. Second, people, unlike computers, do not think in machine language, but rather in human language, which Visual Basic simulates.

Question: Why should I choose Visual Basic over the other available programming languages such as C++ or Java?

Answer: Programmers argue over which programming language is "better" just as people argue about politics. In both cases, it is a matter of opinion. Visual Basic, in its .NET version, supports essentially every feature that the competitive languages support. One important advantage of Visual Basic is its similarity to the English language, making it intuitive and consequently very easy to learn. Another advantage of Visual Basic is a practical one. There already has been much code written in Visual Basic, so with that investment in code already made, it is likely that many businesses will stay with Visual Basic rather than switch to another language.

1-Minute Drill

● What is the basic purpose of a programming language?

● The basic purpose of a programming language is to give instructions to a computer, which then executes those instructions.

Visual Basic .NET Is Used for Writing Windows Applications

While the "Basic" in Visual Basic goes back to 1964, the "Visual" has far more recent origins. Nowadays, the majority of applications are written for at least one if not more of the Windows operating systems, which include Windows 3.x, 9x, NT 4.0, ME, 2000, and XP. Figure 1-1 shows a familiar Windows application, Notepad, which is included by default in the installation of all Windows operating systems.

Although the Windows operating system has virtually taken over the computer world, it has not been with us that long. Windows was not introduced until 1985, more than 20 years after the introduction of BASIC. Prior to then, applications were displayed and ran in a console, or text, mode. As Figure 1-2 shows, applications in a console or text mode have a decidedly different and less rich appearance than Windows applications.

The difference between console and Windows applications is more than skin deep. They also behave very differently. Let's now look at both differences.

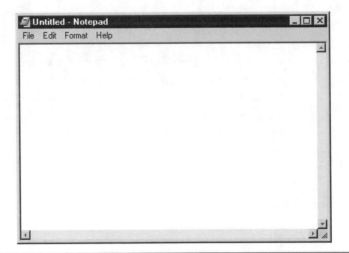

Figure 1-1   Notepad, a Windows application

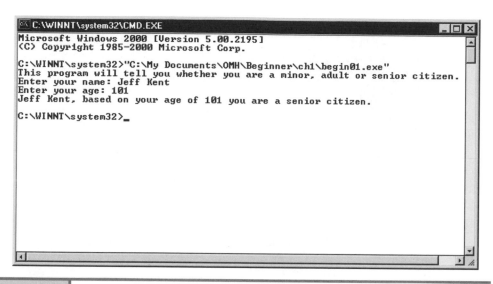

Figure 1-2 A console application

Windows Applications Are Gooey

The hallmark of a Windows application is that the application is displayed in you guessed it, a window. However, there is more to a Windows application than a window. A Windows application has a graphical user interface, which is often referred to by the acronym GUI, pronounced "gooey."

A GUI usually includes a menu, such as the Notepad menu shown previously in Figure 1-1. However, a GUI is not limited to a menu, and normally includes other visual components, such as buttons to click, edit boxes in which to type text, and so on.

The GUI makes Windows applications prettier than console applications, but it serves a more important purpose, which is to make Windows applications easier to use. For example, the menu in Notepad makes it easy for you to open a file. Clicking the File menu and then the Open submenu displays another visual component, the Open dialog box (shown in Figure 1-3), from which you simply pick the file you want to open.

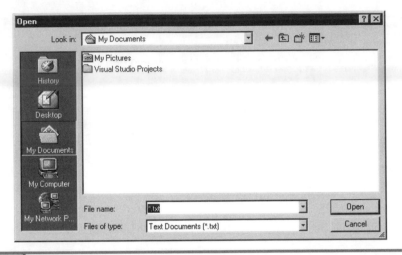

Figure 1-3 The Open dialog box in Notepad

By contrast, if you want to open a file for editing in a console application—for example, a file named *sample.txt* located in the *temp* directory—you would have to type commands at a DOS prompt, first to navigate to the *temp* directory, and then to open the *sample.txt* file for editing, as shown here:

```
C:\>cd temp
C:\temp>edit sample.txt
```

This certainly is doable, but it is hardly as simple or intuitive as opening a file in a Windows application.

Of course, nothing is free in this world. The pretty GUI of a Windows application comes at a programming price. Code, lots of it, and some of it rather complex, is required to create a window, not to mention to create the menu and other controls in the window.

This is where Visual Basic once again eases your task. You do not need to write copious, complex code to create a window. Instead, Visual Basic creates the window for you at literally the click of a button or menu item. Nor do you need to write code to create the controls on the window, which is referred to in Visual Basic as a form. Visual Basic enables you to create a control simply by dragging an icon that represents the control and dropping it on your form. Visual Basic then writes all the code necessary to create the window and controls, so you don't have to. You can view and even fine-tune the code, but you are spared the substantial grunt work of writing the code to create the windows and controls. Visual Basic's ability to do a lot of the hard work for you is a major reason why it's a premier RAD tool.

Windows Applications Are Event-Driven

Console and Windows applications behave differently as well as look different. In console mode applications, the application tells the user what to do. In the program depicted previously in Figure 1-2, the program tells the operating system to print to the screen the text message "Enter your name." The user then inputs their name and presses the ENTER key. The user could not have entered their name before this point, and they had to enter data at this point or the program would not continue. The program then tells the operating system to print to the screen "Enter your age." The user then inputs their age and presses the ENTER key. Once again, the user could not have entered their age before this point, and had to enter data at this point or the program would not continue. Finally, the program tells the operating system to output to the screen a sentence that includes the name and age entered, followed by whether the user is a minor, adult, or senior citizen, based on the age that was entered. Thus, in a console application, the application, not the user, determines the order in which things happen.

Windows applications are just the opposite; the user tells the application what to do. What happens next after you open Notepad? The answer is, "It depends." Specifically, it depends on what you, as the user, do next. If you click the File | Open menu item, the Open dialog box will display as shown previously in Figure 1-3. If instead you click the Help | Help Topics menu item, Notepad Help will display. Of course, you may decide you're tired of Notepad and close it by using the File | Exit menu item or the close button. Thus, in a Windows application, the user's actions, not the application, determine the order in which things happen.

A console application can be analogized to a recipe. The program follows the instructions step by step. By contrast, a Windows application can be analogized to a paramedic. The paramedic waits for a call. When a call comes, the paramedic takes the equipment warranted by the call and goes to the location. When finished, the paramedic waits for the next call, and when it comes, takes the equipment warranted by that call and goes to the next location.

In the parlance of Windows programming, the user's actions create *events* that cause the operating system to send messages to the application. For example, the user's act of clicking Notepad's File | Open menu item is an event that causes the operating system to send a message to the Notepad window that the File | Open menu command has been clicked. When Notepad receives that message, code in Notepad displays the Open dialog box. Since the events resulting from the user's actions drive the application, Windows programming often is referred to as being *event-driven*.

In a Windows application, the unpredictable actions of the user dictate the order of events. This requires the programmer to think more flexibly than with console applications in which the programmer can dictate, and therefore predict, the order of events. However, thinking in event-driven terms will soon become second nature as you start writing programs. Besides, if programming were so easy, everyone would do it! Programming is challenging; that's why programmers make the big bucks!

Ask the Expert

Question: Why would anyone write a console application anymore?

Answer: The GUI of Windows applications does come at a price: higher memory requirements and larger file sizes than console applications. That may not seem important these days with computers having megabytes of RAM in the three digits and gargantuan hard drives, but not all applications are written for desktop and laptop computers. Handheld and pocket-sized computers, such as the Pocket PC, are becoming increasingly popular. Cell phones are now becoming miniature computers through which you can access the Internet, send and receive e-mail, and review your appointments, tasks, and contacts. These devices have far smaller memory and storage capacity than standard computers. Console applications may be the right choice even on a desktop for a simple application that does no more than request and accept text input from the user, such as routine network administration tasks. Nevertheless, though console applications still have a place, particularly because of the trend toward miniaturization of computing devices, the vast majority of the applications you will write likely will be Windows rather than console applications.

1-Minute Drill

● What is the difference between how console and Windows applications look?

● What is the difference between how console and Windows applications behave?

The Visual Basic .NET Programming Language Is Object-Oriented

Most programs keep track of information that has value to the user. Just as we are not simple, single-celled amoebas, but instead complex organisms, the subjects about which information is kept are complex and consist of numerous items. For example, in a sales program, each customer has a name, address, telephone number, order history, and payment history. Each sale to the customer requires information on the item sold, the price, and the quantity purchased. Each item sold has a part number, a source from which it was obtained, the cost of obtaining it, the number of items in stock, and so on.

A programming language needs to be able to handle the fact that the persons, things, and concepts that are the subjects of a program cannot be described with a single item of information. These subjects contain numerous and often related items of information. To solve this problem, programming languages treat persons, things, and concepts as *objects*. For example, when you start writing Visual Basic code, you will refer to the Form object. The Form object is the programming representation of a window. A *programming representation* is the term used in code to refer to an object.

An object may contain other objects. For example, a Car object contains numerous items of equipment, such as a transmission, tires, and gas tank, each of which itself is an object. Similarly, in Visual Basic, a Form object may contain

---

● A Windows application has a window and a graphical user interface (GUI).
● A Windows application is event-driven.

controls, each of which also is an object, specifically a Control object. For example, a menu is a MainMenu object, a toolbar is a ToolBar object, the Open dialog box shown earlier in Figure 1-3 is a FileDialog object, and so on.

While an object may contain other objects, each object has its own unique characteristics. These are described, in programming terms, as *properties*, *methods*, and *events*. A programming language that employs objects, which in turn have properties, methods, and events, may be referred to as *object-oriented*. (OOP, not to be confused with oops, is a common acronym for object-oriented programming.)

There is more to object-oriented programming than just objects and their properties, methods, and events. There also are concepts such as encapsulation, polymorphism, and inheritance, which will be discussed later in this book. However, properties, methods, and events are of immediate importance, for they are the building blocks of the code you will write.

Properties

A property is an attribute of an object. For example, a customer has a name. In Visual Basic code, a Form object has a BackColor property that represents the form's background color, which by default is gray but could be blue, red, or some other color.

Although all objects have properties, objects created from different classes have a different set of properties. For example, both a Form object and a FileDialog object have a Top property that concerns the position of the top edge of the object within another object that contains it. A Form object has a WindowState property that determines if the form starts out minimized, maximized, or normal. A FileDialog object does not have this property, which makes sense since you cannot minimize or maximize the FileDialog object. Conversely, a FileDialog control has a FileName property that reflects the file the user chose from the Open dialog box. A Form object does not have such a property, which again makes sense since you can't choose a file from the form itself.

That objects created from different classes may share some properties but not others is consistent with the real world. For example, both a person and a car may have a Height property. However, a person has an EyeColor property, but a car would not, whereas a car has a Horsepower property that a person does not have.

Methods

A description of an object solely by its attributes is incomplete, because objects also do things. For example, a person may talk, walk, write, and so on.

A method is something that an object does. For example, a Form object has a Move method that enables the form to move from one location to another on the screen. A FileDialog object has a ShowDialog method to display the Open dialog box.

As is the case with properties, objects created from different classes may have some methods in common, but usually would not share the same exact set of methods. Once again, this is consistent with the real world. Both a Person object and a Bird object share a Breathing method since both breathe oxygen to stay alive. However, a Person object has a Write method, but a Bird object does not. Conversely, a Bird object has a Fly method, but a Person object does not (please don't try to prove otherwise, we need the readers).

Events

An event is something that happens to an object, usually as the result of user interaction with the object. For example, a Form object has a Click event that occurs when the user clicks the mouse on the form. As with properties and methods, different objects may have some events in common, but usually would not share the exact same set of events.

As discussed earlier, you write code so the user's action in clicking the File | Open menu item in Notepad will display an Open dialog box that permits the user to choose and open a file. You want this code to execute when, and only when, your application's user clicks the File | Open menu item. You use events to solve this problem, by associating the code that displays the Open dialog box with the Click event of the File | Open menu item object. Module 3 will show you how to associate code with an event, but for present purposes the point is that you use events to "wire" the mouse click of the File | Open menu item to code you want to run when the menu item is clicked.

You use events to determine when your code executes, but your code uses properties and methods to do its work. In the File | Open example, you would use the ShowDialog method of the FileDialog object to display the Open dialog box, and the FileName property of the FileDialog object to return the path to and name of the file chosen by the user from the dialog box. Once again, there will be much more on this subject in Module 3.

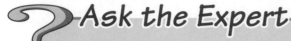

Ask the Expert

Question: How many objects are in Visual Basic?

Answer: There are at least hundreds, if not thousands, of built-in objects. Additionally, you can create your own objects.

Question: With all those hundreds or thousands of objects, not to mention the properties, methods, and events each of these objects have, how can I memorize them all?

Answer: You can't, and there really is no reason to even if you could. Instead, you use the help built into Visual Studio.NET, as well as other reference material. Of course, some memorization is necessary. By analogy, in order to solve algebra problems, you need to do simple arithmetic, which likely requires you to memorize multiplication tables. However, in programming, just as in algebra, understanding and analytical ability are far more important than memorization.

1-Minute Drill

● What is the difference between a property and a method of an object? *Attribute & Do*
Event

● How do you link the running of code with a user action?

Programming with Class

Using OOP concepts, each of us could be regarded as a Person object. There are several billion Person objects on this planet, yet all of us share the same properties, methods, and events of a Person object, such as the Gender property, the Breathe method, and the Pain event. This is because we all are, as the saying goes, "made from the same mold."

You will be creating projects with more than one form. Each form is a Form object, and therefore shares with the other forms the same properties, methods, and events. These Form objects also are made from the same mold. That mold is called a *class*.

● A property is an attribute of an object, such as its color or size, whereas a method is something an object does, such as change its position on the screen.
● You link the running of code with a user action by associating the code with an event.

A class often is analogized to a cookie cutter. A cookie cutter is not a cookie. Rather, it defines the cookie to be produced. A class also can be analogized to a template or pattern for an object.

You use a class to create—or in programming parlance, *instantiate*—an object. For example, you will use the Form class to create Form objects. Every object produced using a given class starts out the same. However, these objects do not have to remain the same, any more than people are all the same. Just as people vary by height, weight, and age, different Form objects may have different sizes, colors, and screen positions.

There are many classes built into Visual Basic, but you are not limited to these classes. You can create your own classes. But whether you use the intrinsic classes or create your own, you will be using classes throughout your code, starting in the next module.

1-Minute Drill

- What is a class?
- What is meant by instantiating an object?
- Can you create classes in addition to the ones built into Visual Basic?

It's Not Just Visual Basic, It's Visual Basic .NET

While the origins of BASIC date back to 1964, Visual Basic has been around only since 1989. Indeed, Visual Basic could not have existed much earlier, as it's used to program Windows applications, and Windows itself was not introduced until 1985. However, Visual Basic has evolved quickly to keep up with the rapid changes in the Windows operating system.

Visual Basic improved with each new version, though the pace of change varied. The changes between some versions, such as between 3 and 4, were very substantial. The changes between other versions, such as between 4 and 5,

---

- A class is a template that defines and describes an object and its properties, methods, and events.
- Instantiating an object is creating an object using a class as a template.
- Yes. The ability to create classes in addition to the ones built into Visual Basic enables you to extend and customize your applications.

or 5 and 6, were more incremental. Programming language changes often are incremental and usually are not regarded as very exciting except by those who teach or preach about the programming language. However, the changes between Visual Basic version 6 and .NET are nothing short of revolutionary. The changes not only are substantial, but also require old-time programmers to unlearn techniques that no longer will work with .NET. Therefore, you picked an excellent time to learn Visual Basic!

Note

.NET also has many new features that affect how you write programs and work with the programming environment. Discussion of these features will be deferred to the ensuing modules when you will be writing programs and working with the programming environment.

Visual Basic's principal claim to fame always has been its RAD capability. You could write a Windows application much faster and more easily in Visual Basic than, for example, in C++. However, Visual Basic also was regarded as not a "serious" programming language because it is not a true object-oriented programming language. Unlike C++ and Java, Visual Basic did not support some of the features of object-oriented programming languages. For this reason—and perhaps also because of jealousy over how Visual Basic eases development of Windows applications—academicians, programming purists, and aficionados of competing languages long have looked upon Visual Basic as a "toy" language.

Though you may not, and perhaps should not, care about the snobbery of academicians, purists, and disgruntled C++ and Java programmers, Visual Basic's lack of support for object-oriented programming had more practical implications. As discussed earlier in this module, an important benefit of object-oriented programming is that it enables you to model your code after the objects in the real world that are the subject of your application. This makes your code more accurately fit the real-world problem you're attempting to solve. Object-oriented programming also makes your code easier to understand and therefore debug, maintain, and improve. Large and complex enterprise and web applications often rely heavily on object-oriented programming concepts.

With successive versions, Visual Basic has moved, or perhaps more accurately, inched toward becoming a true object-oriented programming language. Still, through version 6, it had not yet achieved that goal. With .NET, this no longer is the case. .NET supports all of the features of an object-oriented programming language. Some of those features have already been discussed. Others, such as inheritance, structured exception handling, and overloaded functions, will be discussed as they arise in the ensuing modules.

Summary

Visual Basic is an object-oriented programming language for writing event-driven Windows applications. A programming language gives instructions to a computer, which then executes those instructions.

A Windows application is displayed in a window that has a graphical user interface (GUI), usually including, though by no means limited to, a menu and a toolbar. Additionally, Windows applications are event-driven in that the user's actions, such as clicking a mouse, create events that cause the operating system to send messages to the application. You can write code that will run when those messages are received.

Visual Basic, like other programming languages, represents the persons, things, and concepts that are the subject of an application as objects. Objects have properties, methods, and events. A property is an attribute of an object, such as its height. A method is something that an object does, such as move. An event is something that happens to an object, such as being clicked. You use events to determine when code executes by associating code with the occurrence of an event. However, while you use events to determine when code executes, your code uses properties and methods to do its work, such as changing a form's height or moving the form.

Objects are created, or instantiated, from classes. A class is a template or pattern that defines and describes an object and its properties, methods, and events. There are many classes built into Visual Basic, which you will use, for example, to create forms and the controls on the forms. However, you are not limited to these intrinsic classes. You can also create your own classes.

Finally, Visual Basic, in its .NET version, now is a full-fledged object-oriented programming language.

☑Mastery Check

1. What is the basic purpose of a programming language?

   _____

   _____

2. This type of application is event-driven:

   A. A console application

   ✓ **B.** A Windows application

3. GUI stands for _____.

4. A form's height is:

   ✓ **A.** A property

   B. A method

   C. An event

5. The clicking of a form is:

   A. A property

   B. A method

   ✓ **C.** An event

6. ShowDialog, used by a FileDialog object to display itself, is:

   A. A property

   ✓ **B.** A method

   C. An event

7. You link the running of code with a user action by associating the code with:

   A. A property

   B. A method

   ✓ **C.** An event

Mastery Check

8. What is a class?

_____

_____

9. Creating an object from a class is referred to as _instantiate_ the object.

10. .NET made Visual Basic more object-oriented as a programming language.

✓ **A.** True

B. False

Module 2

Create A Visual Basic .NET Program Without Writing Code

The Goals of this Module

- Understand the relationship between the .NET Framework and Visual Studio.NET
- Identify the version of Visual Studio.NET that is best for you
- Install Visual Studio.NET
- Customize the startup of Visual Studio.NET
- Know how to create a Windows application

When I was an elementary school student (back when dinosaurs roamed the earth, as far as my daughters are concerned), I learned through countless teacher-imposed exercises to multiply and divide several digit numbers in my mind. Fast-forwarding more decades than I care to count, when I now ask my daughters to compute the answers to less complex math homework problems, they whip out their calculators and tell me the answer—quite quickly and accurately, to be sure. When I then ask them instead to calculate the answer in their heads, they look at me as a prehistoric relic and tell me, "Aw, Dad, no one does that anymore."

Calculators do make our lives easier. Imagine the long line at your local fast food outlet if orders had to be calculated by pencil and paper rather than with the calculators built into cash registers. In business, software programs such as Microsoft Excel enable you to perform spreadsheet calculations in minutes that might take you hours with pencil and paper.

Calculators also have a negative side effect, however. Human nature being what it is, if we don't *need* to learn something, we may decide it is not worth the time and trouble. Research suggests that the availability of calculators has contributed substantially to a decline in students' computational skills. Despite calculators, computational skills still are necessary, not just in everyday situations in which a calculator may not be available, but also as a foundation for students to develop skills in creating algorithms and analyzing problems—skills essential in, among other areas, computer programming.

Just as calculators automate computation, Visual Studio.NET automates the creation of applications. For example, creating GUI elements such as menus, toolbars, and other controls strictly through code is difficult, whereas Visual Studio.NET enables you to create these GUI elements simply by dragging and dropping. Indeed, Visual Studio.NET, consistent with prior versions of Visual Studio, enables you to create a Windows application without writing a single line of code! While the resulting Windows application is basic, being no more than a window with default functionality, it also is important in that it is the starting point, or foundation, for all of the Windows applications you will write in the following modules.

There is a danger of Visual Studio.NET doing so much for beginning programmers. They may be seduced by how easy Visual Studio.NET makes creating a Windows application. Consequently, they may just plunge in and start writing programs without really understanding the code they are writing or how the different parts of the program fit together. I have witnessed this with programming students working with prior versions of Visual Studio. They try to write more complex programs, are unable to do so because they don't understand the necessary foundation, become frustrated, and quit.

Because of the importance of understanding the code generated by Visual Studio.NET, this module will analyze that code line by line, as well as show you step by step how to use Visual Studio.NET to build a Windows application. Please resist the temptation to skip the code analysis and race ahead to writing programs in the succeeding modules. The relatively little time you spend now to understand the code will save you much time when you write code later.

You do need to take care of a few minor details before you start using Visual Studio.NET to write programs. First, you need to buy it. This module cannot give you tips on how to come up with the money. However, it will assist you in deciding which of the several versions of Visual Studio.NET is best for you.

You also need to install Visual Studio.NET. Visual Studio.NET is a complex application and has a correspondingly complex installation sequence. This module will walk you through the steps of installing Visual Studio.NET and also give you tips for customizing it once it is installed.

The .NET Framework

You can develop a Visual Basic .NET application without Visual Studio.NET, using a text editor such as Notepad and the command line, though this is the hard way. However, you must install the .NET Framework before you can develop a Visual Basic .NET application. Similarly, you must install the .NET Framework before you can install Visual Studio.NET. In short, there is no .NET without the .NET Framework.

The word "framework" in .NET Framework suggests a supporting structure such as the wood framing of a house. However, the .NET Framework is as much the central nervous system as it is the structural framework of Visual Studio.NET. The .NET Framework has a Common Language Runtime (CLR), system class libraries, compilers, and other tools that are necessary for you to build a .NET application. The CLR, system class libraries, and other components of the .NET Framework will be discussed later in this book. The point for now is that you simply cannot develop a .NET application without the .NET Framework.

Microsoft has committed to provide the .NET Framework for free. So there is no confusion, Visual Studio.NET is not free; only the .NET Framework is.

You can obtain the .NET Framework Software Developer's Kit (SDK) from Microsoft at the MSDN (Microsoft Developer Network) .NET web site (http://msdn.microsoft.com/net/), either as a download or by CD, the latter involving a shipping charge. However, if you have Visual Studio.NET, there is no need to obtain the .NET Framework since it is included in the Visual Studio.NET installation CDs.

Tip

You should install the .NET Framework SDK as part of the Visual Studio.NET installation instead of first installing the .NET Framework separately. The file upgrades required for Visual Studio.NET depend on the operating system and other issues, so it is preferable to perform those upgrades once rather than piecemeal.

The .NET Framework SDK has rigorous system requirements, but no worse than those for Visual Studio.NET, which are discussed in Project 2-1, "Installing Visual Studio.NET."

1-Minute Drill

● What is included in the .NET Framework?

● Do you need to install the .NET Framework to create Visual Basic .NET applications?

Before You Install Visual Studio.NET

Of course, you need to install Visual Studio.NET to start using it, and this module will cover installation. However, before installing Visual Studio.NET, you need to purchase it, and you have several choices of versions. Additionally, you should confirm that your computer and operating system meet the requirements of Visual Studio.NET.

● The .NET Framework has a Common Language Runtime (CLR), system class libraries, compilers, and other tools that are necessary for you to build a .NET application.

● Yes. You need to install the .NET Framework to create Visual Basic .NET applications and also to install Visual Studio.NET. However, the installation program for Visual Studio.NET includes the installation of the .NET Framework.

Visual Studio.NET Versions

You might think that the only problem you will have buying Visual Studio.NET is finding the money to pay for it. However, consistent with prior versions of Visual Studio, Visual Studio.NET comes in several different versions, which vary in price and functionality. It is preferable to buy the correct version the first time rather than try to upgrade later. Additionally, in determining what is the correct version for you, you should consider not just where you are now in your programming career, but where you anticipate being in the next year or two.

Tip

The Professional Edition of Visual Studio.NET and the Standard Editions of Visual Basic .NET and other core languages each will be available in an AE (Academic Edition). The AE versions will be substantially cheaper than their counterparts, and also may include academic-specific features. Educational institutions are eligible to purchase the AE versions; students apparently are not eligible.

Visual Studio.NET System Requirements

While you may be understandably anxious to fire up your installation CD and get started, you first should confirm that your computer is capable of running Visual Studio.NET. Table 2-1 describes the minimum and recommended hardware requirements.

Component	Minimum	Recommended
Processor	Pentium II, 450 MHz	Pentium III, 700 MHz
RAM	128MB	256MB
Hard drive disk space	3GB	NA
Video	800×600, 256 colors	1024×768, high color 16-bit

Table 2-1   Visual Studio.NET Hardware Requirements

Tip

Just as you can't be "too rich or too thin," you can't have too much RAM. Visual Studio.NET consumes prodigious amounts of memory. 128MB really is a bare minimum, and assumes you are not running any other applications at the same time. Additionally, with operating systems such as Windows 2000 Server, 128MB of RAM may not be enough. I believe 256MB is a more reliable minimum. Visual Studio.NET also requires one of the 32-bit Windows operating systems, Windows XP, 2000, NT 4.0, ME, or 98. While Windows 95 is a 32-bit Windows operating system and will run .NET applications, Windows 95 does not support Visual Studio.NET. You can use Visual Studio.NET with Windows NT 4.0, ME, or 98, but only Windows 2000 and XP supports all of the features.

Tip

If you do not currently have one of the requisite operating systems installed, you must upgrade the operating system before, not after, you install Visual Studio.NET. Visual Studio.NET will not work if you do these steps in reverse order.

1-Minute Drill

● Can you run Visual Studio.NET on any modern operating system?

Project 2-1: Installing Visual Studio.NET

The Visual Studio.NET installation consists of five CDs, labeled CD 1, CD 2, CD 3, CD 4, and Windows Component Update. The Windows Component Update CD contains the .NET Framework SDK, which is why, as previously mentioned, you do not need to obtain the SDK separately.

Step-by-Step

1. Place CD 1 in the CD-ROM drive. If the setup program does not start automatically, double-click the setup.exe program in the root directory of the CD-ROM drive. Figure 2-1 displays the startup screen. On an initial installation, only option 1, the Windows Component Update, will be available.

● No. Visual Studio.NET requires one of the following 32-bit Windows operating systems: Windows XP, 2000, NT 4.0, ME, or 98. Of these, only Windows XP and 2000 support all of the features of Visual Studio.NET.

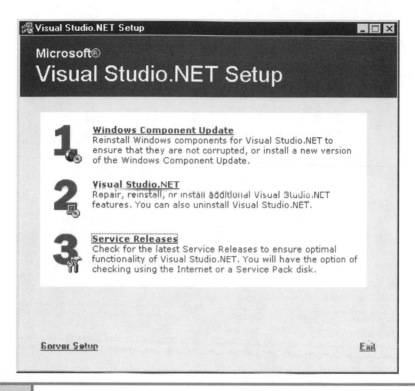

Figure 2-1   The Visual Studio.NET setup screen

2. Click the hyperlink labeled Windows Component Update next to option 1.
As shown in Figure 2-2, you will be prompted to insert the Windows
Component Update CD. Yes, this does mean you will have to take the setup
CD (CD 1) out of the CD-ROM drive while the setup program is running.
Don't worry; this will not cause a problem with the setup program.

3. Remove CD 1 from the CD-ROM drive and place the Windows Component
Update CD in the CD-ROM drive. If necessary, change the location displayed
in the dialog box shown in Figure 2-2, and click OK. When the Windows
Component Update CD starts up, you may be asked to accept a license
agreement. After you agree, Figure 2-3 shows the resulting Windows
Component Update setup screen.

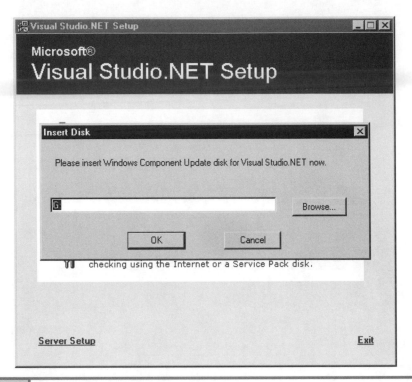

Figure 2-2 Prompt to insert Windows Component Update CD

4. The Windows Component Update requires multiple reboots. If you check Automatically Log On and enter your password, the setup program can automatically start where it left off after each reboot. Otherwise, you have to manually enter your password after each reboot. After you have decided whether to enable automatic log on, click Continue. Figure 2-4 shows the resulting dialog box that lists the actions the Windows Component Update process will perform. The only item listed in Figure 2-4 is the Microsoft .NET Framework. However, the list in your installation may include additional items such as a later version of Microsoft Data Access Components or Internet Explorer if those other items are not already installed on your computer.

5. Click Update Now (which will be called Install Now if there has not been a prior Windows Component Update). The Windows Component Update process will begin. If you enabled automatic log on in step 4, get yourself a

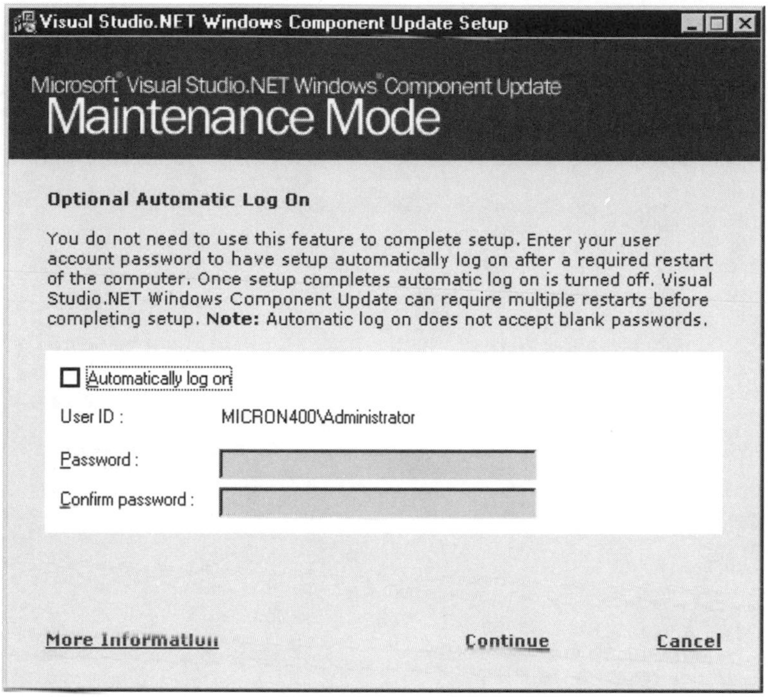

Figure 2-3   The Windows Component Update setup screen

cup of coffee; this process will take a while. If you did not enable automatic log on, you can still get a cup of coffee, but come right back, because you will need to manually log on after each of several restarts. Finally, the Windows Component Update process will finish, and you will see a congratulations screen similar to Figure 2-5.

6. You will be returned to the Visual Studio.NET startup screen shown previously in Figure 2-1 once the Windows Component Update has been completed. You have now installed the .NET Framework SDK and are ready to install Visual Studio.NET. Click the hyperlink labeled Visual Studio.NET next to option 2.

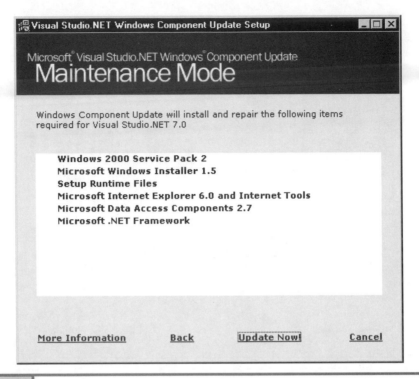

| **Figure 2-4** | List of actions to be taken by Windows Component Update |

7. As is often the case, the first step in proceeding with the installation is to accept the license agreement. After you have accepted, you will be presented with a page similar to Figure 2-6. (It shows the Setup Options page for the Enterprise Architect version.) This page enables you to choose which parts of Visual Studio.NET you want to install.

Tip

Accept the defaults if you have sufficient hard drive space.

8. Once you have completed choosing installation options, click Install Now! This installation also will take some time. You will be shown dialog boxes with status information and lists of features available in Visual Studio.NET. However, other than inserting the remaining CDs when prompted, there really is not much you have to do. The setup program will notify you with a dialog box when the installation is complete. Click Done and you are done. Congratulations! You have installed Visual Studio.NET.

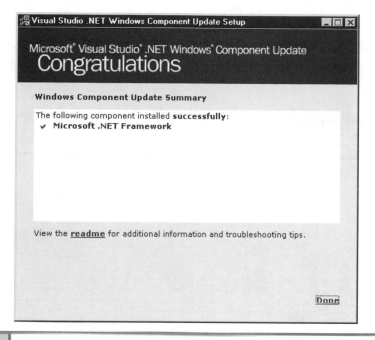

Figure 2-5   Congratulations on installing the Windows Component Update

Tip

If you need to add or repair features in Visual Studio.NET, just put CD 1 in your CD-ROM drive and choose option 2 (Visual Studio.NET) from the dialog box shown previously in Figure 2-1 (the language of this option may change to offering to repair, reinstall, or install additional Visual Studio.NET features once you have completed the installation). You also can check for service releases (option 3).

1-Minute Drill

● Do you need to install the .NET Framework SDK before you install the components of Visual Studio.NET?

● Yes. However, the Visual Studio.NET installation program will prompt you to install or upgrade any .NET Framework SDK components not already installed on your computer.

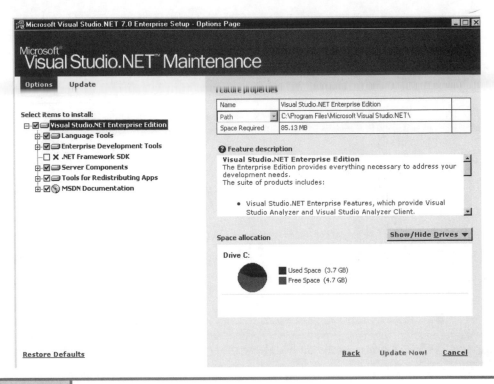

Figure 2-6 The Visual Studio.NET setup options page

Starting and Customizing Visual Studio.NET

You start Visual Basic by clicking Start | Programs | Microsoft Visual Studio.NET 7.0 | Microsoft Visual Studio.NET. This is the first of many changes between Visual Studio.NET and Visual Studio 6.0. Visual Studio 6.0 displayed separate program groups for Visual Basic, Visual C++, and any other programming languages you installed, such as Visual FoxPro or Visual J++. This is because each programming language had a separate IDE. However, with Visual Studio.NET all programming languages share the same IDE.

Figure 2-7 shows the Start Page, labeled the VS (for Visual Studio) Home Page, which, by default, displays when you start Visual Studio.NET. Figure 2-7 also shows existing projects because I couldn't wait to get started before I took this screenshot!

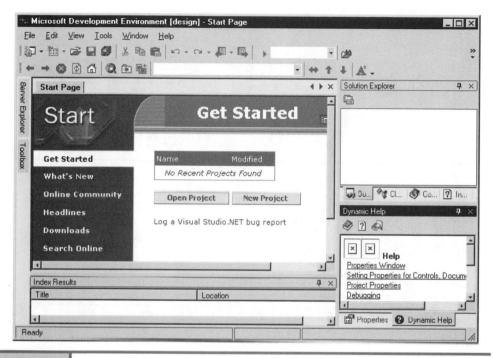

Figure 2-7   The Visual Studio.NET Start Page

You can change the appearance of Visual Studio.NET at startup. Display the Options dialog box (Tools | Options) and then, as shown in Figure 2-8, select a choice from the drop-down box labeled At Startup.

Table 2-2 describes the choices of how Visual Studio.NET will appear at startup.

Choice	Description
Show Start page	This is the default and is shown in Figure 2-7.
Load last loaded solution	Visual Studio.NET will open to the last project you were working on, as it appeared when you closed Visual Studio.NET.
Show Open Project dialog box	Displays the Open Project dialog box, which may also be displayed by the menu command File	Open	Project.
Show New Project dialog box	Displays the New Project dialog box, which may also be displayed by the menu command File	New	Project.
Show empty environment	Displays an empty IDE when you start Visual Studio.NET.

Table 2-2   Options for Visual Studio.NET's Appearance at Startup

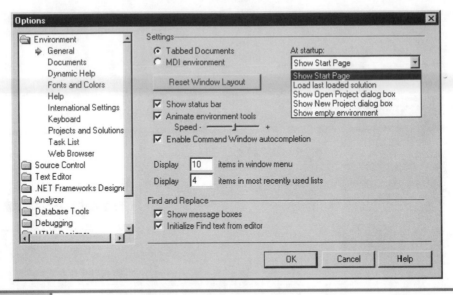

Figure 2-8   Choosing the startup option

We'll stay with the default, the Start Page. However, further customization is possible and indeed desirable.

As stated previously, other Visual Studio.NET programming languages share the IDE with Visual Basic. While overall this is a positive development, one negative aspect is that when, for example, you are using the built-in Help, the IDE does not know whether you are asking from the perspective of a Visual Basic programmer, a C# programmer, or a C++ programmer. This issue will become even more important, as Microsoft is licensing third parties to add languages to those supported by the Visual Studio.NET IDE.

You can tell Visual Studio.NET information about yourself that enables it to customize the IDE to one with which, for example, a Visual Basic programmer would be familiar. The customization provides defaults for the appearance of windows, keyboard shortcuts, Help, and other configuration issues.

You tell Visual Studio.NET information about yourself by choosing My Profile from the Start Page shown previously in Figure 2-7. This will display the My Profile page shown in Figure 2-9.

Choose Visual Basic Developer from the Profile drop-down box. This choice will also change other options such as Keyboard Scheme and Windows Layout.

Figure 2-9   My Profile page

Visual Studio.NET then processes your changes and redisplays the Start Page, now appearing as shown in Figure 2-10.

The Toolbox window on the left in Figure 2-10 is taking up a large amount of screen space. Click its close button. You can later redisplay the Toolbox window when you need it. The appearance of the Start Page now returns to that shown previously in Figure 2-7. Nevertheless, Visual Studio.NET has made configuration changes to the keyboard shortcuts and other items.

1-Minute Drill

● Why should you customize Visual Studio.NET?

● Since other Visual Studio.NET programming languages share the IDE with Visual Basic .NET, the IDE does not know whether you are using the built-in Help, keyboard shortcuts, and such from the perspective of a Visual Basic programmer, a C# programmer, or a C++ programmer. Therefore, you should customize the IDE to one specific to Visual Basic programming.

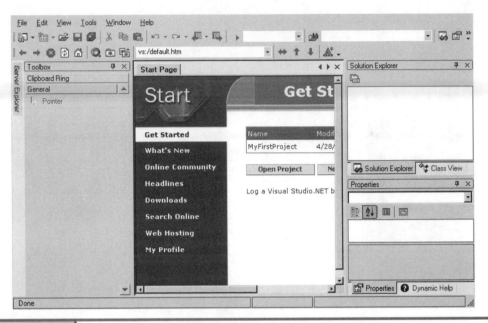

Figure 2-10 The Start Page after changing the profile to Visual Basic Developer

Project 2-2: Creating a Windows Application

Visual Studio.NET enables you to create both console applications and applications having a graphical user interface (GUI). Your three choices are:

- **Windows forms, often called WinForms** Windows forms constitute the user interface for Windows applications, which usually are run from a local computer, though they may be run from a server on the network. Microsoft Word is an example of a Windows application.

- **Web forms** Web forms, which provide a web browser-based user interface, are usually for web applications that run from a web server on the Internet. An example of a web application is an airline web site in which you enter where and when you want to travel and then are provided with a schedule of available flights.

- **Console applications**   Console applications (discussed in Module 1) have been used far longer than Windows applications. Curiously, though, it was difficult to create console applications in prior versions of Visual Basic, which tried to force you to use a Windows interface whether you wanted to or not. Visual Basic .NET supports true console applications.

This section will focus on the first choice, Windows forms, and will describe, step by step, the process of creating a Visual Basic Windows application using the Visual Studio.NET IDE. In the following sections, we will analyze the resulting code generated by Visual Studio.NET.

Step-by-Step

1. On the Start page, choose Create New Project. Figure 2-11 shows the New Project dialog box. You also can display the New Project dialog box by choosing the File | New | Project menu item. In Visual Studio.NET, as in many Windows applications, there usually is more than one way of doing something.

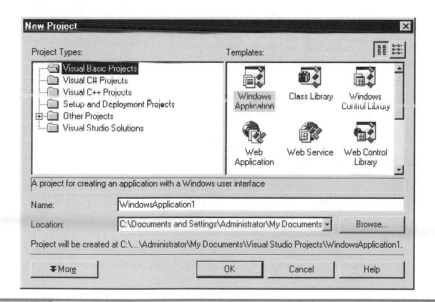

| **Figure 2-11** | The New Project dialog box |

Note

The left or list pane of the New Project dialog box may list other programming languages. The dialog box shown in Figure 2-11 includes, in addition to Visual Basic, Visual C# and Visual C++. Your New Project dialog box may not include Visual C# and Visual C++, or it may include another programming language such as Visual FoxPro, depending on the options you selected when you installed Visual Studio.NET.

2. Since this book is about Visual Basic and not Visual C# or Visual C++, select the Visual Basic Projects folder. The right or contents pane of the New Project dialog box lists the available project templates for a Visual Basic project. A project template helps you get started by creating the initial files and other settings for the selected project. While the New Project dialog box lists many project templates, these project types basically fall within the three categories discussed at the beginning of this section: Windows applications, web applications, and console applications. When you select a template or a project type, the corresponding description appears beneath the Project Types frame. Choose Windows Application. The description beneath the Project Types frame is "A project for creating an application with a Windows user interface."

3. In the Name field, enter the name of the project you want to create. The default project name for your first project is WindowsApplication1, for the second WindowsApplication2, and so on. You should change this default name to one that will help you identify this project later. After you have created many projects, you may not recall what WindowsApplication52 did as opposed to WindowsApplication53. For this example, use the name **MyFirstProject**. When you type the name, Project Will Be Created At changes to show the name of the project. A folder with the same name as the project is also created in the location displayed in the Location field.

4. The Location field contains the parent folder where your project files will be located. For example, if your project will be located in C:\Temp\MyFirstProject, the parent folder displayed in the Location field would be C:\Temp. By default,

new projects are created in the Visual Studio Projects Location, displayed on the Projects And Solutions page, which you can choose from the Environment folder in the Options dialog box, as shown in Figure 2-12. If you don't like that location, you can use the Browse button next to Visual Studio Projects Location to open a Project Location dialog box and navigate to a different location.

5. Once you are satisfied with the name and location of the project, click OK. Visual Studio.NET then generates the files and folders for your first project, and the display changes to that shown in Figure 2-13. These files and folders are shown in Explorer view in Figure 2-14.

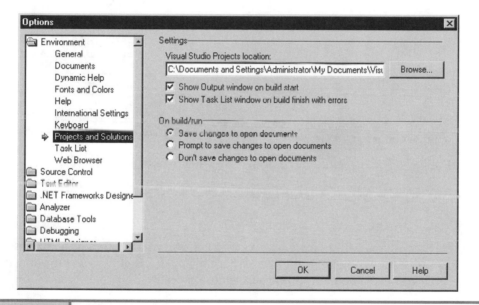

Figure 2-12   Specifying the location of the project

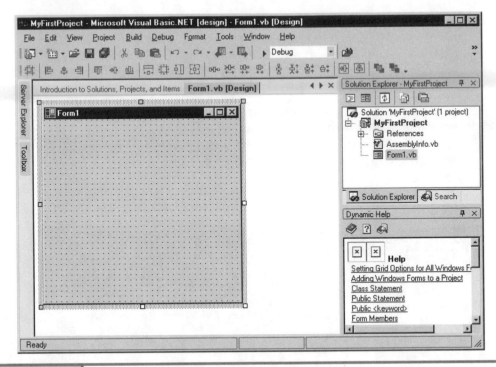

Figure 2-13 The IDE after initial project files and folders are generated

Tip

The IDE is complex, with many windows that perform many different functions. Don't worry about knowing right away what they all do. Each will be introduced, described, and explained in this and succeeding modules.

6. Next, you should build the additional files necessary to run this project as an application by using the menu command Build | Build Solution or Build | Build MyFirstProject. The difference between the two menu commands is

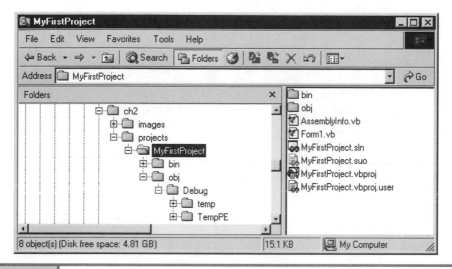

Figure 2-14 Files and folders created for your Windows application

that the first concerns a solution and the second a project. A project contains all the files and links necessary for your application. A solution may contain multiple projects. Since the current application is simple and concerns only one project, there is no practical difference in this instance between the two menu commands.

7. You can now run the project using the menu command Debug | Run or the keyboard command F5. The result is a window named Form1, shown in Figure 2-15.

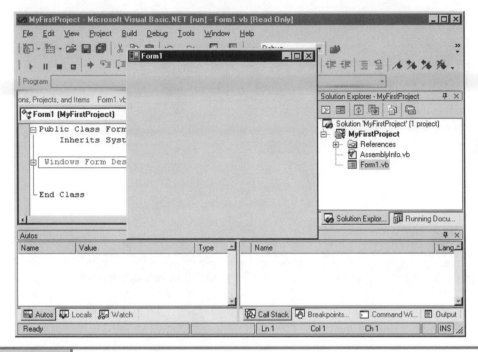

Figure 2-15 The Windows application running

The Code Behind the Scenes

You have created a functioning Windows application. Form1 has the default behavior of a window. For example, you can move Form1 by clicking its title bar and dragging it. You also can resize Form1 by holding your cursor over a border until it becomes a two-headed arrow and then clicking and dragging the border.

Additionally, you created a functioning Windows application without having to write a single line of code. This is impressive since a substantial amount of complex code is required to create a window.

While you did not have to write a single line of code, there is code automatically generated by Visual Studio.NET. You can view the code created by Visual Studio.NET by the menu command intuitively named View | Code, after which you will see the following code:

```
Public Class Form1
    Inherits System.Windows.Forms.Form
+ Region " Windows Form Designer generated code "
End Class
```

Figure 2-16 shows how this code window appears in the IDE.

The plus (+) symbol means that a section is collapsed, similar to collapsing the contents of a drive or folder in Windows Explorer. Normally, you do not need to change this code. In fact, since Visual Studio.NET automatically generates and maintains this code, changing it without knowing exactly what you are doing can result in unpredictable and unwanted consequences. However, analyzing the code is a good learning tool, and we will be careful in changing the code generated by Visual Basic .NET.

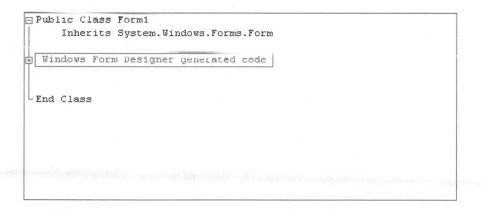

Figure 2-16   The Code window in IDE

Click the plus (+) symbol next to #Region Windows Form Designer Generated Code. The following listing shows the code as expanded:

```
Public Class Form1
    Inherits System.Windows.Forms.Form
- Region " Windows Form Designer generated code "
    Public Sub New()
        MyBase.New()
        'This call is required by the Windows Form Designer.
        InitializeComponent()
        'Add any initialization after the InitializeComponent() call
    End Sub
    'Form overrides dispose to clean up the component list.
    Protected Overloads Overrides Sub Dispose(ByVal disposing As Boolean)
        If disposing Then
        If Not (components Is Nothing) Then
            components.Dispose()
        End If
        MyBase.Dispose(disposing)
    End Sub
    'Required by the Windows Form Designer
    Private components As System.ComponentModel.Container
    'NOTE: The following procedure is required by the Windows Form Designer
    'It can be modified using the Windows Form Designer.
    'Do not modify it using the code editor.
    <System.Diagnostics.DebuggerStepThroughAttribute()>
Private Sub InitializeComponent()
        '
        'Form1
        '
        Me.AutoScaleBaseSize = New System.Drawing.Size(5, 13)
        Me.ClientSize = New System.Drawing.Size(292, 273)
        Me.Name = "Form1"
        Me.Text = "Form1"
    End Sub
#End Region
End Class
```

[handwritten annotations: "Generation of New method by VBN", "Dispose Method", "Assignments", "Generation of Form by VBN"]

While this code may appear complex, with the foundation in object-oriented programming you obtained from Module 1, much of it is understandable. As the following analysis shows, the code is structured around the lifecycle of an object, from birth to death.

Class and Inherits Statements

The code starts with the statements:

```
Public Class Form1
    Inherits System.Windows.Forms.Form
```

As discussed in Module 1, a form is an object representing a window that makes up an application's user interface. Like all objects, a form is created from a template or blueprint called a class. The .NET Framework has a built-in Form class, System.Windows.Forms.Form. This class implements the characteristics and behavior that you would expect of a Windows form.

The Form class is located in a namespace called System.Windows.Forms. A namespace is a grouping of related classes in a .NET system class library. The full class name System.Windows.Forms.Form results from adding the class name Form to the namespace System.Windows.Forms, separating the two by a dot (.).

Each object is an instance of a class. Since you can and often do have more than one form in your application, you need to distinguish one form from another. You do so by giving each object a unique name. Visual Studio.NET has given our form the highly original name Form1. You can change this name, and you should if your application uses more than one form.

The Inherits statement indicates that Form1 will start with all the built-in characteristics and behavior of the Form class. Form1 has the characteristics of a standard window, such as a title bar, a border, and a client area. Form1 also has the behavior of a standard window. You can move Form1 by clicking its title bar and dragging it, and can resize Form1 by holding your cursor over a border until it becomes a two-headed arrow and then clicking and dragging the border.

New Method

As discussed in Module 1, a class is only a blueprint or template for an object. It is not an object itself. Thus, the System.Windows.Forms.Form class is a template for a form, but it is not a form. Since a Windows application does require, after all, a window, you need to create, or *instantiate*, a form from the Form class. Like most aspects of programming, this requires code.

The code that creates an object from a class is called a *constructor*. In Visual Basic .NET, a constructor is always contained in a method that is called New, perhaps because the method creates a new object from the class.

Visual Studio.NET generates the following New method:

```
Public Sub New()
    MyBase.New()
    'This call is required by the Windows Form Designer.
    InitializeComponent()
    'Add any initialization after the InitializeComponent() call
End Sub
```

The code in the New method is executed when the object is instantiated. The first step is to call the New method of the class on which the object is based, in this case the Form class. The MyBase keyword refers to the base (also called parent) class, which is the one specified by the Inherits statement discussed previously. The New method next calls the InitializeComponent method, which is discussed next.

Two of the lines of code start with a single-quote or apostrophe character ('):

```
'This call is required by the Windows Form Designer.
'Add any initialization after the InitializeComponent() call
```

A line of code that begins with a single-quote character is called a *comment*. A comment is not considered part of the code of the application. The compiler ignores comments. Instead, the purpose of a comment is to explain the code.

Tip

You should develop the habit of annotating your code with comments. You will find that you have trouble remembering your reasons for code you wrote only a week or two before. Comments will help you remember. Additionally, when you program for a living, often you will be part of a team, and comments help other members of the team understand your code.

InitializeComponent Method

The InitializeComponent method assigns values to various properties of the form. As discussed in Module 1, a property is an attribute of an object. Each property has a value. For example, a Form object has a BackColor property that represents the form's background color. The actual background color of the form is the value of the BackColor property.

If you do not provide a value for the property, the value is the default—that is, the value given by Visual Studio.NET in the absence of direction from the programmer. For example, the default value of the BackColor property, and thus the background color of the form, is gray. However, the form's background color could be blue, red, or some other color.

The process of giving a property a value is known as *assignment*, as in *assigning* a value to a property. Assignment is performed by the assignment operator, which looks like an equal sign (=). Several assignments of values to properties are performed in the code for the InitializeComponent method, which stripped of comments reads:

```
Private Sub InitializeComponent()
   Me.AutoScaleBaseSize = New System.Drawing.Size(5, 13)
   Me.ClientSize = New System.Drawing.Size(292, 273)
   Me.Name = "Form1"
   Me.Text = "Form1"
End Sub
```

Table 2-3 describes these properties.

The "Ask the Expert" following this section explains how you can obtain a listing and description of the properties of a Form object.

Let's analyze one of the statements:

```
Me.Text = "Form1"
```

The Me keyword refers to the specific instance of the class where the code is executing. In this case, it refers to Form1, a specific instance of the Form class. Text is a property of the Form object. The Text property is the text displayed in the title bar of the Form. Me.Text means that the reference is to the Text property of the instance of the class currently executing, here Form1. The object instance (Me) and the object property (Text) are separated by a dot consistent with the syntax:

```
[Name of Object Instance].[Name of Property]
```

Me   *Text*

Property	Description
AutoScaleBaseSize	A complex property, it relates to how a form adjusts its size and the size of the controls it contains in relation to the height of the font used on the form.
ClientSize	The size of the form's client area. In Microsoft Word, the client area is the area in which you can type, and therefore does not include the menus, toolbars, and so on.
Name	The form's identifier. Discussed in the following text.
Text	The words displayed in the form's title bar. Discussed in the following text.

Table 2-3   Form Properties Used in the InitializeComponent Method

The object instance and property are followed by the assignment operator and the value to be assigned to the property of that object instance. Thus, the entire syntax of the line is:

```
[Name of Object Instance].[Name of Property]= New Value of Property
```

The effect is to give the Text property of Form1 the value on the right side of the assignment operator, "Form1". The value "Form1" on the right side of the assignment operator is the text displayed in the title bar of the form.

The value on the right side of the assignment operator, "Form1", is surrounded by double quotes. This indicates that it is literal text, referred to in Visual Basic .NET as a *string*. By contrast, when the reference is to the object Form1, as in:

```
Public Class Form1
```

The reference stands by itself and is not surrounded by double quotes.

The effect of an assignment of a value to a property is illustrated by changing the code:

```
Me.Text = "Form1"
```

to:

```
Me.Text = "Godzilla"
```

Run the project with the Debug | Run menu command. Figure 2-17 shows the result. The text displayed by the title bar now reads "Godzilla."

The InitializeComponent method is where values are assigned to properties of the object when the object is being created. You will see in the succeeding modules that you can assign values later in the object's lifetime and in other ways.

Dispose Method

The Dispose method corresponds to the New method as death does to life. The New method is called to create an object. The Dispose method is called to destroy the object.

Figure 2-17   The form's title is changed to "Godzilla"

An object should be destroyed when it is no longer needed. The reason is that every object, when created, takes up memory. Memory is a limited resource, and your operating system will crash if it runs too low on memory. Therefore, when the object is no longer needed, the memory used to create it should be released back to the operating system.

The code generated by Visual Studio.NET for the Dispose method is:

```
Protected Overloads Overrides Sub Dispose(ByVal disposing As Boolean)
    If disposing Then
    If Not (components Is Nothing) Then
        components.Dispose()
    End If
    MyBase.Dispose(disposing)
End Sub
```

This code first disposes of any components or controls of the form (though here there are none) and then calls the Dispose method of the class on which the object is based, represented by the MyBase keyword.

Region Directive

A large portion of code is contained within the Region directive, which begins and ends as follows:

```
Region " Windows Form Designer generated code "
'code
#End Region
```

The Region directive tells the code editor the portion of the code to be collapsed and expanded. The text following the initial Region statement, "Windows Form Designer generated code," describes the contained code, and uniquely identifies the region (as you could have more than one region in your code).

While Visual Studio.NET automatically generated this particular region directive, you can create your own region directives. This can be useful to outline your code. You may find this feature useful as your applications become more sophisticated and your code correspondingly longer, since you can hide the code you don't need to examine, enabling you to focus better on the code you do need to analyze.

1-Minute Drill

- Which part of System.Windows.Forms.Form is a namespace and which part is a class?
- What is the difference between the New and InitializeComponent methods?

Ask the Expert

Question: How do you find out the properties of a Form class and what the properties mean?

Answer: You need help—specifically, the Help built into Visual Studio.NET. Choose the menu command Help | Index. This will display the Index dialog box shown in Figure 2-18. Type **form class** in the Look For field, and in the list box, choose Properties under Form Class. This will display Help that lists and describes the Form properties.

- System.Windows.Forms is a namespace, which is a grouping of related classes in a .NET system class library. Form is a class.
- The New method is where an instance of an object or class is created. The InitializeComponent method is where you assign values to properties of the newly created object.

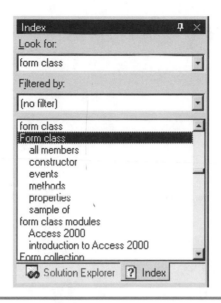

| **Figure 2-18** | The Help Index dialog box |

Summary

While you don't *need* Visual Studio.NET to create Visual Basic .NET applications, it sure helps. Visual Basic .NET automates the task of creating Windows applications. Indeed, Visual Studio.NET enables you to create a basic Windows application without writing a single line of code! This module showed you, step by step, how to use Visual Studio.NET to build a Windows application.

However, it is important to understand the code Visual Studio.NET has generated since that code is the basis of code you will be writing starting with the next module. The code generated by Visual Studio.NET represents the lifecycle of an object, from its creation, the New method, to its death, the Dispose method. In between, the object's properties are assigned values in the InitializeComponent method using the assignment operator.

This module also gave you tips on deciding which of the several versions of Visual Studio.NET is best for you, walked you through the steps of installing Visual Studio.NET, and showed you how to customize Visual Studio.NET.

Mastery Check

1. Visual Studio.NET will not run under which of the following operating systems?

    A. Windows 2000

    B. Windows ME

    √ **C.** Windows 95

    D. Windows NT 4.0

2. You can use *all* of the features of Visual Studio.NET only with the following operating system:

    √ **A.** Windows 2000

    B. Windows ME

    C. Windows 95

    D. Windows NT 4.0

3. The Visual Studio.NET installation program includes the .NET Framework.

    √ **A.** True

    B. False

4. Visual Studio.NET does not support console applications as an interface.

    A. True

    √ **B.** False

5. Which do you *need* to create a Visual Basic .NET application?

    √ **A.** Visual Studio.NET

    B. .NET Framework

    C. Notepad

☑ *Mastery Check*

6. In the statement System.Windows.Forms.Form, Form is a:

   A. Namespace

   B. Property

✓ **C.** Class

   D. Method

7. The method in which values are assigned to a newly created object is:

   A. New

✓ **B.** InitializeComponent

   C. Dispose

8. In the statement Me.Text = "Godzilla", the equal sign (=) is called the _Assignment_ operator.

9. In the statement Form1.Text = "Form1", "Form1" is the object Form1.   *Form's title*

✓ **A.** True

   B. False

10. The value of a property given by Visual Studio.NET if you do not provide a value is the _Default_ value.

Module 3

Event Procedures, Properties, and Controls

The Goals of this Module

- Create event procedures
- Determine and change the value of properties
- Understand the concepts of, and differences between, design time and runtime
- Use the Toolbox to add controls to a form
- Use the Windows Forms Designer to locate, size, and align controls
- Use controls to display dynamic and static information

Module 1 discussed how Windows applications are event-driven: the application user's actions create events, and these events drive the order in which things happen in the application. However, unless you write code for an event, the event usually will be much like a sound with no one to hear it—it might as well not have happened. The application takes an action when a user, for example, clicks a menu item only because a programmer wrote code that ran when the menu item was clicked. That code is inside of an event procedure, which is how Visual Basic .NET connects an event to the code you want to run when the event occurs. This module will explain event procedures and show you how to create them.

It would be pointless to go to the trouble of creating an event procedure if the code inside the event procedure changed nothing. Often the code's purpose is to change the application's current condition, or in programming parlance, *state*. Just as a person's state may be conscious or unconscious, healthy or sick, or standing or sitting or lying down, each of the objects in your application has a state, which is stored in their properties. For example, a form's size and position are stored in the properties Height, Width, Left, and Top. The code inside an event procedure often accesses or changes the values of properties of various objects involved in the application. This module will show you how to do this, both through code and through the Windows Forms Designer.

Thus far we have focused on the Form object. The form is an important control, perhaps the most important one, but it cannot possibly meet all the requirements of a Windows application. The form does not have the functionality to permit typing of text, listing data, selection of choices, and so on. You need other, specialized controls for that additional functionality. Indeed, the form's primary role is to serve as a host, or container, for controls that enrich the GUI of Windows applications, such as menus, toolbars, buttons, text boxes, and list boxes. These controls have their own sets of properties and event procedures. This module will show you how to add controls to your form and use them in your application.

Event Procedures

Module 1 discussed that Windows applications have a graphical user interface (GUI), which may include menus, toolbars, buttons, and other visual components. While the GUI does put a pretty face on Windows, its primary purpose is to enable the application user to give directions to the application, such as to open or save a file or to print a document. For example, if you want to

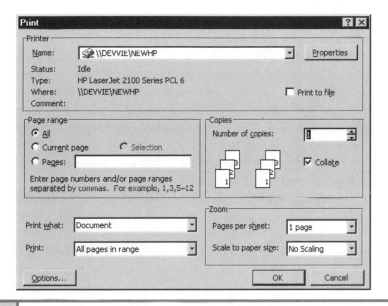

Figure 3-1   The Printer dialog box

print a document, you would display the Print dialog box shown in Figure 3-1, either by the menu command File | Print or by clicking the Print button on the toolbar. The Print dialog box in turn contains drop down lists, radio buttons, a check box, command buttons, and other visual components through which you can choose a printer and other options and then click OK to start printing.

As far as the application user is concerned, the Print dialog box simply appears when they click the File | Print menu command or the Print toolbar button. However, as programmers, we know better. The Print dialog box does not appear magically just because the application user clicked a menu command or toolbar button. Instead, code causes the Print dialog box to appear. That code is inside an event procedure, which is how Visual Basic .NET connects an event to the code you want to run when the event occurs.

When Are Event Procedures Necessary?

Module 1 also discussed that the application user's actions, such as clicking a menu command or toolbar button, create events. Each event causes the operating system to send a message to the application. Thus, when the application user clicks the File | Print menu item, that action is an event that causes the operating system to send a message to the application window that the File | Print menu command has been clicked.

An application usually is bombarded by messages from the operating system. For example, wave your mouse across your browser's window. This action causes the operating system to send numerous messages to the browser window, first that the mouse pointer moved from coordinate 0, 0 to 0, 1, then from 0, 1 to 1, 1, then from 1, 1 to 1, 2, all the way to, for example, 444, 333 or at whatever coordinate the mouse finally stopped.

✓ Fortunately, you do not have to write code to anticipate every possible action by the application user. If you do not write code to handle a particular event, the message resulting from that event is handled by default. The default decides how an application handles a message in the absence of direction (code) by the programmer.

One example of the default handling of an event is when you move your mouse after you have clicked the title bar of an unmaximized window. The default handling of that event is that the window will move with the mouse. Another example is if you hold your mouse cursor over a border of an unmaximized window, the mouse cursor becomes a two-headed arrow, and then clicking and dragging the mouse will move the border and resize the window. However, not all default handling of an event results in something happening. If you click or drag your mouse in the browser window, the default is that nothing will happen to the window.

You, as the programmer, need to decide whether you need to specially handle a particular event. You may decide you do not need to, either because you don't care about the particular event or because you are satisfied with the default handling of the event.

Let's return to the issue of how to display the Print dialog box. You want the Print dialog box to appear when you click the File | Print menu item. The default action when a menu item is clicked is nothing happens. Since that default action will not work for your application, you need to write code to handle the Click event of the File | Print menu item.

Once you have determined that you need to write code, you must answer two questions:

1. What code do you write?

2. Where do you write the code?

Taking the second question first, the answer is an event procedure.

Using the IDE to Create an Event Procedure

As discussed in Module 1, a form, like every visual component in a Windows application, is referred to in programming parlance as an object, and each object recognizes certain events—that is, something that happens to an object, usually as a result of user interaction with the object. For example, a Form object has a Click event that occurs when the user clicks the form.

Visual Basic enables you to connect code to an event so that the code will run when the event occurs. Visual Basic will, on your demand, create an event procedure for each event that an object recognizes. The code in that event procedure will run when, and only when, that specific event occurs to that specific object.

Visual Basic .NET makes creating an event procedure easy. In this example, create a Windows application as discussed in Module 2. Next, switch to the code view of the form. You have several alternatives to get to code view.

- In Solution Explorer, right-click Form1.vb and choose View Code from the context menu as shown in Figure 3-2.

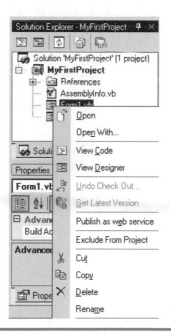

Figure 3-2   Context menu in Solution Explorer

- Select the form in Solution Explorer and choose the View Code button.

- If the form is in designer mode, you can switch to code view by right-clicking the form and choosing View Code or by choosing Code from the View menu.

The code pane has two drop-down boxes. The left one is the class name drop-down box. This box lists the name of all class instances in your form. Currently this box lists only Form1 since there is only one object, the form. The class name drop-down box will list additional names when you add controls to your form. The right drop-down box lists the events that correspond to the name selected in the class name drop-down box.

Listed under and indented to the right of Form1 in the class name drop-down box are:

- **Overrides** This indicates that this procedure overrides an identically named function found in a base class. As will be discussed in later modules, this involves the object-oriented programming principle of polymorphism, in which a function performs different actions depending on which object called it. The data type of the arguments and the return value must exactly match those in the base class procedure.

- **Base class events** These are events of the base class of the Form class.

The event procedure you select depends on what you are trying to accomplish. In the following project, you will be tracking the movement of the mouse over the form. Through code, you will need to determine the current location of the mouse at runtime, since that location will change while the program is running based on the application user's action of moving the mouse. The MouseMove event of the form is the logical event procedure to handle the application user's action of moving the mouse over the form.

Choose Base Class Events from the class name drop-down box and MouseMove from the right drop-down box. The Visual Basic .NET IDE then creates for you the first and last lines of the event procedure, which often is referred to as a *stub*.

```
Private Sub Form1_MouseMove(ByVal sender As Object, _
    ByVal e As System.Windows.Forms.MouseEventArgs) _
    Handles MyBase.MouseMove
End Sub
```

The first line identifies the code as an event procedure, and the last line (End Sub) indicates the end of the event procedure. Actually, the first line is very long, so it is split into three lines to make it more readable. When you split a line of code into multiple lines, you need to advise the compiler that the multiple lines should be regarded as a single line of code. You do so with the line continuation character, which is the underscore (_) preceded by a space.

The first line consists of six parts:

- **Private Sub**   The keyword Sub, which is shorthand for subroutine, indicates that the code concerns a procedure. The keyword Private is explained in later modules, but in essence means that this procedure may be called only from this form module, and not from any other module in your project.

- **Form1**   This identifies by name the specific object to which the event procedure applies. For this example, we will use the default name Form1. However, if your project uses many forms, your code will be more understandable to you and others who read it if you give each form a logical name. Otherwise, you may not recall the difference between Form43 and Form67—and if you as the author cannot recall the difference, think how difficult it will be for another programmer who has to read your code. The name frmMain is a good choice for the main form. The frm prefix indicates the object is a form, and Main indicates it is the main form. This naming convention is a variant of the Hungarian naming convention often used in programming

- **MouseMove**   This identifies by name the specific event to which the event procedure applies. Visual Basic gives the event the name MouseMove, and unlike the name of the object, you cannot change the name of the event.

- The underscore character (_) connects the object name to the event. This underscore character has a different purpose than the one used for line continuation.

- The opening and closing parentheses are used to contain parameters, which are information the event procedure may need. A procedure may have no parameters, one parameter, or many parameters. The MouseMove event has two parameters, separated by a comma. One of these parameters will be used in the following project.

● **Handles MyBase.MouseMove** This indicated that this procedure handles the MouseMove event of the base class of the form.

Writing Code Inside the Event Procedure

While the Visual Basic .NET IDE creates the stub for the event procedure, it will not write the code that goes inside the event procedure. That is your job as the programmer.

An event procedure may contain one line or hundreds of lines of code. Here, however, you need only type one line of code:

```
Debug.Write(e.X & "," & e.Y & " ")
```

When you type this code, the event procedure should read:

```
Private Sub Form1_MouseMove(ByVal sender As Object, _
    ByVal e As System.Windows.Forms.MouseEventArgs) _
    Handles MyBase.MouseMove
        Debug.Write(e.X & "," & e.Y & " ")
End Sub
```

What If You Type the Wrong Code?

Before explaining how this correct code works, you should know what happens if the syntax of your code is incorrect, such as if you misspell or leave out a term. For example, instead of **Write**, you could type **Right** so the code inside the form's event procedure reads:

```
Debug.Right(e.X & "," & e.Y & " ")
```

The term Debug.Right will be underlined with a squiggly line similar to how Microsoft Word highlights misspellings. Additionally, if you hold your mouse over the highlighted code, a ToolTip shows with the warning: "The name 'Right' is not a member of 'System.Diagnostics.Debug'." This warning means that Right is not a method or property of System.Diagnostics.Debug and therefore is not recognized by the compiler.

Undeterred by this warning, you may attempt to build the project, using the Build | Build Solution menu command. The Output window should display with a message box as shown in Figure 3-3, informing you that there were build errors and asking if you want to continue.

3

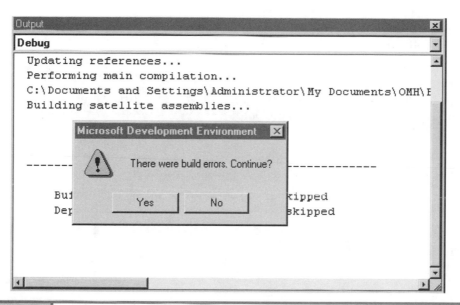

Figure 3-3	Message box warning about build errors

Since the effect of build errors is unpredictable, the prudent course is to just say no to continuing, and instead first fix the problem. The Output window provides further information on the build error and its line number (48 in this case) in the following code:

```
--- Build started: Project: MouseMove, Configuration: Debug .NET ---
Preparing resources...
Updating references...
Performing main compilation...
C:\Documents and Settings\Administrator\My
Documents\OMH\Beginner\ch3\projects\MouseMove\Form1.vb(48) :
error BC30456: The name 'Right' is not a member of
'System.Diagnostics.Debug'.
Building satellite assemblies...
--------------------- Done ----------------------
   Build: 0 succeeded, 1 failed, 0 skipped
```

The Output window is not part of the GUI of your application. Instead, the Output window is part of the Visual Basic .NET IDE. One function of the Output window is for the IDE to provide information to you, including about whether the build was successful. In the next section, you will use the Output window for an additional purpose, which is for your application to give you information about its state.

Tip

If the Output window is not already displayed, you can display it with the menu command View | Other Windows | Output.

Visual Basic .NET also provides you with a Task List, shown in Figure 3-4, which lists the code error as a task you need to resolve.

Tip

If the Task List is not already displayed, you can display it with the menu command View | Other Windows | Task List.

Of course, you still need to correct the code. However, the Visual Basic .NET IDE does give you plenty of warning and information about the syntax error.

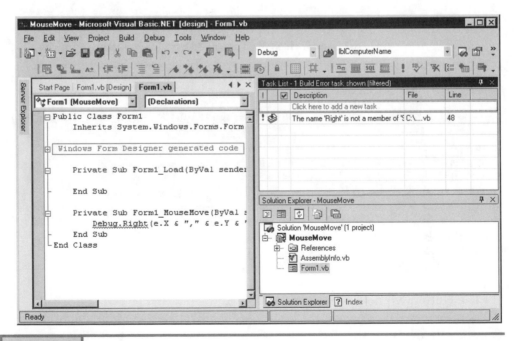

Figure 3-4   Task List

Using the Event Procedure Parameters with the Debug Class

When you run this project—of course, using Debug.Write instead of Debug.Right—the Output window will display the coordinates of the mouse pointer while the mouse is moving over the form. Similar to the concept of coordinates in graphing, mouse coordinates are expressed in two numbers. The first, usually referred to as X, measures a horizontal distance from a reference point. The second, usually referred to as Y, measures a vertical distance from a reference point. In the context of a mouse moving over a form, the reference point is the top left corner of the form. Thus, the X coordinate measures the horizontal distance from the left side of the form, and the Y coordinate measures the vertical distance from the top of the form. The coordinates by convention are expressed with the syntax: X, Y. Therefore, if a coordinate is 60, 77, the mouse is 60 units to the right of the left edge of the form, and 77 units below the top edge of the form. The unit of measurement is a *pixel*, a shortened term for "picture element," a dot that represents the smallest graphic unit of measurement on a screen. Screen resolutions such as 1024×768 are expressed in pixels.

Figure 3-5 shows a number of coordinates in the Output window, though the particular coordinates displayed will vary depending on specifically where over the form the mouse is being moved. Each time the mouse moves, the MouseMove event occurs, and therefore the code inside the event procedure executes.

The code inside the event procedure uses the Write method of the Debug class to output the mouse coordinates to the Output window. The Debug class

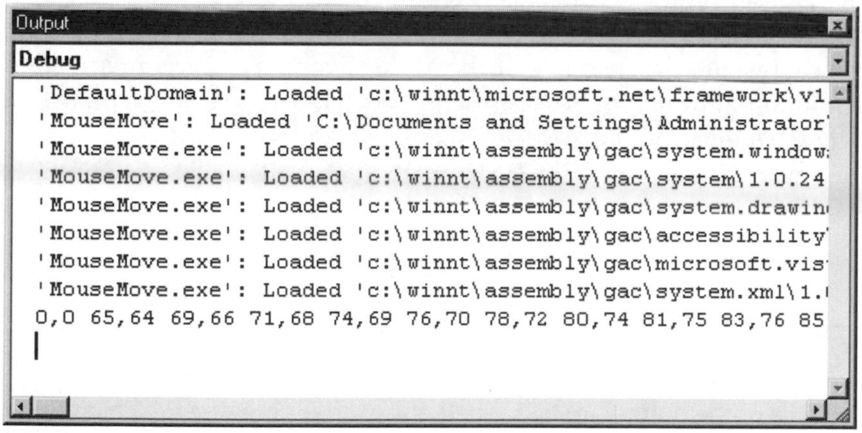

```
Output                                                    [x]
Debug                                                      [v]
  'DefaultDomain': Loaded 'c:\winnt\microsoft.net\framework\v1
  'MouseMove': Loaded 'C:\Documents and Settings\Administrator'
  'MouseMove.exe': Loaded 'c:\winnt\assembly\gac\system.window:
  'MouseMove.exe': Loaded 'c:\winnt\assembly\gac\system\1.0.24
  'MouseMove.exe': Loaded 'c:\winnt\assembly\gac\system.drawin
  'MouseMove.exe': Loaded 'c:\winnt\assembly\gac\accessibility'
  'MouseMove.exe': Loaded 'c:\winnt\assembly\gac\microsoft.vis
  'MouseMove.exe': Loaded 'c:\winnt\assembly\gac\system.xml\1.
  0,0 65,64 69,66 71,68 74,69 76,70 78,72 80,74 81,75 83,76 85
```

Figure 3-5   Output window displaying current coordinates

is built into Visual Basic.NET. Its purpose is to help you debug your code, a concept explained in the following "Ask the Expert."

The Write method of the Debug class writes its parameter to the Output window. For example, the following code would write to the Output window the string "Hello World":

```
Debug.Write("Hello World")
```

In this example, we want to write the mouse coordinates to the Output window as the mouse moves across the application window. You can obtain the mouse coordinates through the second parameter of the MouseMove procedure:

```
ByVal e As System.Windows.Forms.MouseEventArgs
```

This parameter consists of four parts:

- **ByVal**   A keyword that means the parameter represents the value rather than the address of a variable. This is an advanced topic.

- **e**   Holds the value of the parameter.

- **As**   Connects **e** to its data type.

- **System.Windows.Forms.MouseEventArgs**   Designates the data type of the parameter, here an instance of the MouseEventArgs class, which belongs to the System.Windows.Forms namespace.

The MouseEventArgs class has two properties, X and Y, whose values, in the case of the MouseMove event, are the current X and Y coordinates of the mouse. Since e represents the instance of the MouseEventArgs class involved in the current mouse movement, e.X represents the X coordinate of the mouse when the mouse is moved, and e.Y represents the Y coordinate of the mouse when the mouse is moved. Therefore, the Write method of the Debug class outputs e.X and e.Y.

```
Debug.Write(e.X & "," & e.Y & " ")
```

Note

For formatting purposes, a comma (",") and space (" ") are included, and the various parts of the output are tied together by the & operator, which *concatenates*, or combines, parts of a string into one entire string. Don't worry about these details for now; string expressions will be covered in detail in later modules.

1-Minute Drill

- If you did not write an event procedure, does anything happen when an event occurs?
- Can you change the parameters in an event procedure stub?

3

Ask the Expert

Question: What is the difference between a syntax error and a logical error?

Answer: A syntax error prevents your application from building without error. A syntax error is a violation of the spelling or grammar rules of Visual Basic, such as a misspelled or missing word. Using Debug.Right instead of Debug.Write is an example of a syntax error. By contrast, a logical error will not prevent your application from building without error. However, the application may not work as you intended. For example, a logical error could result in 2 + 2 outputting as 22 instead of 4.

Question: What is harder to discover, a syntax error or a logical error?

Answer: No contest; a logical error is much harder to discover. The compiler will flag a syntax error, as shown in the Debug.Right vs. Debug.Write example. However, the compiler will not flag a logical error because the compiler has no way to know what you intend. As far as the compiler knows, since you wrote the code, you must have intended the result of what you wrote.

- If you did not write an event procedure, the event is handled by default. Some default event handlers result in actions visible to you, others do not.
- You cannot change the parameters in an event procedure.

Question: How do I discover the cause of a logical error?

Answer: Through debugging your application. One method of debugging is to use the Output window to output values concerning the application's state. This book will show you many other debugging skills.

Question: Debugging is a strange term. How did it get that name?

Answer: The term "debugging" simply means ridding your program of bugs. A bug is a logical error in your code. The origin of the term "bug" is in dispute. One story is that during the pre-PC era, when mainframe computers ruled the earth, a mainframe was producing illogical results. The programmers checked and rechecked their punch cards but could find no errors. In desperation, they opened up the mainframe. Inside, they saw a small bug fried on one of the circuits.

Viewing and Changing Properties

You often will need to determine the existing value of an object's property or change the value of that property. In programming parlance, you *read* a property to determine its value, and you *write* to a property to change its value. You would read the Text property to obtain the title of a form, and you would write to the Text property to change the title of the form from, for example, Form1 to Godzilla.

You can both read and write to most properties. However, some properties are *read-only*. This means you can access the value of the property, but you cannot change that value. Other properties are *write-once*, which means you can change the property's value, but only once. However, most properties are read and write.

The Name property of a form or control is read-only at runtime. While you can change the value of the Name property at design time, since that property is used by code to refer to the form or control, Visual Basic .NET does not permit you to change that value while your code is running.

An example of a write-once property is an auto-number property, which is used in Microsoft Access. Each object, as it is created, is assigned a unique identifier—the first object 1, the second object 2, and so on. The property is written to when the object is created, but thereafter cannot be changed and is read-only.

You usually have two choices of when you read or write to a property. One choice is at *design time*, which is while you are designing your forms. The Visual Basic .NET IDE provides a user interface, the Properties window, in which you easily can view and change the value of properties at design time. The other choice is at *runtime*, which is when your project is running. With that choice, you use code, which you wrote at design time, to determine or change the value of properties.

Two factors will determine whether you choose to read or write to a property at design time or at runtime. First, you may have no choice. Certain properties may be read or written to at design time but not at runtime, or vice versa. Second, if you do have a choice, then usually you will choose to read or write to a property at design time if the property's value is *static*—that is, it likely will not change during the life of the application. An example would be a property whose value is the total amount of memory installed in your computer. Conversely, usually you will choose to read or write to a property at runtime if the value of the property is *dynamic*—that is, it is subject to change as the application runs. An example would be a property whose value is the amount of memory being used by your computer at a given moment.

This section will show you how to read and write to properties at both design and runtime. After the following section shows you how to add controls to your form, this module will proceed to a project using the Label control, which will provide an example of accessing the same property at both design and runtime, the choice depending on whether the information displayed is static or dynamic.

✓✓ Using the Forms Designer to View and Change Properties

You use the Properties window to view and change a form or control's properties at design time. This section will use the form as the object whose properties are being viewed and changed, but the following discussion would be equally applicable to controls.

You can display the form's Properties windows a number of ways, including by following these steps:

1. Place the form in design mode. In Solution Explorer, you can either right-click Form1.vb and choose View Designer from the context menu, or you can select Form1.vb with your left mouse button and choose the View Designer button.

2. Figure 3-6 shows the form in designer mode. Right-click the form and choose Properties from the context menu to display the Properties window shown in Figure 3-7.

The Properties window has a drop-down box that lists the form and any controls contained in the form. Since you have not yet added any controls to the form, only the form itself is listed.

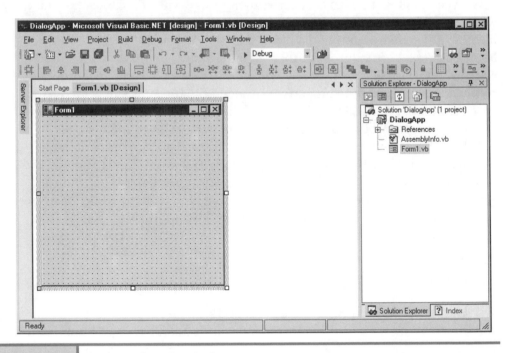

Figure 3-6 Form in designer mode

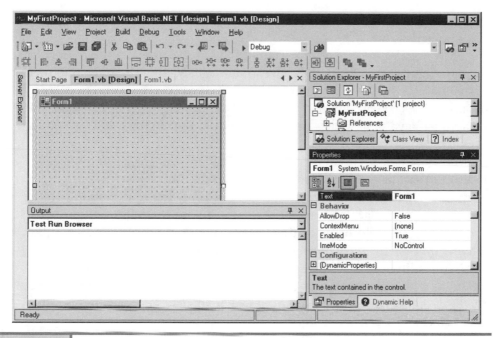

Figure 3-7   Properties window

You should see three enabled buttons below the drop-down box and a multi-column list of information below the buttons. The names and function of the three buttons are:

- **Categorized**   Displays the form or control's design-time properties and events below the button. You can collapse a category to reduce the number of visible properties. When you expand or collapse a category, you see a plus (+) or minus (-) to the left of the category name. Categories are listed alphabetically.

- **Alphabetic**   Displays in alphabetical order the form or control's design-time properties and events.

- **Properties**   Displays the form or control's properties, and for some objects also their events.

Figure 3-7 shows the Properties window after the Categorized button was selected.

The left column displays the names of the properties, and the right column displays their values. Properties have *default values*, the values given to them by Visual Basic .NET in the absence of different directions by you. The reason for default values is that the properties must have *some* value. For example, the form must have some values for its size and location in the event you do not provide values.

You can change the value of a property unless it is grayed-out, which indicates that the property is read-only at design time. The area to the right of the property names has different types of editing fields, depending on the nature of a particular property. For example, the value of the Text property is a literal string. Therefore, the editing field for the Text property is an edit box in which you type the literal string. Since the value of the BackColor property is a color, the editing field for that property is a drop-down box listing various colors. If you click the ellipses (…) in the edit field of another property, Font, the Font dialog box will display, from which you can choose a font, font size, font color, and so on.

Try changing some of these properties. For example, change the BackColor property to another color, such as green. You will notice that the background color of the form changes as soon as you change the color in the Properties window. The Visual Basic .NET IDE usually will give you instantaneous feedback of changes you make through the Properties window. This instant feedback enables you to determine whether you are satisfied with the change without having to run the project.

1-Minute Drill

● How do you view and change the values of properties at design time?

● Should you set properties whose value will be static at design time or runtime?

● You use the Properties window to view and change the values of properties at design time.
● Properties whose value will be static generally should set at design time rather than runtime.

Viewing and Changing Properties Through Code

You also can change a property through code. In this code example, you will change the Text property of the form from the default, Form1, to "Clicked" when the form is clicked. Accordingly, use the Visual Basic .NET IDE to create an event procedure stub for the Click event of the form:

```
Private Sub Form1_Click(ByVal sender As Object, _
    ByVal e As System.EventArgs) Handles MyBase.Click
End Sub
```

You need only type one line of code:

```
Me.Text = "Clicked"
```

This follows the usual syntax for changing the value of a property at runtime:

```
[Object Name].[Property Name] = [Value being assigned]
```

When you type this code, the event procedure should read:

```
Private Sub Form1_Click(ByVal sender As Object, _
    ByVal e As System.EventArgs) Handles MyBase.Click
        Me.Text = "Clicked"
End Sub
```

The title of the form before you run the code is Form1, which is the value of the Form's Text property at design time. When you run this program, and click the form, the title of the form should change to Clicked. You similarly could write code to change the Form's background color, font size, and so on in the Click or another event of the form.

1-Minute Drill

● How do you view and change the values of properties at runtime?

● Should you set properties whose value will be dynamic at design time or runtime?

● You view and change the values of properties at runtime through code.
● Properties whose value will be dynamic generally should be set at runtime rather than design time.

Ask the Expert

Question: You say that properties whose value will be static generally should set at runtime rather than design time. Are there instances in which such properties should be set at runtime?

Answer: Yes. The Form class's Load event, which occurs before a form is displayed for the first time, is a good place to set the initial values of properties, even those that may not change during the application. Your code may even be more readable to another programmer if those values are in code rather than set through the Properties window.

Adding Controls to the Form

The form is a control. It has a specialized purpose, which is to contain other controls. However, its functionality is limited to this purpose. The form does not permit typing of text, listing data, selection of choices, or many other tasks that an application may need to perform. You need other, specialized controls for that additional functionality.

Visual Basic .NET provides numerous specialized controls. For example, the TextBox control enables the application user to type text, such as a password. The Button control cues the application user to click it to perform an action. The ListBox control provides the application user with a list of choices from which to select.

The TextBox, Button, ListBox, and other specialized controls cannot exist on their own. They must be contained, or hosted, in another specialized type of control, a container control. The form is the usual choice for a container control.

Adding controls to a form through code is no easy task. Fortunately, Visual Basic .NET enables you to easily add available controls to a form through the Toolbox.

The Toolbox

Visual Basic uses a Toolbox to display controls that you can add to your form. Figure 3-8 shows the Toolbox, which you can display with the View | Toolbox menu command.

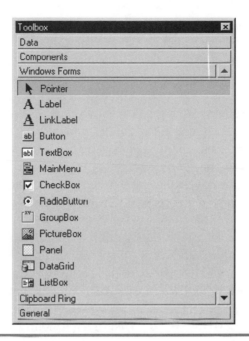

Figure 3-8	Toolbox

The Toolbox has several tabs to organize related items. The Toolbox will always display certain tabs, such as General. The Toolbox will also display other tabs depending on the designer or editor you are using. Since we are using the Windows Forms Designer, the Toolbox also displays the Windows Forms tab.

✓ ┼*Tip* ─────────────

If you do not see the Windows Forms tab, it may be because you are in code view. If so, switch to designer view using the View | Designer menu command and the Windows Forms tab should appear.

The Windows Forms tab contains controls used for Windows Forms. By default, the Windows Forms tab shows the most commonly used controls. However, you may want to change which controls are shown in the Windows Forms tab. You may wish to add a control or, if the tab becomes too crowded with controls, to delete a control from those displayed by the tab.

You use the Customize Toolbox dialog box to change which controls are shown in the Windows Forms tab. Figure 3-9 shows the Customize Toolbox dialog box. You can display the Customize Toolbox dialog box either by the Tools | Customize Toolbox menu command or by right-clicking in the Windows Forms tab area and choosing Customize Toolbox from the context menu.

The Customize Toolbox dialog box has two tabs, COM Controls and .NET Framework Components. Choose the .NET Framework Components tab.

The Name column, as its name suggests, displays the names of available components. There is a check box just before each name. Checking the check box will display the component on the Windows Forms tab when you click OK. Conversely, clearing the check box will remove the component from the Toolbox when you click OK.

You can use the context menu displayed by right-clicking the Toolbox to further customize the appearance of the Toolbox. Figure 3-8 shows the Toolbox in list view. You can toggle the display of the Toolbox between list view and icon view, shown in Figure 3-10, by choosing List View from the context menu. Whether a check mark appears next to List View in the context menu determines whether the Toolbox currently is displayed in list or icon view. The icon view takes up less screen space, but the list view, with its text description of each

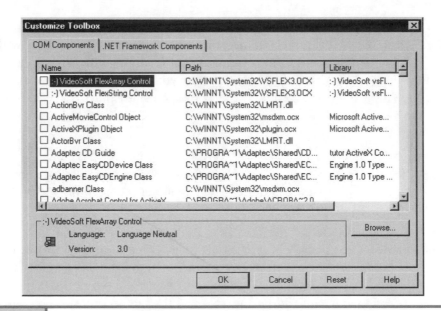

Figure 3-9   Customize Toolbox dialog box

3

Figure 3-10 | Toolbox with icon view

control, may be a better choice until knowing which icons represent which controls becomes second nature for you.

Copying the Control from the Toolbox to the Form

Of course, the reason why you customize the Toolbox is so you can use it more efficiently. You will use the Toolbox primarily to add controls to your form.

You have several methods of adding a control from the Toolbox to your form, including:

- Double-click the control in the Toolbox. The control will appear on the form.

- Click on the control in the Toolbox, drag the control over the form, and then drop the control on to the form.

Use one of these two methods to add the Label control to the form. Figure 3-11 shows the Label control after it is inserted on the form.

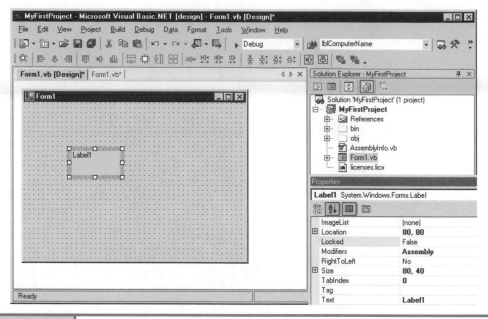

Figure 3-11   The Label control added to the form

Changing the Control's Size and Location Using the Forms Designer

You can use the Forms Designer to change the size or location of the label. Select the label by clicking it. A box then should appear around the label. Figure 3-11 shows the label with that surrounding box.

There are eight small squares on the surrounding box, four at the corners and four halfway between the corners. You can resize the label by holding the mouse over one of these small boxes. The cursor should change to a two-headed arrow. Hold the mouse down and drag it to resize the label.

You can change the location of the label by holding your mouse over the label or the surrounding box. The mouse cursor should change to a four-headed arrow. Click and move the mouse to drag the control to another location.

You can also change the position of the Label control relative to the form by the Format | Center in Form | Horizontally and Format | Center in Form | Vertically menu commands. When a control is selected, it can be moved using the CTRL key plus the arrow keys.

The Code Behind the Scenes

The appearance of the form in the designer is not all that was changed by adding the Label control. Switch to code view (View | Code menu command) and expand the region "Windows Form Designer generated code." The IDE generated additional code for the Label control, starting with:

```
Private WithEvents Label1 As System.Windows.Forms.Label
```

The Label control is an object represented by a Label class. This code declares an instance of the Label control named Label1. The WithEvents keyword specifies that Label1 will respond to the events of a Label control.

System.Windows.Forms.Label indicates that the Label control, like the Form itself, is part of the System.Windows.Forms namespace.

The code then creates an instance of the label:

```
Me.Label1 = New System.Windows.Forms.Label()
```

The Me keyword refers to the current form, Form1. The form is a container for controls such as the Label. Label1 is the name of the Label control being created. The New keyword indicates the creation of an instance of the Label control.

The code then sets various properties of the label, including the label's Name and Text properties:

```
Me.SuspendLayout()
Me.Label1.Location = New System.Drawing.Point(72, 40)
Me.Label1.Name = "Label1"
Me.Label1.Size = New System.Drawing.Size(120, 48)
Me.Label1.TabIndex = 0
Me.Label1.Text = "Label1"
' additional code
Me.ResumeLayout(false)
```

The SuspendLayout method suspends the layout logic of the form as the code still is setting properties of the form's constituent controls. The Label control, like the Form object, has a Text property. However, while a Form object's Text property concerns the text displayed in the form's title bar, the Label control's Text property concerns the text displayed in the label itself. Finally, the ResumeLayout method is called after the code has finished the properties of the form's constituent controls.

1-Minute Drill

- How do you add a control to the Toolbox?
- How do you add a control from the Toolbox to the form?

prj3-1.zip

Project 3-1: Using the Label Control

The Label control has many properties, most affecting its appearance. However, the Label control's most important property is its Text property because the primary role of the Label control is to display text. The text is read-only to the application user, who cannot type on the label to change the label's text. Other controls, in particular the TextBox control, enable the user to type on the control to change the text.

The text displayed by a label usually has one of two purposes, both illustrated by the Print dialog box shown in Figure 3-12.

- Identifying the purpose of another control, such as the Label controls used to identify the purpose of the five drop-down boxes.

- Displaying data, such as the Label controls next to Status, Type, and Where showing the status, type, and location of the printer.

As with the Form object, you can change the value of the Label control's Text property either at design time or through code. You generally will use the Properties window if the purpose of the label is to identify the purpose of another control since that information usually will not change during the running of the application. By contrast, you generally will use code if the purpose of the label is to display data that may change during the running of the application. For example, the Text properties of the labels identifying the status, type, and location of the printer should be set through code because, during the running of the application, the user may change printers, or a printer's status may change, such as going offline.

This project, similar to the earlier example, will display the X and Y coordinates of the mouse pointer while the mouse is moving over the form. This time, however, the coordinates will be displayed on a Label control rather than in the Output window. Figure 3-13 shows what the application looks like

---

- You add a control to the Toolbox using the Components dialog box, which you can display with the Project | Components menu command.
- You add a control from the Toolbox to the form by either double-clicking the control in the Toolbox or dragging the control from the Toolbox and dropping it on to the form.

Displaying data —

Identifying the purpose of another control

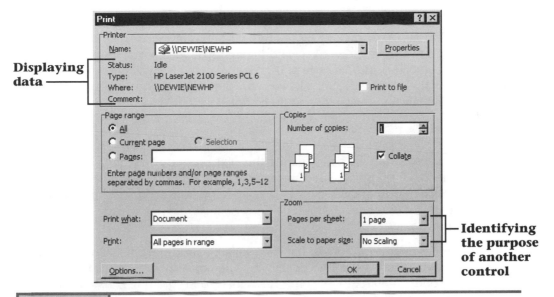

Figure 3 12   Print dialog box

when it is running, though the X and Y coordinates displayed will vary depending on where the mouse is located over the form.

✓✓ Step-by-Step

1. Create a Windows application as described in Module 2.

2. Using the Toolbox, add four labels to the form, one label at a time.

3. Size and align the four labels as shown in Figure 3-13.

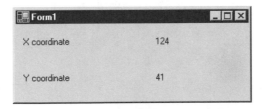

Figure 3-13   The form while the application is running

Tip

You can make labels the same size by selecting all labels involved: click each label while holding down the SHIFT or c key, and then choose the Format I Make Same Size I Both menu command. The size of the label selected last will become the new size of all labels selected. Similarly, you can align the top, bottom, or sides of the controls by selecting the labels and then choosing the Format I Align I Tops (or Middles, Bottoms, Lefts, Centers, or Rights) menu command.

4. Using the Properties window, change the Text properties of the two labels on the left to X Coordinate and Y coordinate, respectively, since the purpose of these labels is to identify the two labels on the right. You are changing the value of this property at design time because it should not change while the project is running.

5. Using the Properties window, change the Name properties of the two labels on the right to lblX and lblY, respectively. The prefix lbl (lowercase L, not the number one) identifies these controls as labels to programmers reading the code. The suffix X and Y notes the purpose of the controls, to display the X and Y coordinates, respectively. It is not so important to rename the two labels on the left as it is unlikely you will need to refer to them in code.

Tip

Be careful when you use prefixes such as lbl that you use a lowercase L and not the number one. Interchanging the two can cause typos that are hard for you to see. Additionally, controls and variable names cannot start with a number.

6. Also using the Properties window, change the default value of the Text properties of lblX and lblY to an empty string so the labels' names won't display in their caption when the project first starts up.

7. Write the following code in the MouseMove event of the form:

```
Private Sub Form1_MouseMove(ByVal sender As Object, _
    ByVal e As System.Windows.Forms.MouseEventArgs) _
    Handles MyBase.MouseDown
        lblX.Text = e.X
        lblY.Text = e.Y
End Sub
```

As in the prior example, the second parameter of the MouseMove procedure is an instance of the MouseEventArgs class. Two of the properties of this class are X and Y, whose values, in the case of the MouseMove event, are the current X and Y coordinates of the mouse. These coordinates are assigned to the Text property of the appropriate Label controls.

Run the project. The information of the X and Y coordinates should change, rapidly, as you move the mouse over the form. The MouseMove event occurs, and therefore the code inside the event procedure executes each time you move the mouse.

Summary

Windows applications are event-driven. The application user's actions create events, and these events drive the order in which things happen in the application. However, without code, the event generally comes and goes as if it never happened. The application takes an action when a user clicks a menu item or selects text only because a programmer wrote code that ran when that event occurred. That code is inside an event procedure, which is how Visual Basic .NET connects an event to the code you want to run when the event occurs.

The purpose of the code inside the event procedure often is to change the application's state, which is reflected in the properties of the application's objects. You can access or change the values of properties of various objects involved in the application both through code at runtime and through the Windows Forms Designer at design time.

The form is perhaps the most important control. However, a single form without controls could only satisfy the requirements of the simplest Windows application. The form does not permit typing of text, listing data, selection of choices, or many other tasks that an application may need to perform. You need other, specialized controls for that additional functionality. Indeed, the form's primary role is to serve as a host, or container, for controls such as menus, toolbars, and buttons, which enrich the GUI of Windows applications. This module showed you how to add controls to your form and to use them in your application.

☑ Mastery Check

1. An event procedure connects an event to the code you want to run when the event occurs.

  √ **A.** True

  B. False

2. If you did not write an event procedure, nothing happens when an event occurs.

  √ **A.** True

  B. False

3. What are inside the parentheses of an event procedure?

  A. Methods

  B. Events

  √ **C.** Parameters

  D. Variables

4. You can change the name of the event in an event procedure stub.

  √ **A.** True

  B. False

5. When you misspell code, such as Debug.Right instead of Debug.Write, it is a:

  √ **A.** Syntax error

  B. Logical error

6. The Debug class is helpful to solve:

  √ **A.** Syntax errors

  B. Logical errors

☑ *Mastery Check*

7. All properties:

   A. Can be read

   B. Can be written to

   ✓ **C.** Have a default value

8. You can use the Properties window to change the value of any property.

   A. True

   ✓ **B.** False

9. When you write to a property at runtime, you use the Properties window.

   A. True

   ✓ **B.** False

10. Properties whose values may change while the application is running are said to be:

   A. Static

   ✓ **B.** Dynamic

11. The Toolbox is used to:

   A. Fix the menu

   B. Add buttons to your toolbar

   ✓ **C.** Add controls to your form

   D. Customize the IDE

3

Part 2

Programming Building Blocks: Variables, Data Types, and Operators

Module 4

Variables and Data Types

The Goals of this Module

- Understand the different data types
- Declare and use variables
- Understand the concepts of variable scope and lifetime
- Declare and use constants

Every day I expectantly wait for my mail, hoping to receive autograph requests from readers of my books. The mail I receive indeed includes many requests for my autograph. Unfortunately, my autograph is requested on checks to pay my mortgage, credit cards, auto insurance, phone service, gas and electricity, and so on.

The banks, insurance, phone, and power companies have thousands of customers. They could not possibly keep track of that many customers using paper and pencil ledgers. Instead, they use computer programs, which harness the computer's unparalleled ability to store and retrieve information and to make computations using that data.

Visual Basic .NET also needs to store and retrieve data to run your projects. Each property of each object in your project stores a value that Visual Basic .NET retrieves when you run your project. For example, the title of a form is stored in the Text property of the Form class, which Visual Basic .NET retrieves and displays in the title bar of the form when you run the project. Similarly, the height of the form is stored in the Height property, which Visual Basic .NET retrieves to display the form at that height.

The data used by Visual Basic .NET may be a number, such as the value of the Height property of the Form class, or alphabetic characters, such as the value of the Text property of the Form class. The data may even be an object. The type of data, whether number, character, or object, is referred to as the data type. This module will explain the different available data types.

While Visual Basic .NET provides you with many built-in properties and parameters as information storage locations, Visual Basic .NET also enables you to create your own information storage locations, called *variables*. This module will show you how and where to create variables.

Finally, certain values never change during the life of the program. These unchanging values are represented by *constants*. This module will show you how to declare and use constants.

Data Types

Visual Basic .NET has a number of predefined data types. You also can create your own data types using structures and classes. However, even those custom data types build on the predefined ones covered in this module.

Visual Basic .NET has three categories of predefined data types:

- **Numeric**   Numbers, whether whole numbers such as 5 or –5, or fractional ones such as –.5, .5, or 5.5

- **Character**   A single character, such as A or 1, or a number of characters, such as those contained in this sentence

- **Miscellaneous**   The remaining data types, Boolean, Date, and Object

Table 4-1 lists and describes the predefined data types.

Type	Bytes	Range
Boolean	2	True or False
Byte	1	0 to 255
Char	2	0 to 65535
Date	8	January 1, 0001 to December 31, 9999
Decimal	12	+/–79,228,162,514,264,337,593,543,950,335 with no decimal point +/–7.9228162514264337593543950335 with 28 places to the right of the decimal smallest non-zero number is +/–0.0000000000000000000000000001
Double (double-precision floating-point)	8	–1.79769313486231E308 to –4.94065645841247E-324 for negative values, 4.94065645841247E-324 to 1.79769313486232E308 for positive values
Integer	4	–2,147,483,648 to 2,147,483,647
Long (long integer)	8	–9,223,372,036,854,775,808 to 9,223,372,036,854,775,807
Object	4	Any type can be stored in a variable of type Object
Short	2	–32,768 to 32,767
Single	4	–3.402823E38 to –1.401298E-45 for negative values, 1.401298E-45 to 3.402823E38 for positive values
String	10 bytes + 2 bytes for every character in the string	0 to approximately 2 billion (2 ^ 31) characters

Table 4-1   Predefined Visual Basic .NET Data Types

Your first task is to memorize everything in this table. Just kidding. As has been stressed in previous modules, memorization is not important; understanding the concepts is. Unless I was looking at this book at the time, I would not know that the highest value of the Long data type is 9,223,372,036,854,775,807. Nor would I need to know that specific piece of information, as I could easily look it up. Rather, it is important to understand the concepts such as variable size and range, to which we now turn.

Bits and Bytes

Table 4-1 has a column for bytes. For those of you who like movies in which the hero has a Transylvanian accent, don't get your hopes up. A byte is not Dracula's contribution to computer programming. Instead, a *byte* is eight *bits*.

A bit is a 1 or a 0. While we usually express numbers in decimal, or base 10, computers often deal with numbers in binary, or base 2. Binary numbers are a series of 1s and 0s; 1 in decimal is 1 in binary, 2 in decimal is 10 in binary, 3 in decimal is 11 in binary, 4 in decimal is 100 in binary, and so on. As discussed in Module 1, early computers essentially were a series of switches, 1 representing on, 0 representing off. While today's computers are far more complex, they still "think" fundamentally in 1s and 0s.

While computers may think in bits, they cannot process information as small as a single bit. The smallest unit of information a computer can process is 8 bits (1 byte). Thus, no data type may be smaller than 1 byte. Many data types are larger than 1 byte. However, the number of bytes is always a whole number. You cannot have a data type whose size is 3.5 bytes because .5 byte, or 4 bits, is too small for the computer to process.

You cannot change the number of bytes required to store a data type. That number is specified by the operating system. Therefore, you do not need to specify the number of bytes. Visual Basic knows from the data type you specify how many bytes are needed.

Though you cannot change the number of bytes required to store a data type, and do not need to specify this information in your code, nevertheless you should know the number of bytes associated with a data type in order to choose the right data type for your programming task.

The number of bytes required to store a data type determines the *range* of that data type. The range is, in essence, the difference between the lowest and highest possible values the data type may hold. The range, in decimal, is 2^n, n equaling the number of bits (not bytes) of the size of the data type. For example, since the size of the Byte data type is 1 byte (which makes sense), or 8 bits, the range of the Byte data type is 2^8, which is 256. As Table 4-1 shows, the lowest possible value of the Byte data type is 0 and the highest is 255. This means the Byte data type, between its lowest and highest possible values, may have 256 different values.

To take another example, since the size of the Integer data type is 4 bytes, or 32 bits, the range of the Integer data type is 2^{32}, which is 4,294,967,296. As Table 4-1 shows, the lowest possible value of the Integer data type is –2,147,483,648 and the highest is 2,147,483,647, which is 4,294,967,296 different values.

The range of the data type is important because you cannot go below or above the range. If you do, you will get an error, referred to as an *overflow error* because you are overflowing the boundaries of the range of the data type. If the compiler can detect the error while building the project, such as assigning the value 256 to a variable of the Byte data type, it will report the error as follows: "error BC30439: This constant expression produces a value that is not representable in type 'Byte'."

If the error only occurs when the project is running, such as the value 256 is assigned by user input to a variable of the Byte data type, your application will come to an inglorious halt, displaying the message box shown in Figure 4-1 reporting an unhandled exception of the type System.OverflowException. In Visual Basic .NET, the term *exception* is synonymous with an error that occurs while your program is running (as opposed to a compile error).

Since an Integer data type can represent any whole number that you can represent with a Byte data type, and has a far greater range, you could avoid, or

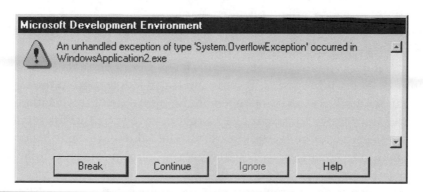

Figure 4-1 | Overflow error while project is running

at least minimize, overflow errors by always using the Integer data type instead of the Byte data type. However, there is a downside to this solution. While the Byte data type only requires 1 byte of memory, the Integer data type requires 4. The difference between 1 and 4 bytes might seem insignificant in these days of computers with acres of hard drive space and wheelbarrows full of RAM. However, consider an application that tracks 1 million bank customers, each of whom has an Age property that could be represented by either the Byte or Integer data type. The choice between the two data types then would not be between 1 and 4 bytes, but instead between 1 million and 4 million bytes. That difference may well have a measurable impact on the performance of your application. Therefore, the general rule is, all other things equal, to use the smallest data type—that is, using the least number of bytes possible without encountering an overflow error.

Tip

Of course, all other things are not always equal. Visual Basic .NET is optimized for the Integer data type for calculations involving whole numbers and for the Single data type for floating point calculations. Part of a programmer's life is tradeoffs, such as between size and speed.

Numeric Data Types

Table 4-2 lists and describes the predefined Visual Basic .NET numeric data types.

These data types fall within one of two categories. The *integral* types represent only whole numbers, whereas the *floating point* types represent numbers with both integer and fractional parts.

Table 4-2 uses *E notation*, which is a helpful and shorter way of expressing numbers with many digits either to the left or right of the decimal point. The letter E in E notation stands for exponent. The number before the E is called the *mantissa*, which is always expressed as having a single digit to the left of the decimal point, and usually several digits on the right side of the decimal point. The number after the E is a power of 10, which may be positive for very large numbers or negative for very small fractions. The value of the expression is the mantissa multiplied by the power of 10. Table 4-3 shows some examples of using E notation.

Table 4-2 also has a column for whether a number is *signed* or *unsigned*.

Type	Bytes	Signed?	Range
Byte	1	No	0 to 255
Decimal	12	Yes	+/–79,228,162,514,264,337,593,543,950,335 with no decimal point, +/–7.9228162514264337593543950335 with 28 places to the right of the decimal; smallest non-zero number is +/–0.0000000000000000000000000001
Double	8	Yes	–1.79769313486231E308 to –4.94065645841247E-324 for negative values, 4.94065645841247E-324 to 1.79769313486232E308 for positive values
Integer	4	Yes	–2,147,483,648 to 2,147,483,647
Long	8	Yes	–9,223,372,036,854,775,808 to 9,223,372,036,854,775,807
Short	2	Yes	–32,768 to 32,767
Single	4	Yes	–3.402823E38 to –1.401298E-45 for negative values, 1.401298E-45 to 3.402823E38 for positive values

Table 4-2 Numeric Data Types

A signed number may be positive or negative; the sign shows which. For example, the signed number 1 can be positive or negative. The negative or – sign (as in –1) indicates the number is negative. The positive or + sign (as in +1) indicates the number is positive, though if the sign is omitted, as in 1, then by convention a signed number is positive.

By contrast, an unsigned number can never be negative. Since an unsigned number always is positive, no sign is necessary.

Number	E Notation	Same as ...
2,900,000	2.9E6	$2.9 * 10^6$
247.91	2.4791E2	$2.4791 * 10^2$
0.00072	7.2E-4	$7.2 * 10^{-4}$

Table 4-3 E Notation

Note

Zero also is an unsigned number. Some may disagree whether zero is a positive number, but the point here is that while the number 1 can be positive or negative, zero cannot be; zero is zero. Therefore, no sign is necessary in the case of zero.

The highest positive value of an unsigned number is 2 to the power of the number of bits of its data type, minus 1. For example, the highest positive value of the Byte data type, whose size is 8 bits, is $2^8 - 1$, or 255. The reason for the minus one is that zero also is included in the range of the Byte data type, so the 256 possible values of the Byte data type are 0 to 255 instead of 1 to 256.

A number being signed reduces its highest positive value, though not its range, by a power of 2. For example, the Short data type is 2 bytes, or 16 bits. However, the largest number is not $2^{16} - 1$, but instead $2^{15} - 1$, or 32,767. The reason is the Short data type is signed, and the sign takes up 1 bit, leaving 15, not 16, for the number. However, the range of the Short data type remains 2^{16}, as there are 2^{16} or 65,536 possible values between –32,768 and 32,767.

Integral Types

Table 4-4 lists the integral data types, which represent whole numbers.

Since integral data types represent whole numbers, they cannot hold fractions, such as 5.9. No error will occur if you attempt to assign a fractional number to an integral data type. However, the fractional number will be rounded off, such as 5.9 becoming 6. Depending on the context, this rounding off could represent a loss of data or result in an inaccurate calculation. If you were writing a program for a bank to track deposits and withdrawals, integral

Type	Bytes	Signed?	Range
Byte	1	No	0 to 255
Integer	4	Yes	–2,147,483,648 to 2,147,483,647
Long	8	Yes	–9,223,372,036,854,775,808 to 9,223,372,036,854,775,807
Short	2	Yes	–32,768 to 32,767

Table 4-4 Integral Data Types

numbers would be a poor choice as all deposits and withdrawals would be rounded off to the nearest dollar!

Of the four integral data types, only the Byte data type is unsigned. The other three all are signed, the only distinction between them being the number of bytes, and therefore the range, of the data type.

Floating Point Types

Table 4-5 lists the *floating point* data types, which represent numbers with both integer and fractional parts. All of the floating point numeric data types are signed.

The Decimal data type supports up to 28 *significant digits*, which in the context of floating point numbers is the number of digits that may be displayed to the right of the decimal point. The Decimal data type is particularly suitable for financial and other calculations that require a large number of digits but cannot tolerate rounding errors.

The Single and Double data types each has a larger range than the Decimal data type. However, the Single and Double data types are more prone to rounding errors because they support fewer significant digits than the Decimal data type. The Single data type supports 7 significant digits, the Double data type 15, as compared to 28 for the Decimal data type.

Type	Bytes	Range
Decimal	12	+/–79,228,162,514,264,337,593,543,950,335 with no decimal point, +/–7.9228162514264337593543950335 with 28 places to the right of the decimal; smallest non-zero number is +/–0.0000000000000000000000000001
Double	8	–1.79769313486231E308 to –4.94065645841247E-324 for negative values, 4.94065645841247E-324 to 1.79769313486232E308 for positive values
Single	4	–3.402823E38 to –1.401298E-45 for negative values, 1.401298E-45 to 3.402823E38 for positive values

Table 4-5   Floating Point Data Types

Character Data Types

Visual Basic provides two *character* data types. *Char* is used for a single character. The character may be a letter of the alphabet, a punctuation mark, a digit, or even a space. *String* is used to contain any number of characters, such as the characters comprising this paragraph. The following "Ask the Expert" discusses how characters are stored by the computer and covers the ANSI/ASCII and Unicode character sets.

A digit often is used for a numeric data type. The phrase "call 911" contains digits, but as characters, not as numbers. As a general rule, a digit appearing as part of a unit that also includes non-numeric characters usually are stored as characters, not numeric data types. Consequently, phone numbers, street addresses, or ZIP codes, though they are comprised mostly of digits, usually are stored as characters.

Tip

As a general rule, you store digits as numbers rather than as a String data type if you intend to perform an arithmetic calculation with the number. You may perform arithmetic calculations based on a person's age, but you are unlikely to do so with street addresses, ZIP codes, or phone numbers.

Miscellaneous Data Types

There are several remaining predefined data types: Boolean, Date, and Object. A Boolean variable is stored as a 16-bit number, but it can only have one of two values, True or False. True and False are keywords used to assign a value to a Boolean variable, such as:

```
Private blnVisible As Boolean
blnVisible = True
```

Many properties have a Boolean data type. For example, in previous projects the ControlBox property of the Form object has been set to False. False is the default value of a Boolean variable.

Since the Boolean data type is essentially a number, 0 is considered False. All non-zero numbers are considered True, though True is stored internally as –1.

Date variables represent a date and time between 12:00 A.M. on January 1, 0001 to 23:59:59 on December 31, 9999 (we should live so long). Date variables are stored internally as Long integers, each increment representing 100 nanoseconds of elapsed time since 12:00 A.M. on January 1, 0001.

Date literals—that is, a value that is literally a date and usually is intended to be assigned to a Date variable—must be enclosed within number signs (#) and be in the format m/d/yyyy, such as:

```
Private SomeDate As Date = #5/4/2001 7:48 AM#
```

The Object data type is the root type in Visual Basic .NET. This means that all other data types and object types are derived from it, either directly or ultimately. It also means that any other data type can be converted to Object. Consequently, you could use Object as the universal data type. This is called *loose typing*, which is not a commentary on the morals of the data type, but rather a reflection of the use of a one-size-fits-all data type (Object) rather than a specific data type. The following example illustrates the flexibility of loose typing:

```
Dim V As Object
V = "17"        ' V contains the 2-character string "17".
V = V - 15      ' V now contains the integer value 2.
V = "H" & V     ' V now contains the 2-character string "H2".
```

Tip

While loose typing is flexible, it also has its drawbacks, not the least of which is it makes your code hard to read. Since every variable is an object, the reader of your code doesn't know if a variable is intended as a number or string. My recommendation is to avoid loose typing, use specific data types, and only use Object when there are good reasons to do so, such as that the appropriate data type may not be known until the project is running.

Default Values

In Module 3 you may have noticed that in the Properties window most of the properties of the form (or control) already had values. These values are referred to as default values—that is, values provided by Visual Basic .NET in the absence of direction from you, the programmer. Default values are necessary. When you first run your project, the form has to have some height, width, background color, and so on, even if you have not specified the values of these properties.

Variables similarly have default values. The default value of all numeric variables, whether whole numbers or floating point, is zero (0). The default value for Boolean is False, which also evaluates to zero. The default value for a String is an empty string, noted by a pair of double quotes with no space in between ("").

Ask the Expert

Question: Why is the size of the Char data type 2 bytes?

Answer: Fundamentally, computers work with numbers, so they store letters and other characters by assigning a number for each one. For the English language, the character set adopted by ANSI (American National Standards Institute) and ASCII (American Standards Committee for Information Interchange) used the numbers 0 through 255 to cover all alphabetical characters (upper- and lowercase), digits and punctuation marks, and even characters used in graphics and line drawing.

Of course, the world does not end at the shores of the United States. In addition to other languages such as German, French, and so on that share our basic alphabet but have characters that do not exist in English, there are languages such as Russian and Chinese with totally different alphabets. Different encoding systems were used to translate the characters in those locations to corresponding numbers.

With the increasing globalization of the economy, software was written for use in many different countries. The problem arose that a number may mean one character under ASCII/ANSI but another character in another country that used a different encoding standard.

The solution was Unicode. Unicode provides a unique number for every character, no matter which language. Of course, 256 numbers (2 ^ 8, or 1 byte) no longer was sufficient for all these characters. Therefore, the size of the Char data type in Visual Basic .NET is 2 bytes (2 ^ 16 or 65,536).

1-Minute Drill

● What is the main difference between the data types Integer and Long, on the one hand, and Single and Decimal on the other?

● What is a signed number?

● Which data type is the parent or root type in Visual Basic .NET?

● Integer and Long data types represent whole numbers, whereas Single and Decimal data types may represent a fractional number.

● A signed number can be a positive or negative number, as opposed to an unsigned number, which can only be positive.

● The Object data type is the root data type in Visual Basic .NET.

Variables

A *variable* is used to store information, or data, similar to how properties are used to store information about an object, such as its background color or size. The data stored in the variable then can be accessed later in the program, similar to how you can access the value of a property of an object.

The primary difference between a variable and a property is that a property is built into Visual Basic .NET whereas you, as the programmer, create a variable. The property also has a built-in role designated by Visual Basic .NET that you cannot change. For example, the Text property of a Form represents the caption of a form. You cannot change that property so it instead represents the width of a form or the name of your best friend. By contrast, a variable represents what you decide it should represent.

4

Option Explicit

You declare a variable by a statement that tells the Visual Basic .NET compiler that you intend to create a variable. Visual Basic .NET by default requires you to declare variables explicitly, but permits you to change this default to declare variables implicitly.

You implicitly declare a variable just by using it, such as:

```
somevariable = 10
```

The compiler assumes *somevariable* is a variable, since it is not otherwise defined as an object or a property, and you are assigning it a value, which is something you could do with a variable. The data type of the variable, since it is not declared, is Object, which, as discussed in the previous section on data types, is the root data type.

By contrast, with explicit declaration, before you assign a value to a variable, you need to declare it, such as the following code excerpt.

```
Dim drQuit As DialogResult
```

The following example will show why you should configure your programs to require explicit declaration. Assume you declare a variable intVar and then misspell it as intJar when attempting to assign a value to it:

```
Dim intVar as Integer
intJar = 10
```

If Option Explicit is on, the attempted assignment to intJar will result in an error when you build your project because intJar was never declared as a variable. If Option Explicit is off, the attempted assignment to intJar will not result in an error when you build your project because, with Option Explicit off, you do not have to declare variables before you use them.

That you receive a build error when Option Explicit is on, but not when it is off, at first may appear to be a good reason to turn Option Explicit off instead of on. However, the opposite is true. For example, if Option Explicit is off, later in your code you may assume intVar has a value of 10. However, it doesn't, because you assigned 10 to intJar, not intVar. Therefore, your code may have a logic error, and result in illogical input, because of your understandable but mistaken assumption that intVar has a value of 10. You will find it very time-consuming, especially in a project with many lines of code, to trace through the code to figure out why your program is providing unexpected and illogical results.

In comparison, if you have turned Option Explicit on, the compiler would catch that you misspelled intVar as intJar. You only would need seconds to correct the code, and the problem would be solved.

Although programmers cringe when the compiler reports errors, the compiler is your friend. You can solve errors much faster if the compiler catches them than if you have to trace through your code to find the error.

Now that I hopefully have convinced you to turn Option Explicit on, you need to know how to do it. One way is through the project's Property Pages dialog box, shown in Figure 4-2.

You can display the project's Property Pages dialog box by right-clicking the project in Project Explorer and choosing Properties. Once the dialog box is displayed, choose Build under Common Properties. The value of Option Explicit in Figure 4-2 is set to On, the default. When Option Explicit is turned on, you must declare values explicitly. Conversely, when Option Explicit is turned off, you may declare variables implicitly, though you still can (and should) declare them explicitly if you want.

You also can set the value of Option Explicit through code. All you need to do is simply make the Option Explicit statement the first line in your module, before the class declaration:

```
Option Explicit On ' or Off
Public Class Form1
    Inherits System.Windows.Forms.Form
```

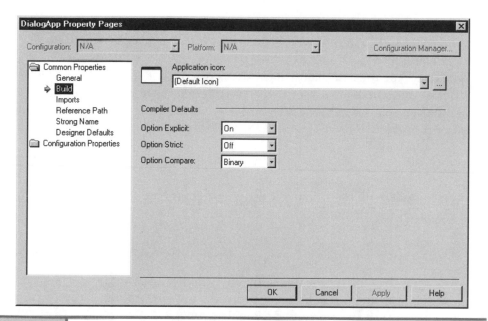

Figure 4-2   The Project Property Pages dialog box

Note that the Option Explicit statement really is the first line of code before the class declaration. You make the Option Explicit statement the very first line of code by choosing the project name from the left drop-down box in code view and Declarations from the right or Methods drop-down box.

Option Strict

Another option shown in Figure 4-2 is Option Strict. Option Strict, like Option Explicit, requires you to declare a variable. Unlike Option Explicit, Option Strict also requires that when you declare a variable, you explicitly declare its data type.

Like Option Explicit, you can turn Option Strict on or off. If you turn Option Strict on, you do not need to include an Option Explicit statement in your code, because an Option Strict On statement includes turning Option Explicit on. Instead, you would put the Option Strict On statement in the same place that you would have placed the Option Explicit On statement:

```
Option Strict On
Public Class Form1
    Inherits System.Windows.Forms.Form
```

Option Strict is off by default, as shown in Figure 4-2. Even if it is off, you still may, and should, declare the data type of the variable. If you do not, the compiler will choose a data type for you.

The data type the compiler will choose if you do not specify the data type depends on the value you assign to the variable. For example, the compiler will cast a variable assigned a whole number as an Integer, as in the following statement:

```
Dim x = 100
```

The compiler will cast a variable assigned a fractional number as a Double, as in the following statement:

```
Dim x = 100.1
```

Of course, the data type assigned by the compiler may not be the best choice for your program and can even cause problems in your program. Therefore, you should turn Option Strict on and declare data types.

Turning Option Strict on also affects type conversions, which are discussed in Module 5.

Scope

The location in code view that you wrote the Option Explicit On statement is called the *module level*. The term *module* refers to the code module. Each form in your project has its own code module. The area is called module level because it is above, or before, the event procedures in the code module.

You can declare a variable either at module level or inside a procedure. A variable declared inside an event procedure is also referred to as a *local variable*.

You declare a variable at module level by placing the declaration right after the class declaration that follows the Option Explicit statement:

```
Option Explicit On
Public Class Form1
   Inherits System.Windows.Forms.Form
   Private x As Integer
```

You declare a variable inside an event procedure by placing it between the title of the event procedure and the End statement:

```
Private Sub Form1_Click(ByVal sender As Object, _
   ByVal e As System.EventArgs) Handles MyBase.Click
      Dim x As Integer = 0
End Sub
```

If you declare a variable at module level, you can refer to it (such as by assigning it a value) anywhere in that module. You also may be able to refer to it outside the module, depending on the access specifier you use. That issue will be covered in the next section.

By contrast, if you declare a variable inside an event procedure, you can only refer to it inside that event procedure. If you refer to the variable outside the event procedure (such as in another, separate event procedure), if Option Explicit is on, you will get an error just as if you had attempted to use the variable before declaring it.

The reason is that the scope of the variable is limited to the event procedure in which it is declared. If it is referred to outside the event procedure, it is as if the variable was not declared at all. In other words, the variable can be "seen" only inside the event procedure.

Declaring a variable inside an event procedure does not necessarily mean that it can be seen throughout the event procedure. In Visual Basic .NET, a variable declared inside a block, such as an If ... End If block has scope only inside the block, and is not accessible outside the block. Therefore, in the following code, the variable x can be referenced throughout the entire event procedure. However, since the variable z was declared inside the If ... End If block, it can only be referenced inside that block. Thus, while the assignment $z = 2$ inside the block is legal, the assignment $z = 6$ outside the block will cause a build error because, outside the block, z is an undeclared variable:

```
Private Sub Form1_Click(ByVal sender As Object, _
   ByVal e As System.EventArgs) Handles MyBase.Click
      Dim x As Integer = 0
      If x = 0 Then
        Dim z As Integer
        z = 2
      End If
      x = 3
      z = 6 ' error - undeclared variable
End Sub
```

Given the potential for compiler errors resulting from variables being referenced outside their scope, the temptation is to give your variables the widest possible scope. This is not a good idea. Indeed, as a general rule, you should give your variables the least amount of scope possible. Every place in your program from which a variable can be accessed is another place from which the value of that variable can be changed, and changing the value of a variable overwrites (destroys) the previous value of the variable. If the variable can be accessed only from one location in your program, you only need to check the code in that one place to confirm that the new value is valid and whether you should first save the old value before overwriting it. If the variable can be accessed from ten locations in your program, you need to check the code in all ten places, as well as determine the effect of any interrelationships between the ten locations. In other words, the less amount of scope the variable has, the easier your task as a programmer. Why make your job harder than it has to be?

Of course, there will be circumstances in which a variable should have module-level scope, or even greater scope. The point is that, in determining whether to declare a variable in an event procedure or module level, do not declare it at module level unless you can justify to yourself why you need to do so.

Declaring a Variable

You declare a variable to create it and specify its name and data type. The syntax of declaring a variable is:

```
[Access Specifier] [Variable Name] As [Data Type]
```

This syntax will be analyzed from right to left. The reason is that access specifiers are the most complex of the three syntax elements, and having already covered the other two syntax elements will permit code illustrations of the access specifiers.

Choosing a Data Type

You do not need to declare the data type of the variable if Option Strict is off, as it is by default. If you do not declare the data type of the variable, then, as discussed in the preceding section on Option Strict, the compiler will choose a data type.

You can choose any data type you want when you declare a variable. Logically, you should choose a data type that is appropriate for the purpose of the variable. For example, if the variable represents someone's name, you likely will choose String as the data type.

Naming the Variable

The primary limitations on how you can name a variable are that the variable name:

- Cannot begin with any character other than a letter of the alphabet (A–Z or a–z) or an underscore (_)

- Cannot contain embedded spaces, such as *My Variable,* or punctuation marks other than the underscore character (_), such as ?,.\(/)

- Cannot be longer than 255 characters

- Cannot be the same as a keyword, such as *Private* or *Public*

- Cannot have the same name as the name of another variable of the same scope

4

The last limitation merits brief discussion. You can declare a module-level variable and declare a variable of the same name inside an event procedure because they do not have the same scope. However, as your mother may have told you, just because you can do something doesn't mean you should do it. While the compiler easily can differentiate between two variables of the same name but with different scope, you or some other programmer reading your code may find it confusing that you have given two variables the same name.

Besides these limitations, you can name a variable pretty much whatever you want. However, it is a good idea to give your variables names that are meaningful.

For example, more than once while assisting students in my college's computer science lab, I have been asked by a student to help them figure out why their program is not working the way it should. I then review their code and see that they have declared variables such as var1, var2, var3 through var17 (or TextBox1 through TextBox13). When I ask the student what var9 is, they furrow their brow, frown, and finally answer, "I don't remember. What do you think?" I then respond with my teenage daughter's favorite saying: "I have no clue." And I don't, as I then continue with one of *my* favorite sayings: "I may be psycho, but I'm not psychic."

Actually, my reaction is relatively benign compared to what you may find when programming in the real world. If you really want to see psychotic behavior, tell an overworked, stressed-out programmer tasked to review your code, "I don't remember. What do you think?" when they ask you what var9 is.

In order to preserve your sanity, or possibly your life in the case of enraged fellow programmers, I recommend you use a naming convention when naming your variables. A naming convention simply is a consistent method of naming variables (as well as objects, methods, and so on). A number of naming conventions are in use, and it is not particularly important which naming convention you use. What is important is that you use one and stick to it.

Naming conventions already have been used in previous modules, in particular for naming controls. The control name starts with a prefix that indicates its control type, followed by a name that suggests its purpose. For example, a command button whose purpose is to cancel could be named cmdCancel.

Similarly, variables may be named with a prefix (usually all lowercase and consisting of three letters) that indicates its data type, followed by a word, first letter capitalized, that suggests its purpose. For example, in Module 4, the variable that was assigned the return value of the Show method of the MessageBox class was named drQuit. The prefix dr indicated that its data type was DialogResult (since that was the data type of the return value of the Show method), and the name Quit indicated that its purpose was to determine if the user has chosen the Quit button in the message box.

Tip

If you need more than one word to describe the variable's purpose, you should combine the word into one word (since you cannot have embedded spaces) but capitalize the first letter of each word, such as drDidUserQuit.

Table 4-6 lists prefixes for the various data types.

You also can take this naming convention one step further by adding to the prefix a letter that indicates the scope of the variable, such as m for module level or l (that is a small L, not the number 1) for local. While this makes the name more informative, it also makes it more complex. How you evaluate this tradeoff is up to you. There is no one correct naming convention. However, you should decide on a naming convention and use it consistently.

Type	Prefix
Boolean	bln
Byte	byt
Char	chr
Date	dat
Decimal	dec
Double	dbl
Integer	int
Long	lng
Object	obj
Short	sht
Single	sng
String	str

Table 4-6   Prefixes for the Data Type of Variables

4

Access Specifiers

The available access specifiers, and their effect, depend on whether the variable is local or module level.

Local Variables   If you declare a variable inside an event procedure, you would use the access specifier Dim or Static.

The scope of a variable is identical under Dim or Static; since you are declaring the variable inside an event procedure, you will not be able to access the variable outside the event procedure. Instead, the difference between Dim and Static concerns the lifetime of the variable.

To illustrate the difference between Dim and Static, start a new Windows application and create the following event procedure for the Click event of the default form:

```
Private Sub Form1_Click(ByVal sender As Object, _
    ByVal e As System.EventArgs) Handles MyBase.Click
        Dim i As Integer
        Debug.Write(i)
        i = i + 1
End Sub
```

The first time you click the form, the Debug window will display 0 (zero), the default value of an integer variable. The integer variable i then is incremented (increased) by 1 so it now has the value 1, and the procedure ends. However, the second time you click the form, the Debug window still will display 0. Indeed, no matter how many times you click the form, the Debug window will still display 0.

The variable i does not remember its previous value of 1. The reason is that the lifetime of the variable is limited to the running of the procedure. Each time the procedure ends, the variable i is destroyed. Each time the procedure is called (by clicking the form), a new variable i is created, with the default integer value of 0.

Now change the code so you use the keyword Static instead of Dim, the event procedure code now being:

```
Private Sub Form1_Click(ByVal sender As Object, _
   ByVal e As System.EventArgs) Handles MyBase.Click
      Static i As Integer
      Debug.Write(i)
      i = i + 1
End Sub
```

As with the Dim keyword, the first time you click the form, the Debug window will display 0 since that is the default value of an integer variable, the integer variable i then is incremented by 1, and finally the procedure ends. However, the second time you click the form, the Debug window will display 1, the third time, 2, the fourth time, 3, and so on. The variable i does "remember" its previous value. The reason is that the lifetime of a variable declared as Static is not limited to the running of the procedure, but rather, it survives as long as your application continues running.

Static variables can be very useful. For example, they often are used to keep track of a running total.

Module-Level Variables   If you declare a variable at module level, you could use the access specifiers Dim, Private, Public, or Shared.

There is no difference between Private and Dim. The Dim keyword is a carry-over from previous versions of Visual Basic. While the compiler doesn't care, I recommend you use Private instead of Dim for module-level variables (you cannot use Private for local variables, as discussed in the preceding section) as the Private keyword is more descriptive of the effect of the access specifier, which is to keep the variable private to the module in which it is declared, and hidden from other modules of the project or other code components that may be accessing your project.

A variable declared with the Private access specifier can be accessed only within its module. Any attempt to reference in one form a variable declared as Private in another form will result in a build error. This is similar to the build error that occurs, as discussed in the preceding section on scope, when you attempt to reference outside an event procedure a variable declared inside an event procedure.

You still could access in one form a variable declared as Private in another form, though not directly by reference to the variable, but instead by using a Property Get procedure, as shown in Module 10.

By contrast, a variable declared with the Public access specifier can be accessed throughout the project, not just in its own module. Thus, a variable declared as Public in the first form could be referenced in the code of the second form, using the syntax:

```
[FormObjectVariable].[Variable Name]
```

This will be illustrated in Project 4-1.

As stated in an earlier section, "Scope," as a general rule, it's recommended that you should give your variable the least amount of scope possible, since the fewer places in your program a variable can be affected, the less code you need to check to determine if the variable is being affected in a manner you did not intend. For similar reasons, you should declare module-level variables as Private instead of as Public unless you can justify to yourself why the variable may need to be accessed outside the current module. Of course, there may be circumstances in which the variable will need to be accessed outside of the current module. The point is that you make a conscious decision that such is the case before using the Public keyword.

The Shared keyword does not affect the scope of the variable. By default, a Shared variable is Private, but you can make a Shared variable Public simply by putting the Public keyword in front of the Shared keyword, as in:

```
Public Shared [variable name] As [Data Type]
```

Instead, the effect of the Shared keyword is that it is a class variable instead of an instance variable.

By way of example, assume you place two buttons on a form, for OK and Cancel, respectively. Both buttons come from the same Button class, and each is a separate instance of that class. While each button has a Text property, the value of one button's Text property is "OK" whereas the value of the other button's Text property is "Cancel." Changing the text of one button would not affect the text of the other button. The value of a property of one instance of a button is separate and independent of the value of the same property in the other instances of the Button class.

By contrast, when a variable is Shared, each separate instance of the class does not have a separate copy of the variable. Instead, all of the instances of the class share one copy, which is held by the class itself. Therefore, a change to the value of the shared variable affects all instances of the class.

Declaring Multiple Variables

You can declare more than one variable of the same data type on a line. Instead of:

```
Private strName As String
Private strSSN As String
Private strAddress As String
```

You can declare them all in one line:

```
Private strName, strSSN, strAddress As String
```

The syntax is almost the same as declaring a single variable, but instead of one variable name, you have several, delimited (separated) by commas.

However, the multiple variables declared on one line must be of the same data type. If you have several integer variables, declare them on a different line than you declare the multiple string variables.

prj4-1.zip

Project 4-1: Shared Variable

One common use of a shared variable is to keep track of the number of class instances that have been created. This project will use one form, the main form shown in Figure 4-3. The main form has three integer variables, Private, Public, and Shared, which start at 0, and are increased by 1 each time the

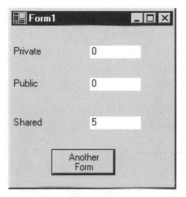

| **Figure 4-3** | The main form after the dialog box has been displayed five times |

Another Form button is clicked. Clicking the Another Form button creates another instance of the main form, and displays the values of that new instance's Private, Public, and Shared integer variables. Figure 4-3 shows the main form after the Another Form button has been clicked five times. While the values of the Private and Public variables are still at 0, the Shared variable's value is 5. The reason is that the Private and Public variables are instance variables. In the new instance of the main form, these variables were initialized at 0 and never increased since the button on the newly created form was never clicked. By contrast, the shared variable is a class variable, so the increase in its value in the default form is shared by all other instances of the main form.

Step-by-Step

1. Create a Windows application, which creates the first form by default.

2. Declare the following module-level variables in the Declarations section of the form:

```
Private intPrivate As Integer = 0
Public intPublic As Integer = 0
Shared intShared As Integer = 0
```

This code declares three variables, which are Private, Public, and Shared. All three are of the Integer data type. Each variable is explicitly initialized to 0. The term *initialize* refers to assigning a value to a variable at the same time it is declared.

Tip

Technically, it is not necessary to initialize integer variables to 0 since, by default, the value of integer variables is 0. However, initializing the variables does make your code more readable, especially to someone else who may not recall the default value of integer variables.

3. Create a Button control in the form and set its properties as follows:

- **Name** btnShowForm2
- **Text** Show Form2

4. Create six labels on the form with the properties indicated in Table 4-7, after which the form should resemble Figure 4-3 (without the values 0, 0, and 5).

5. Write the following code for the Click event of btnAnotherForm:

```
Private Sub btnAnotherForm_Click(ByVal sender As
System.Object, _
    ByVal e As System.EventArgs) Handles btnShowForm2.Click
        Dim frm As New Form1()

        intPrivate = intPrivate + 1
        intPublic = intPublic + 1
        intShared = intShared + 1
        lblPrivateValue.Text = frm.intPrivate
        lblPublicValue.Text = frm.intPublic
        lblSharedValue.Text = frm.intShared
End Sub
```

The first line of code inside the event procedure creates another instance of the main form. The next three lines of the code increase the value of each variable by 1. The last three lines of the code inside the event procedure update the labels with the corresponding values of the Private, Public, and Shared variables in the newly created form, represented by the object variable frm.

6. Run the code. Every time you click the Another Form button, the value of the Shared variable increases by 1. However, the values of both the Private and Public variables remain at 0.

Name	Text	BackColor	Purpose
lblPrivateText	Private	Control	Identifies label to right as displaying the value of the Private variable
lblPrivateValue	(Blank)	HighlightText	Displays the value of the Private variable
lblPublicText	Public	Control	Identifies label to right as displaying the value of the Public variable
lblPublicValue	(Blank)	HighlightText	Displays the value of the Public variable
lblSharedText	Shared	Control	Identifies label to right as displaying the value of the Shared variable
lblSharedValue	(Blank)	HighlightText	Displays the value of the Shared variable

Table 4-7 Label Controls in the First Form

The Public and Private variables are instance variables. The labels reflect the values of these variables in the newly created form. In the new instance of the main form, these variables were initialized at 0, and never increased since the button on the newly created form has never been clicked.

By contrast, the Shared variable is a class variable, so the increase in its value in the default form is shared by all other instances of the main form.

1-Minute Drill

● What does it mean when Option Explicit is on?

● What does it mean when Option Strict is on?

● When Option Explicit is on, you have to declare variables before you use them.
● When Option Strict is on, you have to declare the data type when you declare the variable.

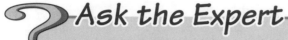

Ask the Expert

Question: Where does the word *explicit* in Option Explicit come from?

Answer: The term *explicit* in Option Explicit comes from the fact that Option Explicit, when on, forces you to explicitly declare all variables in that module.

Question: Are there circumstances when a programmer should not use Option Explicit?

Answer: No. It always is a good idea to explicitly declare all variables in that module. Implicitly declaring variables only saves you one line of code, but can greatly increase your time and trouble in finding errors that your compiler would have caught had you turned Option Explicit on.

Constants

A *constant* is similar to a variable, except that a constant's value cannot change during the life of the program. The syntax of a constant is also similar to a variable:

```
[Access Specifier] Const [Constant Name] As [Data type] = [literal]
```

For example, the following statement declares a constant MAXSCORE whose value, 100, is the maximum score that can be obtained on a test:

```
Public Const MAXSCORE As Integer = 100
```

The main difference in syntax between declaring a variable and declaring a constant is that a constant must be initialized when it is declared. The reason is that the value of a constant cannot be changed after it is declared. Therefore, a constant must be given a value when it is declared.

Additionally, the value to which the constant is initialized must be a literal. A literal is a value that literally is as it states. For example, 111 and "Jeff Kent" both are literals. By contrast, a variable is not a literal. Consequently, a constant cannot be initialized to the value of a variable.

Other than the requirement that a constant must be initialized when it is declared, the rules governing declaring a variable apply to declaring a constant. Constants, like variables, can be declared within an event procedure or at module level. The effects of Private, Public, and Option Strict also are the same. The available data types for constants are slightly more limited than for variables. A constant may be a Boolean, Byte, Char, Date, Decimal, Double, Integer, Long, Short, Single, or String data type; it cannot be an Object data type.

Since a constant's value cannot be changed during the life of the program, even attempting to assign a value to a constant will cause an error:

4

```
Public Const MAXSCORE As Integer = 100
MAXSCORE = 200 'error
```

The naming convention for constants is different than for variables. By convention, constant names are entirely descriptive, uppercase, and use an underscore character to separate words, as in BRIBE_PAID. Unlike variables, by convention, constant names do not have a prefix to specify data type and scope.

While it is important to know how a constant differs from a variable and how to declare constants, an important issue remains: why use constants at all? The reason is that constants make your code easier to read and maintain.

For example, you may have pleasant (or unpleasant) memories of the mathematical symbol π, or pi (pronounced "pie"), which is used in formulas such as calculating the area of a circle (area = πr^2). The value of π can be carried to an infinite number of digits, so by necessity it must be rounded off at a given number of digits. Since the value of π does not change, it is a good candidate for a constant, where it could be declared as:

```
Public Const PI As Decimal = 3.141592653589793
```

Thus, in code, instead of using:

```
3.141592653589793 * (r * r)
```

you can use:

```
PI * (r * r)
```

Using the constant PI makes your code easier to read. The reader of your code may not grasp that 3.141592653589793 refers to π. The reader is far more likely to understand what PI refers to. Additionally, using the constant PI makes errors less likely. If you have to refer to π throughout your code, it is far easier on you to type PI ten times than to type 3.141592653589793 ten times. It would be easy to mistype 3.141592653589793, and the compiler would not flag your mistyping as an error as long as you typed some legal number. Typing PI is easy, and once you properly declare the constant, even if you mistype it later in your code as PIE, the compiler would catch the error as long as you had turned Option Explicit on.

While constants are useful for values such as π that never will change, constants perhaps are even more useful for values that someday may change. For example, we've all paid sales tax on purchases. Assuming the tax rate is 8 percent, the amount of the tax is price * .08. Thus, throughout your code for a store, you may have calculations such as:

```
[price variable] * .08
```

One day, the government decides to increase the sales tax to 8.25 percent. Now you have to find all of the places in your code where you referred to the sales tax rate and change all of those references from .08 to .0825. This not only is a pain, but prone to error.

Alternatively, you could have declared the sales tax rate as a constant:

```
Public Const SALES_TAX_RATE As Single = .08
```

Thus the tax calculation in your code would be:

```
[price variable] * SALES_TAX_RATE
```

Then, when the government increases the sales tax to 8.25 percent, you only have to make the change in one place in your code, and you're done.

```
Public Const SALES_TAX_RATE As Single = .0825
```

Thus, the value of a constant may change by your changing the code at design time. A constant's value just cannot change during the life of the program. While the sales tax may change from year to year, it will not change while the program is running, so you can, and should, use a constant for the sales tax rate.

1-Minute Drill

- Do you have to initialize the value of a constant when you declare it?
- Can the value of a constant be changed while the program is running?
- Can you change the value of a constant when modifying the code at design time?

Summary

Data is stored in different data types. These types primarily are either numeric, such as 3, 3.5, and −35, or character-based, such as Jeff, J, and 911. There are other data types, such as Boolean (which is True or False), Date, and Object, which is the root type of all other data types.

Visual Basic .NET uses many built-in properties and parameters as information storage locations. You may also create your own information storage locations, called variables. You should, and if Option Explicit is on you must, declare variables before you use them. The scope and lifetime of variables depends on how and where they are declared.

Finally, certain values never change during the life of the program. These unchanging values are represented by constants, which are declared similarly to variables. However, unlike variables, constants must be initialized when they are declared, and their value cannot thereafter change during the lifetime of the program.

- Yes.
- No.
- Yes.

☑ *Mastery Check*

1. Which data type is the root type in Visual Basic .NET?

    A. Single

    B. Double

    C. Object

    D. String

2. Which type of number may be negative?

    A. Signed

    B. Unsigned

3. Which data type may hold the value 3.5?

    A. Long

    B. Single

    C. Byte

    D. Boolean

4. You have to declare variables before you use them when Option Explicit is off.

    A. True

    B. False

5. You have to declare the data type of a variable when:

    A. Option Explicit is on

    B. Option Explicit is off

    C. Option Strict is on

    D. Option Strict is off

✓ Mastery Check

6. You have to initialize the value of a constant when you declare it.

   A. True

   B. False

7. You can change the value of a constant:

   A. While the program is running

   B. In code view at design time

   C. Never

4

Module 5

Assignment and Arithmetic Operators

The Goals of this Module

- Understand the assignment operator
- Know type conversions, their risks, and the effect on them of Option Strict
- Understand the arithmetic operators
- Use the InputBox function and its return value

While variables must be declared, since the purpose of a variable is to store a value, a declared variable without an assigned value is like me in my high school dating years: all dressed up but no place to go. While there was no solution for my problem, assigning a value to a variable or property is easy using the *assignment operator*.

There is overlap among data types. For example, there are several data types that may represent a whole number. Intentionally or unintentionally, you may attempt to assign a value of one data type to a variable or property of a similar but not identical data type. To perform this assignment, the data type of the value must be converted to that of the variable or property. This is called *type conversion*, and it can be tricky. This module will show you the rules involved.

Computers, in addition to being able to store vast amounts of data, can calculate far faster and more accurately than we can. You harness the computer's calculating ability using *arithmetic operators*.

Finally, instead of supplying in code the value that is assigned, you can use the InputBox function to enable your application's user to input that value, which then, as the *return value* of the function, is assigned to a variable or property.

The Assignment Operator

The equal sign (=) performs double duty in Visual Basic .NET. This section will examine its role as an assignment operator. The section later in this module on logical operators will discuss its other role, comparing two values for equality.

Tip

An operator, such as the equal sign, that is used for two different purposes is referred to as *overloaded*. Visual Basic .NET has other overloaded operators, several of which are discussed in this module.

The assignment operator was used in Module 2 to change the title of the form from the default Form1 to the more interesting Godzilla, using the following statement:

```
Me.Text = "Godzilla"
```

The syntax of the assignment operator is:

```
[Variable or Writable Property] = [Value]
```

This entire code statement, using an assignment operator, is referred to as an *assignment statement*.

The Location of the Assignment Statement

You can assign a value to a variable at the same time as you declare the variable:

```
Dim intVar As Integer = 1
```

In that event, the assignment can take place wherever the variable is declared, at the module level or procedure level.

By contrast, if you assign a value to a variable after you declare it, the assignment statement can only be within a procedure, regardless of whether you declared the variable at module level or procedure level. The following module-level assignment statement will generate a compiler error that a declaration is expected:

```
intVar = 22 'compiler error at module-level
```

Similarly, an assignment to a property must take place within a procedure.

The Left Side of the Assignment Statement

The purpose of the assignment statement is to change the value of the variable or property on the left side of the assignment statement. Therefore, the variable or property on the left side of the assignment statement must be capable of having its value changed.

A variable is always capable of having its value changed. Indeed, that is the very quality that distinguishes the variable from its close relation, the constant. For this reason, a constant cannot be on the left side of an assignment statement. Similarly, a literal, such as 123 or "Jeff", cannot be on the left side of an assignment statement.

Unlike variables, not all properties are writable—that is, capable of having their values changed. For example, all controls, including a form, have a CanSelect property, a Boolean value that indicates whether the control can be selected, usually with a mouse. Most controls can be selected, though a few cannot, such as labels and progress bars. A form object's CanSelect property is

5

True because you can select a form by, for example, clicking its title bar. Therefore, the following code outputs True to the Debug window:

```
Private Sub Form1_Load(ByVal sender As System.Object, _
    ByVal e As System.EventArgs) Handles MyBase.Load
        Debug.Write(Me.CanSelect)
End Sub
```

However, Visual Basic .NET, not the programmer, determines whether a control can be selected. Therefore, you cannot change the value of the CanSelect property by code, such as by inserting the following statement in the preceding event procedure:

```
Me.CanSelect = False
```

The compiler will object that the CanSelect property is read-only. You can access its value, as we did with the Debug.Write statement, but you cannot change its value.

If the property is writable, the syntax of assigning a value to it is similar to assigning a value to a variable, except that properties have to be preceded with the object variable representing the instance of the class to which the property belongs. This was the syntax used in Module 2 and again at the start of this module to change the title of the form from the default Form1 to Godzilla:

```
Me.Text = "Godzilla"
```

The Right Side of the Assignment Statement

The value on the right side of the assignment statement can be anything that has a value, including a property, a variable, a constant, a literal, or an expression, such as 2 + 2. The only qualification is that, in the case of a property, it must be capable of being read at runtime, which almost always is the case. Properties often may not be writable at runtime, but they almost always are readable at runtime.

The issue that arises with the right side of the assignment statement is that the property, variable, constant, literal, or expression must be of a data type that can be stored in the variable or property on the left side of the assignment statement. This is not an issue if the data types on the two sides of the assignment statement are identical. However, if they are not, then whether the assignment will be successful depends on (1) whether the value can be converted to the data type of the property or variable and, if so, (2) whether Visual Basic .NET will permit the conversion.

For example, the Form class has a Visible property, having a Boolean data type, which indicates whether or not the form is visible (True) or hidden (False). This property is writable, so you could assign True or False to it, as in:

```
Me.Visible = False
```

This assignment clearly will work because both the value and the property have the same data type, Boolean.

The following assignment statement would not work because you cannot convert the string "Jeff" into a Boolean. Instead, you would get an unhandled exception (error) that a cast (conversion) from the string "Jeff" to Boolean is not valid:

```
Me.Visible = "Jeff"
```

In contrast, while the following assignment statements also do not use the same data type on both sides of the assignment statement, the value can be converted, or cast, to the Boolean data type of the Visible property:

```
Me.Visible = 22
Me.Visible = "True"
```

As discussed in Module 4, a non-zero number (such as 22) will be evaluated as True. Similarly, the string representation of True ("True") will be evaluated as True when an assignment is attempted to a Boolean property or variable. Therefore, the remaining issue is whether Visual Basic .NET will permit the conversion. The rules Visual Basic .NET follows in allowing (or not allowing) a conversion are analyzed in the very next section, "Type Conversions."

1-Minute Drill

- Can any property be on the left side of an assignment statement?
- Can an assignment statement be located at module level?

- No. The property must be writable.
- Yes, but only if the assignment is combined with the declaration of a variable.

Type Conversions

As discussed in the preceding section on the assignment operator, a type conversion is the conversion of a value from one data type to another. Such conversions are possible because many values can be stored by more than one data type. For example, the value 1234567891 can be stored in either an Integer or Long data type.

This section will discuss the two types of conversions, *widening* and *narrowing*, and how conversion may be performed *implicitly* or *explicitly*.

A widening conversion is when a value is being converted to a data type with a larger number of bits, such as from an Integer (32 bits) to a Long (64 bits). Conversely, a narrowing conversion is when a value is being converted to a data type with a smaller number of bits, such as from a Long (64 bits) to an Integer (32 bits).

Widening conversions may be performed implicitly—that is, Visual Basic .NET performs the conversion automatically, and you do not need to write any extra code to accomplish the conversion. An implicit conversion also is referred to as coercion or type coercion.

Narrowing conversions may be performed implicitly only if Option Strict is off. If Option Strict is on, narrowing conversions must be performed explicitly— that is, with required extra code, specifically a *type conversion keyword*.

That's a lot of concepts for a few paragraphs! Let's examine with examples how these concepts work, and why you should turn on Option Strict.

Widening Conversions

The value 1234567891 can be stored in either an Integer or Long data type. The following code assigns that value to both an Integer and a Long variable, using a type conversion:

```
Dim MyBigInt As Integer = 1234567891
Dim MyReallyBigInt As Long = MyBigInt
```

The first line of code assigns the value 1234567891 to a 32-bit Integer variable MyBigInt. This presents no problem, since 1234567891 is within the range of an Integer variable. However, the second line of code attempts to assign the value that is stored in the 32-bit Integer variable MyBigInt to a 64-bit Long variable MyReallyBigInt. This does present a problem, as a 64-bit value, not a 32-bit value, should be assigned to a 64-bit variable. Therefore, to accomplish this assignment, Visual Basic .NET first converts the 32-bit value stored in MyBigInt to a 64-bit value before it is assigned to the 64-bit variable MyReallyBigInt. MyBigInt remains a 32-bit Integer variable; only the value assigned to MyReallyBigInt is converted from 32 bits to 64 bits.

This is a widening conversion since it increases the number of bits, here from 32 to 64 bits. A widening conversion is considered safe in terms of the risk of losing data. For example, any value stored in a 32-bit Integer variable also can be stored in a 64-bit Long variable.

Table 5-1 shows the standard widening conversions.

Narrowing Conversions

The following code is the converse of the above code. A value that is represented by the 64-bit Long variable MyReallyBigInt is being assigned to the 32-bit Integer variable MyBigInt, again using a type conversion:

```
Dim MyReallyBigInt As Long - 1234567891
Dim MyBigInt As Integer = MyReallyBigInt
```

The first line of code assigns the value 1234567891 to a 64-bit Long variable MyReallyBigInt. So far so good, since 1234567891 is within the range of a Long variable. However, the second line of code attempts to assign the value that is stored in the 64-bit Long variable MyReallyBigInt to a 32-bit Integer variable

Data Type	Widens to Data Types
Byte	Short, Integer, Long, Decimal, Single, Double
Short	Integer, Long, Decimal, Single, Double
Integer	Long, Decimal, Single, Double
Long	Decimal, Single, Double

Table 5-1   Widening Conversions

MyBigInt. This does present a problem, as a 32-bit value, not a 64-bit value, should be assigned to a 32-bit variable. Therefore, to accomplish this assignment, Visual Basic .NET first converts the 64-bit value stored in MyReallyBigInt to a 32-bit value before it is assigned to the 32-bit variable MyBigInt. MyReallyBigInt remains a 64-bit Long variable; only the value assigned to MyBigInt is converted from 64 bits to 32 bits.

This is a narrowing conversion since it decreases the number of bits, here from 64 to 32 bits. Narrowing conversions are not considered safe because not all values that can be stored in a data type with a larger number of bits also can be stored in a data type with a smaller number of bits. The Integer data type only has a range of -2,147,483,648 to 2,147,483,647, compared to a range of -9,223,372,036,854,775,808 to 9,223,372,036,854,775,807 for the Long data type. An error could result if the value of the Long variable was outside the -2,147,483,648 to 2,147,483,647 range of the Integer variable. For example, the following code will result in an overflow error because the 2147483648 value being assigned is higher (by 1) than the high range of an Integer variable:

```
Dim MyReallyBigInt As Long = 2147483648
Dim MyBigInt As Integer = MyReallyBigInt
```

The adverse consequences of a narrowing conversion are not limited to an overflow error. Another risk is a loss of data. Consider the following code:

```
Dim MyDouble As Double = 142.72
Dim MyInt As Integer = MyDouble
```

The integer variable MyInt cannot store the value 142.72 that is assigned to it because integer variables can store only whole numbers. Therefore, the value being assigned to MyInt would be rounded off to 143, resulting in a loss of data. The significance of this loss of data depends on the context of the code. If the code is calculating a person's weight, whether that weight is 142.72 or 143 pounds probably is not important (though I'd prefer to have my weight rounded down rather than up). However, if you are writing code for a program that tracks deposits and withdrawals in a bank, rounding off is a very bad idea, and likely will result in your salary being rounded off to zero.

The standard narrowing conversions include the reverse directions of the widening conversions in Table 5-1. Conversions in either direction between Boolean and any numeric type also is considered narrowing. However, the narrowing conversion that is not intuitively obvious, yet very common in code, is in either direction between String and any numeric type, Boolean, or Date. For example, the Shared variable example earlier in this module employed the following code:

```
lblPrivateValue.Text = frm.PrivateValue
lblPublicValue.Text = frm.intPublic
lblSharedValue.Text = frm.ShareValue
```

Each of the three lines of code involves a narrowing conversion. The value being assigned is an Integer variable, and the property to which the value is being assigned has a String data type. These conversions work because a number also can be represented as text.

The Effect of Option Strict on Conversions

Option Strict has no effect on widening conversions. Since widening conversions are considered safe, whether Option Strict is on or off, Visual Basic .NET permits widening conversions to be performed implicitly. Visual Basic .NET performs the conversion automatically; you do not need to write any extra code to accomplish the conversion.

Option Strict in contrast has a major effect on narrowing conversions. Since narrowing conversions are potentially unsafe, if Option Strict is on, the compiler will not permit narrowing conversions. In the narrowing conversion example used in the previous section:

```
Dim MyReallyBigInt As Long = 1234567891
Dim MyBigInt As Integer = MyReallyBigInt
```

The compiler would report the following build error: "Option Strict disallows implicit conversions from Long to Integer."

This result only will occur if Option Strict is on. If Option Strict instead were off, the compiler would not complain about a narrowing conversion. Of course, then there would be a risk of loss of data or a runtime error.

Type Conversion Keywords

As the compiler message states, Option Strict disallows implicit narrowing conversions. Option Strict does allow explicit narrowing conversions, however.

A narrowing conversion is performed explicitly using a type conversion keyword. Performing an explicit conversion also is known as *casting* an expression to a given data type. This code uses the type conversion keyword CInt to convert, or cast, the value of MyReallyBigInt to an integer before assigning that value to the integer variable MyBigInt:

```
Dim MyReallyBigInt As Long = 1234567891
Dim MyBigInt As Integer = CInt(MyReallyBigInt)
```

Table 5-2 lists the type conversion keywords.

Type Conversion Keyword	Converts an Expression to Data Type	Allowable Data Types of Expression to be Converted
CBool	Boolean	Any numeric type, String, Object
CByte	Byte	Any numeric type, Boolean, String, Object
CChar	Char	String, Object
CDate	Date	String, Object
CDbl	Double	Any numeric type, Boolean, String, Object
CDec	Decimal	Any numeric type, Boolean, String, Object
CInt	Integer	Any numeric type, Boolean, String, Object
CLng	Long	Any numeric type, Boolean, String, Object
CObj	Object	Any type
CShort	Short	Any numeric type, Boolean, String, Object
CSng	Single	Any numeric type, Boolean, String, Object
CStr	String	Any numeric type, Boolean, String, Object
CType	Type specified following the comma (,)	When converting to an elementary type, the same types as allowed for the corresponding conversion keyword

Table 5-2 Type Conversion Keywords

The syntax of using the type conversion keywords, with the exception of CType, is:

```
[Property or variable] = [Type conversion keyword](value being converted)
```

Thus, in the preceding example, the type conversion keyword CInt converts (casts) the value stored in the Long variable MyReallyBigInt to an integer before assigning that value to the integer variable MyBigInt:

```
Dim MyBigInt As Integer = CInt(MyReallyBigInt)
```

The CType keyword uses a different syntax, with two arguments instead of one. The first argument is the expression to be converted, and the second argument is the destination data type or object class. The following example demonstrates the use of CType:

```
Dim MyBigInt As Integer = CType(MyReallyBigInt, Integer)
```

Using a type conversion keyword will not prevent overflow errors or rounding off. For example, the use of the CInt type conversion keyword does not prevent the overflow error discussed above with the same code absent the CInt type conversion keyword:

```
Dim MyReallyBigInt As Long = 2147483648
Dim MyBigInt As Integer = CInt(MyReallyBigInt)
```

Thus, the type conversion keyword does not alter the necessity that the source value (the value being assigned) must be valid for the destination data type. An error will occur if the value being assigned is not valid for the destination data type, such as here where the value being assigned is too large for the destination Integer data type, resulting in an overflow error.

Instead, the value of Option Strict is to ensure that you are aware that you are performing a narrowing conversion. In other words, it is Visual Basic .NET's way of asking you, as the programmer: "Are you really, really sure you want to do this?" If you do not use a type conversion keyword, the compiler will report to you an error such as: "Option Strict disallows implicit conversions from Long to Integer." If you do use a type conversion keyword, you necessarily must be aware that you are performing a narrowing conversion, for otherwise there would be no reason for you to use a type conversion keyword.

5

By contrast, without Option Strict, you could be performing narrowing conversions without knowing it. The result would be a runtime error, or perhaps even worse, a logic error in your code caused by, for example, rounding off.

While beginning programmers shy away from tools such as Option Strict that increase the number of build errors reported by the compiler, experienced programmers know that the compiler is the programmer's friend (perhaps only friend in the case of some antisocial programmers I know). You can resolve a build error quickly. By contrast, it might take you many hours to hunt down a logic error caused by an unwise narrowing conversion, assuming you even realize there is a problem at all.

1-Minute Drill

● What effect does Option Strict have on type conversions?

● What does a type conversion keyword permit you to do when Option Strict is on?

Arithmetic Operators

Visual Basic .NET can do your arithmetic, and since a computer is involved, much faster and more accurately than any human could! Even better, the code is relatively easy to write, as the syntax for arithmetic is quite similar to how you would write the arithmetic calculation on paper.

Table 5-3 lists and describes the arithmetic operators:

Table 5-3	Arithmetic Operators

● Option Strict prohibits implicit narrowing conversions.
● A type conversion keyword permits you to explicitly perform narrowing conversions when Option Strict is on.

These arithmetic operators are binary—that is, they need two operands, one on the left of the operator, one on the right. For example, in the arithmetic operation:

```
2 + 3
```

2 and 3 are operands, and + is the operator.

The addition, subtraction, and multiplication operators work exactly as you would expect them to. The exponent operator may not be as familiar, but its use is simple: 4 squared (4^2) is expressed as 4 ^ 2.

+Note

An operator that is unary (that requires only one operand, to its right) is the minus or negative sign (–), as in –33. The – sign is yet another overloaded operator, since it serves both as the unary negation operator and the binary subtraction operator.

The Division Operators

The operators /, \, and Mod all involve division. However, one important difference among the three division operators is how they report the results of the division.

Using as an example 11 divided by 4, the result is 2, remainder 3. The 2 is the quotient, the 3 the remainder. The results reported by the three division operators are:

- The / operator reports the entire result, 2 remainder 3, expressed as a decimal, 2.75.

- The \ operator reports only the quotient, 2, and drops the remainder. Integer division does not round off. If it did, 11 \ 4 would be 3, not 2.

- The Mod operator reports only the remainder, 3, and drops the quotient.

Another important difference among the three division operators concerns the data types of their operands. The operands in floating point division may be either whole or floating point numbers. By contrast, the operands in integer division should be whole numbers.

Note

The consequences of using a floating point operand in integer division depend on whether Option Strict is on. If an operand in integer division is a floating point number, it first must be coerced to a whole number before integer division can be performed. If Option Strict is on, such implied coercion is not permitted, and a compiler error results. If Option Strict is off, the implied coercion of the floating point number to a whole number is permitted. However, given the limitations of a whole number, one result of the conversion is that the part of the number to the right of the decimal point is lost. Thus, 3.93 \ 2.2 would be regarded as 3 \ 2, with the result of 1.

The Mod operator, like floating point division, may have as operands either whole or floating point numbers. If both operands are whole numbers, the remainder necessarily will be a whole number. For example, 10 Mod 5 is 0, and 10 Mod 3 is 1. However, if either operand is a floating point number, the remainder may be a floating point number. For example, 12.5 Mod 5 is 2.5.

You often will use the / operator, which performs floating point division, as it provides you with the complete result. However, the Change Machine Project later in this module shows you that the \ and Mod operators can also be very useful.

Tip

Programmers sometimes find it difficult to recall which of the / and \ operators is floating point division and which is integer division. One mnemonic is that the / is a forward slash, and the "f" in forward corresponds to the "f" in floating point. Another memory technique is that the / looks more like the normal arithmetic division operator than does the \, and floating point division produces the normal quotient and remainder result of arithmetic division, whereas integer division does not.

Concatenation Operators

Concatenation is a fancy term for combining or appending two strings. For example, concatenating the strings "Jeff" and "Kent" results in the string "Jeff Kent". Indeed, concatenation is a form of addition involving strings.

The following example uses the & operator to concatenate a string literal ("Hello ") and a string variable (myStr) to output "Hello World":

```
Dim myStr As String
myStr = "World"
Debug.Write("Hello " & myStr)
```

The concatenation operator is required to append the string stored in the string variable myStr to the string literal. String literals are enclosed in double quotes, but string variables are not. If you enclose the string variable in double quotes, Visual Basic .NET will interpret the reference to myStr as a string literal, and the output will be the name of the variable, not its value. For example, the following example will output "Hello myStr".

```
Dim myStr As String
myStr = "World"
Debug.Write("Hello myStr")
```

The concatenation operator permits you to separate the part of the "Hello World" string that is a string variable from the part that is the string literal.

Similarly, you can use the concatenation operator to separate a literal from an expression. The following statement will output "2 squared is 4":

```
Debug.Write("2 squared is " & 2^2)
```

Similarly, the following statement will output "2 squared is 4 and 2 cubed is 8":

```
Debug.Write("2 squared is " & 2^2 & " and 2 cubed is " & 2^3)
```

You also can use the + operator to concatenate strings. The + operator is overloaded, performing both addition of numbers and concatenation of strings. I recommend that you use only the & operator, and not the + operator, to concatenate strings. Using the + operator for string concatenation as well as numerical addition creates an ambiguity whether addition or string concatenation is intended or will occur.

Type Conversions Revisited

The operands for arithmetic operations must evaluate as a number. Though some of my students may want to subtract me from their lives, Visual Basic .NET cannot perform the subtraction "Jeff" −"Kent".

Nevertheless, Visual Basic .NET will try to perform arithmetic on string representations of numbers. If Option Strict is off, the following code will write 5 to the Debug window:

```
Private Sub Form1_Load(ByVal sender As System.Object, _
    ByVal e As System.EventArgs) Handles MyBase.Load
        Dim str1 As String = "22"
        Dim str2 As String = "17"
        Debug.Write(str1 - str2)
End Sub
```

This code will not compile only if Option Strict is on, instead generating the compiler error "Option Strict disallows implicit conversions from String to Double." To perform the subtraction, Visual Basic .NET must first convert the string representation of the number to an actual number, and as discussed in Module 4, Option Strict does not permit this narrowing conversion to be performed implicitly.

Of course, Option Strict will permit explicit narrowing conversions, so the following statement would work:

```
Debug.Write(CInt(str1) - CInt(str2))
```

The + operator presents a special case. Even with Option Strict turned on, the overloaded nature of the + operator may cause you to use it inadvertently for concatenation when your intention is addition. For example, assuming you have a calculator program, clicking the add button (cmdAdd) will add the numbers entered in two text boxes (txtFirstNum and txtSecondNum) and display their sum in a label control, lblResult:

```
Private Sub cmdAdd_Click(ByVal sender As System.Object, _
    ByVal e As System.EventArgs) Handles cmdAdd.Click
        lblResult.Text = txtFirstNum.Text + txtSecondNum.Text
End Sub
```

If you enter 2 in the two text boxes and click the add button, the result is that 2 + 2 = 22, not 4. Since the operands are strings rather than numbers, Visual Basic .NET assumes you intend to concatenate the two strings, as opposed to adding the two numbers represented by the strings. This likely is not the result you intended.

Note

Turning Option Strict on would not have prevented this problem. There is no type conversion. The data types on both sides of the assignment statement are the same, String.

The lesson is to use type conversion keywords to the extent necessary to ensure that the operands are numbers when you intend additions and strings when you intend concatenation.

Operator Precedence

Does the arithmetic expression 2 + 3 * 4 equal 20 (by performing addition before multiplication) or 14 (by performing multiplication before addition)? One and only one of these two answers can be correct. Rules of operator precedence are necessary to determine which of the two answers is correct.

Table 5-4 lists the order of precedence, or priority, among arithmetic operators:

Thus, 2 + 3 * 4 equals 14, because multiplication has a higher priority than addition and therefore is performed first.

Since multiplication and division have equal priority, when both operators occur together in an expression, priority goes from left to right, so whichever of the two operators is on the left is performed before the one on the right. The same left-to-right priority rules applies between addition and subtraction.

Priority	Operator(s)	Description
1	^	Exponent
2	–	Unary negation operator (not subtraction)
3	*, /	Multiplication and floating point division
4	(	Integer division
5	Mod ()	Modulus (remainder)
6	+, –	Addition and subtraction, string concatenation (+)
7	&	String concatenation (&)

Table 5-4 Operator Precedence

5

Parentheses can be used to override the order of precedence and force some parts of an expression to be evaluated before others. Operations within parentheses are always performed before those outside the parentheses. Within parentheses, however, operator precedence is maintained.

Combining Arithmetic and Assignment Operators

The following code, in the third statement, adds the values of two variables, intFirst and intSecond, and assigns the sum, 7, to one of the variables, intFirst:

```
Dim intFirst As Integer = 5
Dim intSecond As Integer = 2
intFirst = intFirst + intSecond
```

Addition is performed before assignment because all arithmetic operators have precedence over the assignment operator.

The third statement can be shortened and still accomplish the same result:

```
intFirst += intSecond
```

The combined arithmetic/assignment operators are shown in Table 5-5.

Operator	Use	Statement
+=	Incrementing	intSomeVariable += 1
-=	Decrementing	intSomeVariable -= 1
*=	Doubling	intSomeVariable *= 2
/=	Halving	intSomeVariable /= 2
\=	Halving	intSomeVariable \= 2
^=	Squaring	intSomeVariable ^= 2
&=	Appending	strName &= strAppendName

Table 5-5   Arithmetic/Assignment Operators

These shorthand arithmetic/assignment operators make your code more readable. The statement

```
intSomeVariable += 1
```

is more apparent as incrementing than the statement:

```
intSomeVariable = intSomeVariable + 1
```

The Mod operator has no corresponding arithmetic/assignment operator because the remainder of a variable divided by itself is always 0.

1-Minute Drill

- What is the purpose of the concatenation operator?
- Which arithmetic operator returns the remainder of division?

prj5-1.zip

Project 5-1: Change Machine Project

My mother was not above using a change machine to distract cranky or mischievous young grandchildren. The youngsters poured hundreds of pennies into the top of the machine, and watched with fascination (fortunately children are easily fascinated) as the machine sorted the pennies into amounts of change which could be taken to the bank and exchanged for dollars, quarters, and so on. The grandchildren were motivated as well as fascinated, since guess who got to keep the quarters?

The entire code for this project will be placed in the Load event of the form and write the result to the Debug window. However, you could easily modify this project to display the result in label controls on the form.

- The concatenation operator combines two strings.
- The Mod arithmetic operator returns the remainder of division.

Step-by-Step

1. Create a Windows application, which creates the first form by default.

2. Insert the following code in the Load event of the default form:

```
Private Sub Form1_Load(ByVal sender As System.Object, _
    ByVal e As System.EventArgs) Handles MyBase.Load

    Dim intDollars, intQuarters, intDimes, _
        intNickels, intLeftover As Integer
    Const DOLLAR As Integer = 100
    Const QUARTER As Integer = 25
    Const DIME As Integer = 10
    Const NICKEL As Integer = 5
    intLeftover = CInt(InputBox("Enter total number of pennies"))
    Debug.Write("Change for " & intLeftover & " pennies " & vbCrLf)
    intDollars = intLeftover \ DOLLAR
    intLeftover = intLeftover Mod DOLLAR
    intQuarters = intLeftover \ QUARTER
    intLeftover = intLeftover Mod QUARTER
    intDimes = intLeftover \ DIME
    intLeftover = intLeftover Mod DIME
    intNickels = intLeftover \ NICKEL
    intLeftover = intLeftover Mod NICKEL
    Debug.Write("Dollars - " & intDollars & vbCrLf)
    Debug.Write("Quarters - " & intQuarters & vbCrLf)
    Debug.Write("Dimes - " & intDimes & vbCrLf)
    Debug.Write("Nickels - " & intNickels & vbCrLf)
    Debug.Write("Pennies - " & intLeftover & vbCrLf)
End Sub
```

3. The program starts with an input box, shown in Figure 5-1. Type a positive number in the edit area of the input box and then click OK. If, for example, you enter 364 in the input box, the Debug window should output:

```
Change for 364 pennies
Dollars - 3
Quarters - 2
Dimes - 1
Nickels - 0
Pennies - 4
```

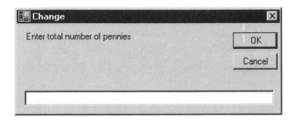

Figure 5-1   The input box

Now let's analyze the code.

The InputBox Function and Return Value

The input box is a form, but one built into Visual Basic .NET, so you do not have to design it. Instead, you display it by calling the InputBox function, and dismiss it by clicking its OK or Cancel button.

The syntax of the InputBox function is:

```
[Variable or Writable Property] = _
   InputBox( [Prompt], [Title], [Default Value]
```

Table 5-6 lists and describes the parameters of the InputBox function:

Name	Required?	Purpose
Prompt	Yes	The text informing the user what to enter, such as "Enter total number of pennies" in Figure 5-1.
Title	No	The title of the input box. If omitted, the name of the project is used as the title.
Default Value	No	The value displayed in the input box when it is first displayed. If omitted, nothing (an empty string) is displayed.

Table 5-6   Parameters of the InputBox Function

The InputBox function works quite similarly to the previous examples of assignment statements. The function is called on the right side of an assignment statement. The user then has the opportunity to enter text. If the user clicks the OK button, whatever the user types is assigned to a variable or writable property on the left side of the assignment statement. If instead the user clicks the Cancel button, whatever the user typed is ignored, and an empty string ("") is assigned to a variable or writable property on the left side of the assignment statement.

Tip

The project code assumes that the user typed a positive integer in the input box and clicked the OK button. In a real-world project you would want to write error-checking code to make sure that the user did so before continuing with code that makes that assumption. The next module, on control structures, will show you how.

The essential difference between the InputBox function and the previous examples of assignment statements is that in the prior examples the right side of an assignment statement was a value, whereas here it is a function. However, the difference is only one of timing. When the execution of the code reaches the statement that calls the InputBox function, the first thing that happens is that the *InputBox* function executes, displaying the input box. When the user clicks either the OK or Cancel button, dismissing the input box, a value is returned to the right side of the assignment statement, either the entered text if the OK button was clicked or an empty string if the Cancel button was clicked. That return value, referred to as the *function return value*, is assigned to a variable or writable property on the left side of the assignment statement. Therefore, the end result of calling the InputBox function is that a value on the right side of the assignment statement is assigned to a variable or writable property on the left side of the assignment statement, just as in the previous examples.

Caution

Assuming the user typed a positive integer in the input box and clicked the OK button, what the user typed is not really a number, but rather a String representation of a number. This distinction is important if Option Strict is on, since you then cannot implicitly assign the String value on the right side of the assignment statement to the Integer variable on the left side of the assignment statement. Instead, you first need to convert the value to an Integer, using the CInt type conversion function discussed in Module 5.

The Algorithm

The next step is to convert the pile of pennies into neater stacks of dollars, quarters, dimes, nickels, and pennies.

When you divide the number of pennies (stored in intLeftover) by 100 (the number of pennies in a dollar), the quotient is the number of dollars in the pennies, and the remainder is the number of pennies left over. Integer division provides you with the quotient but no remainder, and the Mod Operator provides you with the remainder:

```
intDollars = intLeftover \ DOLLAR
intLeftover = intLeftover Mod DOLLAR
```

5

The quotient, representing the number of dollars in the pile of pennies, is stored in the variable intDollars for later retrieval. The remainder is stored in intLeftover, which will be used for further division. The constant DOLLAR is used instead of 100 to make the code more readable.

Next, you follow the same procedure, this time using QUARTER (a constant with the value 25) as the divisor and intLeftover (the number of pennies left after the division by DOLLAR) as the dividend (the number to be divided):

```
intQuarters = intLeftover \ QUARTER
intLeftover = intLeftover Mod QUARTER
```

The same process is followed, using DIME as the divisor, then NICKEL. The number of pennies left over after division by NICKEL cannot be converted into any higher change, so there is no need for further division. There is no need for a separate variable intPennies (similar to intNickels, intDimes, and so on) because intLeftover stores the number of pennies left.

The concept of dividing the total number of pennies by the number of pennies in a dollar, storing the quotient in a variable holding the number of dollars, and dividing the remainder by the number of pennies in a quarter and so on, is known as an algorithm. An algorithm is a step-by-step logical procedure for solving a problem. You frequently will need to create and implement algorithms. Implementing algorithms in your code is computer programming. Creating algorithms is a skill that can be developed from any field that requires analytical thinking, including but not limited to mathematics as well as computer programming.

Outputting the Result

The final step is to output, here to the Debug window using the Write method of the Debug object, the number of total pennies and then the number of constituent dollars, quarters, and so on, with the output (assuming an input of 364) of:

```
Change for 364 pennies
Dollars - 3
Quarters - 2
Dimes - 1
Nickels - 0
Pennies - 4
```

The first step is to output the total number of pennies:

```
Debug.Write("Change for " & intLeftover & " pennies" & vbCrLf)
```

The final part of the argument to the Write method, vbCrLf, is a constant built into Visual Basic .NET that outputs a carriage return and line feed, so the following output will be on a new line rather than continue on the same line.

As discussed earlier in this module, this code uses the concatenation operator to separate literal strings "Change for" and "pennies" from the variable intLeftover and the constant vbCrLf. The literal string "Change for" also has a space built in so there is a space before the following output of the number of pennies.

Note

The output of the total number of pennies must be output before that total is divided by DOLLAR, QUARTER, and so on. The reason is that the value of the variable storing the total number of pennies, intLeftover, will be overwritten by the division, so instead of storing the total number of pennies, it will store the total number of pennies left over from the division.

The output of the total number of dollars, quarters, and so on follows the same technique of using the concatenation operator to separate literal strings from the variable and the constant, such as:

```
Debug.Write("Dollars - " & intDollars & vbCrLf)
```

Summary

The purpose of a variable is to store a value. You use the assignment statement to assign a value to a variable or property. The left side of the assignment statement is either a variable or a writable property. The right side of the assignment statement is any value, which can be a variable, constant, expression, literal, or a readable property.

Many of the data types overlap. For example, there are several data types that may represent a whole number. Often intentionally, but sometimes unintentionally, you will be converting a value between similar but not identical data types. This conversion between data types is called type conversion. Widening conversions, those that increase the number of bits, also are permitted. By contrast, if Option Strict is turned on, narrowing conversions, those that decrease the number of bits, are only permitted if done explicitly, using type conversion keywords.

Computers, in addition to being able to store vast amounts of data, are much faster and more accurate than we are in performing arithmetic calculations. You harness the computer's calculating ability using arithmetic operators. Most of the arithmetic operators are familiar, such as addition and subtraction, but a few may not be, such as integer division, which returns the quotient but not the remainder, and the Mod operator, which returns the remainder but not the quotient. You also can use the concatenation operators to combine two string values.

Finally, instead of your supplying in code the value that is assigned, you can use the InputBox function to enable your application's user to input that value. That value, as the return value of the function, is assigned to a variable or property.

5

✓ *Mastery Check*

1. Which is a true statement of what can be on the left side of an assignment statement?

A. Any property or variable

B. Any property but only writable variables

C. Any variable but only writable properties

D. Only writable variables and writable properties

✓ Mastery Check

2. Can an assignment statement be located at module level?

   A. Always

   B. Never

   C. Only if combined with the declaration of a variable

   D. Only on national holidays

3. Option Strict prohibits:

   A. Explicit widening conversions

   B. Implicit widening conversions

   C. Explicit narrowing conversions

   D. Implicit narrowing conversions

4. Type conversion keywords permit the following when Option Strict is on:

   A. Explicit widening conversions

   B. Implicit widening conversions

   C. Explicit narrowing conversions

   D. Implicit narrowing conversions

5. A type conversion that converts a value from a numeric data type to a string is:

   A. A widening conversion

   B. A narrowing conversion

   C. Prohibited

   D. Acceptable only if Option Explicit is on

6. Which of the following is a type conversion keyword?

   A. Boolean

   B. Option Strict

✓ Mastery Check

C. CInt

D. Option Explicit

7. Which of the following operators is not overloaded?

A. +

B. –

C. *

D. =

8. Concatenation means:

A. Adding numbers

B. Adding strings

C. Subtracting numbers

D. Subtracting strings

9. Which arithmetic operator returns the remainder of division?

A. /

B. \

C. Mod

D. ^

10. What is the result of 3 + 4 * 5?

A. 35

B. 60

11. An algorithm is:

A. Named after Al Gore

B. Used to combine two strings

C. A logical procedure for solving a problem

D. Used to call a function

5

Module 6

Comparison and Logical Operators

The Goals of this Module

- Understand comparison operators
- Be familiar with the differences between numerical, object, and string comparisons
- Understand logical operators and how they enable you to combine comparisons

So far, the flow of the programs has followed a relatively straight line. The program took a predetermined action based on the user's choice. However, as programs become more sophisticated, they often branch in two or more directions based on whether a condition is True or False. For example, in a calculator program, your code would need to determine whether the user chose addition, subtraction, multiplication, or division before performing the indicated arithmetic operation. Your code would make that determination by comparing the user's choice with the various alternatives. That comparison would be made using a comparison operator.

Comparisons also are often used for error prevention. For example, in the calculator program, before performing division, the program should compare the divisor to zero, because division by zero is illegal and, if performed, will result in a runtime error. If the divisor is equal to zero, the user should be warned and the division not performed. Otherwise, the division may be performed.

There are comparison operators to test for equality, inequality, whether one value is greater (or less) than another, and other tests. Comparison operators may be used not only to compare numerical values, but also for strings or even objects.

A comparison operator can make only one comparison at a time. Sometimes you need to combine several comparisons. To determine if someone is eligible to vote, you have to compare both their age to the minimum voting age and their country of citizenship to being the United States. In this case, both comparisons must evaluate as True or the person is not allowed to vote. However, in other comparisons, only one of two conditions need be True. For example, you may be permitted to attend a movie free if you are either a child or a senior citizen.

You use logical operators to combine several comparisons. The logical operators include And, when both comparisons must evaluate as True for an action to be taken, and Or, when only one of two comparisons must evaluate as True for an action to be taken.

The comparison and logical operators lay the groundwork for the following modules: Module 7 on control structures and Module 8 on loops, which use these operators to determine if a condition, or a combination of conditions, evaluate as True or False.

Comparison Operators

Often your programs will need to compare two values. The comparison may be whether the two values are equal, or whether one value is greater (or less) than another. Regardless of which comparison is being made, the comparison may have only one of two possible results, either True or False.

The syntax of a comparison is:

```
[Expression1] [comparison operator] [Expression2]
```

The two expressions may be anything that has a value that can be compared: literals, constants, variables, or readable properties. Table 6-1 lists and describes the comparison operators and the circumstances under which they evaluate to True or False.

6

Operator	Meaning	True If	False If
<	Less than	expression1 < expression2	expression1 >= expression2
<=	Less than or equal to	expression1 <= expression2	expression1 > expression2
>	Greater than	expression1 > expression2	expression1 <= expression2
>=	Greater than or equal to	expression1 >= expression2	expression1 < expression2
=	Equal to	expression1 = expression2	expression1 <> expression2
<>	Not equal to	expression1 <> expression2	expression1 = expression2
Is	Do two object variables refer to same object?	Both object variables refer to same object	The two object variables do not refer to same object
Like	A string matches a specified pattern	The string matches the specified pattern	The string does not match the specified pattern

Table 6-1   Comparison Operators

The following expressions each evaluate as True:

- 4 = 4
- 4 < 5
- 4 <= 5
- 4 > 3
- 4 >= 3
- 4 <> 3

By contrast, the following expressions each evaluate as False:

- 4 <> 4
- 4 = 5
- 4 > 5
- 4 >= 5
- 4 < 3
- 4 <= 3

Tip

As with other operators, you should be careful to compare values of the same data types. For example, when an expression of the Decimal data type is compared with an expression of the Single or Double data type, the Decimal expression will be converted to the Single or Double data type. The result may be that any fractional value less than 1E-28 may be lost. Consequently, the two values may compare as equal when they are not. For this reason, care should be taken when using equality (=) to compare two floating-point variables.

The equality comparison operator (=) is overloaded, also serving as an assignment operator as discussed in Module 5. The compiler can tell whether you are using the = operator for assignment or comparison based on the context in which the operator is used. The = operator will be used for comparison in Module 7 on Control Structures and Module 8 on Loops.

Comparing Objects

The Is comparison operator is used to determine if one object variable refers to the same object as another object variable, returning True if the two object variables refer to the same object, and False if they do not.

The following code, which you can place in the Form_Load event procedure of a standard Windows application project, illustrates how the Is operator works:

```
Dim frm1 As New Form1()
Dim frm2 As New Object()
Dim frm3 As New Object()
frm2 = frm1
Debug.Write(frm2 Is frm1) 'outputs True
Debug.Write(frm3 Is frm1)    'outputs False
```

The first line of code, Dim frm1 As New Form1(), creates an object variable frm1 that refers to the default form (Form1) generated when you create a Windows program. The next two lines of code create two object variables, frm2 and frm3, that simply refer to some object in memory.

Note

The object variables frm2 and frm3 do not need to be created with the New keyword since they simply are used to refer to an existing object rather than create a new object. Therefore, the statements Dim frm2 as Object() and Dim frm3 as Object() would be sufficient.

The fourth line of code, frm2 = frm1, uses the assignment operator differently than before. Previously, we used the assignment operator to assign the value of the expression on the right side of the assignment statement to a variable or writeable property on the left side of the assignment statement. Here the assignment operator has a different effect. The object variable on the left side of the assignment statement will refer to the same object as the object variable on the right side of the assignment statement. Consequently, the result of the statement is that frm2 now also refers to the default form Form1. Therefore, the statement:

```
Debug.Write(frm2 Is frm1)
```

6

outputs True, since the two object variables refer to the same object. However, the statement:

```
Debug.Write(frm3 Is frm1)
```

outputs False, since frm3 does not refer to Form1 as does frm1.

The TypeOf … Is expression is related to the Is operator, and in essence combines the Is operator with the TypeOf keyword. The TypeOf … Is expression is used to check whether an object variable refers to a particular type of object, returning True if it does, and False otherwise. The syntax is:

```
TypeOf [object variable] Is [type of object]
```

The following code determines if an object variable named ctrl refers to an object that is (or inherits from) a Button control:

```
TypeOf Ctrl Is Button
```

Often in code, you may know only that an object is a control, but not what kind of control it is. The TypeOf … Is expression may be used to determine through code whether a control is a Button, a Label, a TextBox, or something else.

Comparing Strings

Comparing two strings is quite similar to comparing two expressions having a numerical value. For example, "Jeff" = "Jeff" evaluates to True, whereas "Jeff" = "Kent" evaluates to False.

String comparisons are based on the Unicode values of the characters in the string. As discussed in Module 4, for the English language, the character set adopted by ANSI (American National Standards Institute) and ASCII (American Standards Committee for Information Interchange) use the numbers 0–255 to cover all alphabetical characters (upper- and lowercase), digits and punctuation marks, and even characters used in graphics and line drawing. Since 255 characters is not sufficient for all of the different alphabets used in this wide world, the Unicode standard was adopted, permitting (in Visual Basic .NET) potentially 65,536 different characters. However, the values of commonly used characters are the same in ASCII and Unicode. Table 6-2 lists the ASCII values of commonly used characters.

Characters	**ASCII Value**
0 through 9	48–57 (0 is 48, 9 is 57)
A through Z	65–90 (A is 65, Z is 90)
a through z	97–122 (A is 97, Z is 122)

Table 6-2 | ASCII Values of Commonly Used Characters

The result of the comparison of string representations of numbers may not always be what you expect. As you might suspect, "5" is greater than "4" since the ASCII value of 5 (53) is greater than the ASCII value of 4 (52). However, "5" also is greater than "4444" for the same reason. In comparing two strings, if the value of the first character of one string is greater than the first character of the other, the values of the remaining characters of the two strings do not matter. Thus, the string "ZAAA" is greater than "AZZZ." Only if the values of the first characters are the same is there a comparison to the second characters, or if necessary to the third, to break the tie.

Additionally, string comparisons involve two issues not involved with numerical comparison: whether the comparison is case sensitive, and the use of the Like operator.

Option Compare

As Table 6-2 shows, the ASCII values of lowercase alphabetical characters are greater than their uppercase counterparts: a is greater than A. The default in Visual Basic .NET is that string comparisons are case sensitive—that is, they distinguish whether a character is uppercase or lowercase. Consequently, jeff is greater than, rather than equal to, Jeff.

Depending on the context of your program, you may want to make case-insensitive comparisons—that is, comparisons in which whether a character is uppercase or lowercase is irrelevant. In validating a user who is attempting to log on, for example, usernames often are not case sensitive (whereas passwords usually are).

You use the Option Compare statement to declare the default comparison method to use when string data is compared. The Option Compare statement may be one, but only one, of the following:

```
Option Compare Binary
Option Compare Text
```

Option Compare Binary is the default, and is a case-sensitive comparison. Option Compare Text is a case-insensitive comparison. Thus, under Option Compare Binary, aaa is greater than AAA. However, under Option Compare Text, aaa is equal to AAA.

You can override the Option Compare setting by using the built-in functions UCase and LCase.

The UCase function takes a character or string as an argument. It converts all lowercase letters to uppercase; all uppercase letters and nonletter characters remain unchanged. For example, if the string "Hello World 1234" is the argument for the UCase function, the function would return the string "HELLO WORLD 1234":

```
Debug.Write (Ucase("Hello World 1234"))    ' Writes "HELLO WORLD 1234".
```

The LCase function is the converse of the UCase function, converting all uppercase letters to lowercase, with all lowercase letters and nonletter characters remaining unchanged. For example, if the string "Hello World 1234" is the argument for the LCase function, the function would return the string "hello world 1234".

The UCase and LCase functions may be used to override the Option Compare setting by converting the strings being compared to either all lowercase or all uppercase before making the comparison, thus eliminating case as a factor in the comparison.

The Option Compare statement must be declared at the module level, before any procedures.

Like Operator

The Like operator is used to determine if a string matches a given pattern, returning True if the string does match the pattern, and False if it does not. The syntax is:

```
[string] Like [pattern]
```

The following statement will return True:

```
Debug.Write ("F" Like "F") 'return True
```

The following statements will return False:

```
Debug.Write ("FF" Like "F") 'return False
Debug.Write ("F" Like "FF") 'return False
```

The following statement will return True if Option Compare is Text, and False if Option Compare is Binary:

```
Debug.Write ("F" Like "f") True if Option Compare Text, otherwise False
```

In the previous examples, the Like operator operates no differently than the equality operator. The real power of the Like operator is using pattern matching.

Pattern matching is often used in everyday computing activities. For example, in searching for a file on your computer that you know starts with "msado" and has the extension .dll, you could do a search for the file msado*.dll, using the wildcard character *.

Table 6-3 lists the pattern matching characters supported by Visual Basic .NET.

The wildcard character * is commonly used for searches, particularly when not all of the details of the string being searched for are known or remembered. The following statement returns True because "aBBBa" has an "a" at the beginning, an "a" at the end, and any number of characters in between:

```
"aBBBa" Like "a*a"
```

The wildcard character ? provides for a more focused search than * because, while the * wildcard character can represent zero or more characters, the ? wildcard character represents one character, no more and no less. The following statement returns True because "BAT" starts with a "B," ends with a "T," and has exactly one character in between:

```
"BAT" Like "B?T"
```

Characters in Pattern	Matches in String
?	Any single character
*	Zero or more characters
#	Any single digit (0–9)
[charlist]	Any single character in charlist
[!charlist]	Any single character not in charlist

Table 6-3   Characters for Pattern Matching

The wildcard characters ? and *, like others, can be combined. The following statement returns True because "BAT" starts with a "B," followed by any single character, followed by a "T," and finally zero or more characters of any type.

```
"BAT123khg" Like "B?T*"
```

The wildcard character # provides for an even more focused search than the wildcard character ? because, while the ? wildcard character can represent any character, the # wildcard character can only represent a character that signifies a digit. The following statement returns True because "a2a" begins and ends with an "a" and has exactly a single digit number in between:

```
"a2a" Like "a#a"
```

A group of one or more characters (charlist) enclosed in brackets ([ ]) can be used to match any single character in a string and can include almost any character code, even digits. The following statement returns True because "F" occurs in the set of characters from A to Z:

```
"F" Like "[A-Z]"
```

Note

When a range of characters is specified, they must appear in ascending sort order, from lowest to highest. Thus, [A-Z] is a valid pattern, but [Z-A] is not.

An exclamation point (!) at the beginning of charlist means that a match is made if any character except the characters in charlist is found in the string. The following statement returns False because "F" occurs in the set of characters from A to Z:

```
"F" Like "[!A-Z]"
```

Precedence

Comparison operators rank lower than the arithmetic operators discussed in Module 5 and higher than the logical operators discussed in the next section, "Logical Operators." All comparison operators are of equal precedence, and are evaluated from left to right.

1-Minute Drill

- What is the data type returned by the comparison operators?
- What statement determines if a string comparison is case sensitive?

Logical Operators

A comparison operator can only make one comparison at a time. Sometimes you need to combine several comparisons. To determine if someone is eligible to vote, you have to compare their age to being greater than or equal to 18, and their citizenship status to being True. In that case, both comparisons must evaluate as True or the person is not allowed to vote. To determine if a buyer is eligible for a discount that encourages large purchases (as most discounts do), you may have to compare if the total of all of their purchases is greater than $500 or if any one purchase is greater than $100. In that case, the buyer is eligible for the discount as long as at least one of the two comparisons evaluates as True.

The combining of comparisons in either the conjunctive (and) or disjunctive (or) involves logical operators named, not surprisingly, And and Or, respectively.

Note

Many of the same operators used as logical operators, which compare Boolean expressions, also can be used as bitwise operators that compare two numeric expressions. As discussed in Module 1, computers "think" in 1s and 0s, and often numbers are expressed in binary, or base 2. In bitwise comparisons, two binary numbers are compared, bit by bit, with either a 1 or a 0 in that bit resulting from the comparison. This module will focus on logical rather than bitwise operators because Module 7 and Module 8 use logical rather than bitwise operators.

The And Operator

The And operator performs a logical conjunction operation on two Boolean expressions and returns a Boolean value which, as Table 6-4 shows, is False unless both of the Boolean expressions being compared are True.

- Boolean.
- Option Compare. Option Compare Binary means the comparison is case sensitive; Option Compare Text means the comparison is case insensitive.

6

If First Expression Is	And Second Expression Is	Result Is
True	True	True
True	False	False
False	True	False
False	False	False

Table 6-4 The And Operator with Boolean Expressions

The following code shows how the And operator works with Boolean expressions:

```
Dim A As Integer = 10
Dim B As Integer = 8
Dim C As Integer = 6
Dim myCheck As Boolean
myCheck = A > B And B > C    ' Returns True.
myCheck = B > A And B > C    ' Returns False.
```

The voting eligibility example discussed at the beginning of this module is a good example of when you would use the And operator, since both conditions (adult age and citizenship) must be True or the result (eligibility to vote) is False.

The AndAlso Operator

The AndAlso operator is almost identical to the And operator in comparing two Boolean expressions. As Table 6-5 shows, the only difference is that if the first expression is False, the second expression is not evaluated. The following "Ask the Expert" discusses the consequences of the second expression not being evaluated and why you might use the AndAlso operator instead of the And operator.

If First Expression Is	And Second Expression Is	Result Is
True	True	True
True	False	False
False	(not evaluated)	False

Table 6-5 The AndAlso Operator

Note

The AndAlso operator, unlike the And operator, only performs a logical comparison of two Boolean expressions, and cannot be used to perform a bitwise comparison of two numeric expressions.

The Or Operator

The Or operator performs a logical disjunction operation on two Boolean expressions and returns a Boolean value which, as Table 6-6 shows, is True unless both of the Boolean expressions being compared are False.

The following code shows how the Or operator works with Boolean expressions:

```
Dim A As Integer = 10
Dim B As Integer = 8
Dim C As Integer = 6
Dim myCheck As Boolean
myCheck = A > B Or B > C    ' Returns True.
myCheck = B > A Or B > C    ' Returns True.
myCheck = B > A Or C > B    ' Returns False
```

The free movie ticket example discussed at the beginning of this module is a good example of when you would use the And operator, since if either condition (minor or senior citizen) is True, the result (get in free) is True. Only if both conditions are False do you have to pay.

If First Expression Is	And Second Expression Is	Result Is
True	True	True
True	False	True
False	True	True
False	False	False

Table 6-6 The Or Operator with Boolean Expressions

The OrElse Operator

The OrElse operator is to the Or operator what the AndAlso operator is to the And Operator. As Table 6-7 shows, the only difference between the OrElse operator and the Or operator is that if the first expression is True, the second expression is not evaluated. The "Ask the Expert" following this section discusses the consequences of the second expression not being evaluated and why you might use the OrElse operator instead of the Or operator.

Note

As with the AndAlso operator, the OrElse operator, unlike the Or operator, only performs a logical comparison of two Boolean expressions, and cannot be used to perform a bitwise comparison of two numeric expressions.

The Xor Operator

The Xor operator performs a logical exclusion operation on two Boolean expressions and returns a Boolean value, which as Table 6-8 shows, is True if one and only one of the expressions evaluates to True, but otherwise is False.

The following code shows how the Xor operator works with Boolean expressions:

```
Dim A As Integer = 10
Dim B As Integer = 8
Dim C As Integer = 6
Dim myCheck As Boolean
myCheck = A > B Xor B > C    ' Returns False.
myCheck = B > A Xor B > C    ' Returns True.
myCheck = B > A Xor C > B    ' Returns False.
```

If First Expression Is	And Second Expression Is	Result Is
True	(not evaluated)	True
False	True	True
False	False	False

Table 6-7   The OrElse Operator

If First Expression Is	And Second Expression Is	Result Is
True	True	False
True	False	True
False	True	True
False	False	False

Table 6-8   The Xor Operator with Boolean Expressions

The Xor operator is useful when you want to determine that one or the other condition is True, but not both.

The Not Operator

The Not operator performs a logical negation operation on two Boolean expressions and returns a Boolean value, which as Table 6-9 shows, is True if the expression evaluates to False, but otherwise is False.

The Not operator is useful in situations in which Not True appears more natural than False. For example, in the calculator program discussed at the start of this module, in verifying whether the divisor is equal to zero (division by zero being illegal), it may be intuitive to say that division may be performed if the divisor is not equal to zero.

Precedence

Logical operators rank lower than the comparison operators discussed earlier in this module. Table 6-10 lists the order of precedence among comparison operators.

If Expression Is	Result Is
True	False
False	True

Table 6-9   The Not Operator

6

Priority	Operator(s)	Description
1	Not	Negation
2	And, AndAlso	Conjunction
3	Or, OrElse	Disjunction
4	Xor	Exclusion

Table 6-10   Precedence Among Logical Operators

If the logical operators of equal priority appear in the same statement, precedence between them is from left to right.

1-Minute Drill

● What logical operator works with only one operand rather than two?
● Which logical operator returns False if both operands are True?

Summary

As programs become more sophisticated, they often branch in two or more directions based on whether a condition is True or False. As discussed at the beginning of this module, a calculator program, before performing division, should check to see if the divisor is equal to zero (division by zero being illegal and if performed would result in a runtime error). The program branches by performing the division if the divisor is not equal to zero, but warning the user if the divisor is equal to zero.

You use comparison operators to determine if the divisor is equal (or is not equal) to zero. There are comparison operators to test for equality or inequality, or whether one value is greater or less than another. Comparison operators may be used to compare not only numerical values, but also strings or even objects.

A comparison operator can make only one comparison at a time, and sometimes you need to combine several comparisons. For example, to determine if someone is eligible to vote, you have to compare both their age to the minimum voting age, and their country of citizenship to the United States. In this case, both comparisons must evaluate as True or the person is not allowed to vote.

● Not.
● Xor.

Ask the Expert

Question: What difference does it really make that the AndAlso operator does not evaluate the second expression if the first expression is False, or that the OrElse operator does not evaluate the second expression if the first expression is True?

Answer: There is no real difference if the second expression is simply a comparison. However, the second expression may be more complex, such as a function call that changes values before returning a Boolean result. In that event, variables may have different values depending on whether the second expression was evaluated.

Question: Why would you use the AndAlso operator instead of the And operator, or the OrElse operator instead of the Or operator?

Answer: If the second expression is complex, you may want to save processor time by not evaluating it. However, normally the decision regarding whether to use the AndAlso operator instead of the And operator, or the OrElse operator instead of the Or operator, depends on the logic of your program. As discussed in the preceding answer, when the second expression is complex, such as a function call that changes values before returning a Boolean result, variables may have different values depending on whether the second expression was evaluated. You need to determine if the logic of your program dictates that those changes be made regardless, or only if the first expression evaluates as True (or False, as the case may be). There is no hard and fast answer; it all depends on the logic of your program.

However, in other comparisons, only one of two conditions need be True. For example, you may be permitted to attend a movie without having to pay for a ticket if you are either a child or a senior citizen.

You use logical operators to combine several comparisons. The logical operators include And, when both comparisons must evaluate as True for an action to be taken, and Or, when only one of two comparisons must evaluate as True for an action to be taken. There are other logical operators as well.

The comparison and logical operators lay the groundwork for Module 7 and Module 8, which use these operators to determine if a condition, or a combination of conditions, evaluate as True or False.

☑ *Mastery Check*

1. What data type do the comparison operators return?

  A. Boolean

  B. Byte

  C. Integer

  D. String

2. Which data type does the Like comparison operator compare?

  A. Boolean

  B. Byte

  C. Integer

  D. String

3. Which comparison operator compares references to objects?

  A. >

  B. <>

  C. Is

  D. Like

4. Which statement affects whether a string comparison is case sensitive?

  A. Option Explicit

  B. Option Compare

  C. Option Strict

  D. Stock Options

☑ Mastery Check

5. Which of the following is not used in pattern matching in string comparisons?

    A. #

    B. ^

    C. ?

    D. *

6. Comparison operations rank, in precedence:

    A. Higher than arithmetic operators but lower than logical operators

    B. Lower than arithmetic operators but higher than logical operators

    C. Higher than both arithmetic and logical operators

    D. Lower than both arithmetic and logical operators

7. Which of the following logical operators works with only one operand rather than two?

    A. And

    B. Or

    C. Not

    D. Xor

8. Which of the following logical operators returns False if both operands are True?

    A. And

    B. Or

    C. Not

    D. Xor

6

☑ *Mastery Check*

9. Which of the following logical operators has the highest priority?

    A. And

    B. Or

    C. Not

    D. Xor

10. Which of the following logical operators will not evaluate the second expression if the first one is True?

    A. And

    B. AndAlso

    C. Or

    D. OrElse

Part 3

Controlling the
Flow of the Program

Module 7

Control Structures

The Goals of this Module

- Understand If statements
- Understand Select Case statements
- Use the CheckBox and RadioButton controls with If and Select Case statements

Comparison and logical operators, featured in the previous module, are used to evaluate expressions as True or False. This module will show you how to structure your code using control structures, specifically an If statement or a Select Case statement, so that different blocks of code execute depending on whether an expression evaluates as True or False.

The application user interacts with your code, including If and Select Case statements, through the GUI of your application. This module will demonstrate two controls that are used with If and Select Case statements. The CheckBox control is used when a particular decision has only two choices, as in True or False, Yes or No, and so on. The CheckBox control also is useful when more than one option can be selected, such as various toppings for a pizza, of which you could choose all, none, or any combination. The RadioButton control is used when there are multiple, mutually exclusive choices.

If Statements

The If statement comes in several varieties, depending on the structure of the alternative blocks of code. The most basic structure is the If…Then statement, which you use if you want a block of code to execute should a condition be True, but no block of code to execute if the condition is False.

You use the If…Then…Else statement if you want one block of code to execute if the condition is True, and a second, different block of code to execute if the condition is False. This code structure often is used when there are two alternatives, such as Yes or No, or Male or Female, each with their separate block of code to execute. This module also will cover the IIf function, which is quite similar to the If…Then…Else statement.

The If…ElseIf statement is more complex. You use this statement if you want one block of code to execute if its condition is True, but if instead that condition is False, a second, different block of code to execute if its condition is True, and if that condition is False, optionally a third (or fourth, or fifth, and so on) block of code to execute if its condition is True, and optionally a final block of code to execute if none of the preceding conditions were True. For example, assume a student's overall percentage in a class is represented by the variable avg. If avg >= 90, the grade would be an A, else if avg >= 80, the grade would be a B, else if avg >= 70, the grade would be a C, else if avg >= 60, the grade would be a D, else the grade would be an F. If avg is 99, the conditions avg >= 90 and avg >= 60 both are True, but the student gets an A, not a D, since only the first block of code whose condition is True executes.

The If...Then Statement

You use an If...Then statement to execute code if, and only if, a condition is True. If the condition is False, the code dependent on the If...Then statement does not execute. After the If...Then statement finishes, execution continues with the code, if any, following the statement.

The syntax of an If...Then statement depends on whether the code to be executed is only one line or more than one line.

If the code to be executed is only one line, you have two choices in syntax. The first syntax choice is to put the entire statement on one line:

```
If [condition] Then [Code]
```

For example, the following code writes "The date is earlier than today" to the Output window if a given date is earlier than today. The code assumes that datMyDate is a Date variable that already has been declared and assigned a value. The Today property, which is read-only, returns the current date.

```
If datMyDate < Today Then Debug.Write "The date is earlier than today"
```

If the line is long, you can use a line continuation character, in which case the compiler still regards the statements as being on a single line even though visually the statement is on two lines:

```
If datMyDate < Today Then _
    Debug.Write "The date is earlier than today"
```

The second syntax choice is to put the code to be executed in an If...End If block:

```
If [condition] Then
    [Code]
End If
```

This syntax results in the following code:

```
If datMyDate < Today Then
    Debug.Write "The date is earlier than today"
End If
```

7

The compiler permits you to choose between the two syntaxes if only one line of code is being executed. If more than one line of code is being executed, you have no choice in syntax. You must use the second (If...End If block) syntax:

```
If MyDate < Today Then
    Debug.Write "The date is earlier than today"
    Debug.Write "But tomorrow is another day"
End If
```

Tip

I recommend that you don't use the one-line If...Then statement even though the compiler might permit you to do so. The End If statement usually is necessary, and programmers should be consistent in the syntax they use.

The If...Then...Else Statement

You use the If...Then...Else statement if you want one block of code to execute if the condition is True, and a second, different block of code to execute if the condition is False. This differs from the If...Then statement in that some code in the If...Then...Else statement will be executed; the only question is which. By contrast, with the If...Else statement, if the condition is False, no code dependent on the If...Then statement executes.

After the If...Then...Else statement finishes, execution continues with the code, if any, following the statement.

The syntax of an If...Then...Else statement is:

```
If [condition] Then
    [Code]
Else
    [Code]
End If
```

No express condition follows the Else statement because the condition is implied as being the negation of the condition following the If statement. In other words, the code following the Else statement executes if the condition following the If statement is not True.

Caution

The one-line syntax of an If...Then statement is not possible with an If...Then...Else statement even if only one line of code follows the If condition.

The following code illustrates the use of the If...Then...Else statement. As before, the code assumes that datMyDate is a Date variable that already has been declared and assigned a value.

```
If datMyDate < Today Then
   Debug.Write "The date is earlier than today"
Else
   Debug.Write "The date either is today or after today"
End If
```

While you can have an If without an Else, as with the If...Then statement, you cannot have an Else without an If.

The IIf Function

The peculiarly named IIf function is quite similar to an If...Then...Else statement. The first parameter is an expression that must evaluate to a Boolean value. The second parameter is the value the function returns if the expression is True, and the third parameter is the value the function returns if the expression is False. The syntax is:

```
IIf([Expression], [Return Value if True], [Return Value if False]
```

For example, assume a variable named intHeight previously was declared and assigned a person's height in inches. Anyone over 78 inches is too tall to fit inside a car, so the following function would return a string "too tall" or "not too tall" depending on the value of intHeight:

```
Dim strMsg
strMsg = IIf(intHeight > 78, "Too tall", "Not too tall")
Debug.Write strMsg
```

7

The If...ElseIf Statement

You use the If...ElseIf statement if you have more than two alternative blocks of code, the maximum possible with an If...Then...Else statement.

With an If...ElseIf statement, the first block of code whose condition is True executes, and all following blocks of code are skipped. The first block of code follows the If clause, and each succeeding block of code coupled with a condition is an ElseIf clause. You can have as many ElseIf clauses as you want. Finally, you may optionally have an Else clause, which, as with an If...Then...Else statement, acts as "none of the above." Also as with an If...Then...Else statement, after the If...ElseIf statement finishes executing, execution continues with the code, if any, following the statement.

The syntax of an If...ElseIf statement is:

```
If [condition] Then
    [Code]
ElseIf [condition] Then
    [Code]
Else
    [Code]
End If
```

The following code illustrates the use of the If...ElseIf statement. Once again, the code assumes that datMyDate is a Date variable that already has been declared and assigned a value.

```
If datMyDate < Today Then
    Debug.Write "The date is earlier than today"
ElseIf datMyDate > Today Then
    Debug.Write "The date is after today"
Else
    Debug.Write "The date is today"
End If
```

While you can have as many ElseIf clauses as you want, none can appear after an Else clause. The Else clause is optional; it serves the function of "none of the above."

As is the case with the Else clause, while you can have an If without an ElseIf, you cannot have an ElseIf without an If.

The comparisons may also use logical operators, as in the following code which validates a test score (represented by the variable intScore) as between 0 and 100. The code assumes that intScore is an Integer variable that already has been declared and assigned a value.

```
If intScore >= 0 And intScore <= 100 Then
   Debug.Write "The test score is valid"
ElseIf intScore < 0 Then
   Debug.Write "Test score cannot be less than zero"
Else
   Debug.Write "Test score cannot be greater than 100"
End If
```

You also can nest If statements inside other If statements. The preceding code could be changed to read:

```
If intScore < 0 Or intScore > 100 Then
   If intScore < 0 Then
      Debug.Write "Test score cannot be less than zero"
   Else
      Debug.Write "Test score cannot be greater than 100"
   End If
Else
   Debug.Write "The test score is valid"
End If
```

7

Tip

The preceding example shows the importance of indenting your code.

1-Minute Drill

● The IIf function most closely resembles which of the If statements?

● Which of the If statements may use the most blocks of code?

● The If…Then…Else statement.
● The If…ElseIf statement.

Controls Used for If Statements

The application user interacts with your code, including If statements, through the GUI of your application. Two controls in particular are used in conjunction with If statements. The CheckBox control is used when a particular decision has only two choices, as in True or False, Yes or No, and so on. The CheckBox control also is useful when more than one option can be selected, such as various toppings for a pizza, of which you could choose all, none, or any combination. The RadioButton control is used when there are multiple, mutually exclusive choices.

CheckBox Control

CheckBox controls are commonly used in Windows applications. For example, in the Print dialog box, there are check boxes for Print To File and Collate. CheckBox controls are often used because they are ideal for situations in which there are only two choices. The CheckBox control being checked is considered True or Yes, unchecked False or No. Each CheckBox control is independent of the others. They may all be checked, or all unchecked, or any combination of checked and unchecked.

RadioButton Control

RadioButton controls also are commonly used in Windows applications. Taking again the example of the Print dialog box, there are radio buttons for Print to all pages, current page, or selected pages.

The primary difference between CheckBox and RadioButton controls is that while each check box is independent, all radio buttons in a group are related in that only one of them can be chosen at any one time. Therefore, the RadioButton control is ideal for situations in which there are more than two choices.

All radio buttons on a form usually constitute a single group. In this situation, only one radio button on the form may be selected at one time. However, if radio buttons are contained within a GroupBox control, those radio buttons are a group independent of any other radio buttons on the form. In this situation, the selection of a radio button within the GroupBox control would not affect your ability to select a radio button outside the GroupBox control. The converse also is true; the selection of a radio button outside the GroupBox control would not affect your ability to select a radio button inside the GroupBox control. This is useful when you want different groups of radio buttons on a form to be independent of each other. For example, one group of radio buttons may concern age, another group income level, and so on. The GroupBox control also has another purpose, an aesthetic one, to place a frame around radio buttons (or other controls).

The Arithmetic Calculator project at the end of this module uses radio buttons and the GroupBox control.

prj7-1.zip

Project 7-1: Tuition Calculator

This project calculates the cost of tuition. This cost is based on the amount of units, which the application user inputs, and the cost per unit, which is $11 per unit for residents and $50 per unit for nonresidents. Before calculating tuition, the application confirms that the user entered a positive whole number for the number of units, and if not, notifies the user instead of calculating tuition. Figure 7-1 shows the project in action.

This project uses the CheckBox control for the user to input whether the student is a resident. The project code also uses a number of concepts discussed in this and the previous module, including If...Then...Else statements and nesting one inside another, comparison operators, and logical operators such as Not and OrElse. It also introduces the built-in IsNumeric function to check if the user entered a number, and the StatusBar control for the display of messages to the application user.

7

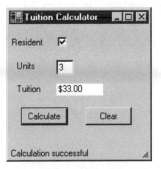

Figure 7-1   Tuition calculation application

Step-by-Step

1. Create a Windows application.

2. From the Toolbox, add to the default form (the only one used in this project) a CheckBox control with the following changes in its default properties:

- Name: chkResident
- CheckAlign: MiddleRight. This property determines the location of the check box inside the control. This control consists of two components: the check box itself and identifying text. *Middle* refers to its vertical position, *Right* to its horizontal position. The check box is aligned to the right of the control so that the text will appear to its left and be aligned with identifying text (using labels) of other controls.
- Text: Resident
- TextAlign: MiddleLeft

3. Add two labels whose Text properties are Units and Tuition, respectively. You do not need to change the default names of these labels (Label1, Label2, and so on) as you will not be referring to them in code.

4. To the left of the label captioned Units, add a TextBox control with the following properties:

- Name: txtUnits
- Text: "" (empty string)
- MaxLength: 2. This property limits the number of characters that can be entered in the text box. The assumption is that a student would not be taking more than 99 units at one time so there is no need for more than two characters. We will use code to make sure each character is a digit.

5. To the left of the label captioned Tuition, add another Label control with the following properties:

- Name: lblTuition
- Text: "" (empty string)
- BackColor: HighlightText. This value gives the label control a white background. This is not required; it just gives the label an appearance consistent with the text box above it.

6. Add a StatusBar control to the bottom of the form. You can keep the default name of StatusBar1 (since there only will be one status bar in the program), but set the Text property to an empty string. StatusBar controls are common in Windows programs. In Microsoft Word, for example, they display the page and line on which the cursor is located, as well as whether you are in overtype mode. The StatusBar control, while informative, is unobtrusive in that it need not be dismissed by user action, as is the case with dialog and message boxes.

7. Add two CommandButton controls, one named cmdCalculate and captioned Calculate, and the other named cmdClear and captioned Clear.

8. Place the following code in the Click event procedure of the cmdCalculate command button, which is used to calculate tuition:

```
Private Sub btnCalculate_Click(ByVal sender As Object, _
    ByVal e As System.EventArgs) Handles btnCalculate.Click

    Const RESIDENT As Integer = 11
    Const NONRESIDENT As Integer = 50
    If Not IsNumeric(txtUnits.Text) _
        OrElse CInt(txtUnits.Text) < 0 Then
        If Not IsNumeric(txtUnits.Text) Then
            StatusBar1.Text = "Number of units must be numeric"
        Else
            StatusBar1.Text = "Number of units must be positive"
        End If
    Else
        If chkResident.Checked Then
            lblTuition.Text = Format(CInt(txtUnits.Text) *
RESIDENT, "c")
        Else
            lblTuition.Text = Format(CInt(txtUnits.Text) *
NONRESIDENT, "c")
        End If
        StatusBar1.Text = "Calculation successful"
    End If

End Sub
```

9. Place the following code in the Click event procedure of the cmdClear command button, which is used to clear the values for units and tuition:

```
Private Sub btnClear_Click(ByVal sender As Object, _
    ByVal e As System.EventArgs) Handles btnClear.Click

    chkResident.Checked = False
    txtUnits.Text = ""
```

7

```
        lblTuition.Text = ""
        StatusBar1.Text = ""

End Sub
```

This code simply returns the controls to default values for the program.

Run the code. If you type a nonnumeric value in the text box and click the Calculate button, the status bar will read "Number of units must be numeric," and no tuition will be calculated. If you type a numeric but negative value in the text box and click the Calculate button, the status bar will read "Number of units must be positive," and again no tuition will be calculated. If you type a positive number in the text box and click the Calculate button, the program will calculate tuition, at $11 per unit if the Resident check box is checked, and at $50 per unit if it is not. The status bar will read: "Calculation successful."

How It Works

Constants first are declared for the cost per unit for residents and nonresidents respectively. The actual values (11 and 50) could have been used in the code instead. However, using constants makes the code easier to change if the cost per unit ever changes, since only one change would need to be made (the value of the constant) rather than changing the value everywhere it is used in the code.

The remaining code branches in two directions, depending on whether the input of the number of units is valid (a positive number) or not (nonnumeric or a negative value). Since the input is either valid or not, an If...Then...Else statement works well. The If clause handles when the input is not valid, and the Else clause handles the circumstances in which the input is valid.

The If condition combines the Not operator with the OrElse operator:

```
If Not IsNumeric(txtUnits.Text) _
    OrElse CInt(txtUnits.Text) < 0 Then
```

The first condition is whether the input is a string representation of a number. The IsNumeric function is built into Visual Basic .NET. It returns True if the string that is its parameter (here the text entered in the text box) is a string representation of a number, and False if it is not. By using the Not operator, the first condition evaluates as True if the input is not numeric.

The second condition is whether the input is a negative number, and therefore invalid input. The type conversion keyword CInt, discussed in Module 5, is used before the comparison to convert the value of the text box control to an Integer.

The two conditions are in the disjunctive (or) rather than the conjunctive (and) because if the input is invalid if it either is not a number or is negative. The OrElse rather than Or operator is used because the CInt type conversion keyword in the second condition would cause an error if the first condition is True (the input is not a string representation of a number). For example, you could not use CInt to convert "Jeff" into an integer. With the OrElse operator, the second condition will not be evaluated if the first condition is True, avoiding this problem, which could cause an error if the Or operator were used instead.

If the If clause evaluates to True, it could be because the input either is not a number or is negative. Therefore, another If...Else statement is nested within the If Clause to handle both circumstances and output the appropriate message to the StatusBar control:

```
If Not IsNumeric(txtUnits.Text) Then
    StatusBar1.Text = "Number of units must be numeric"
Else
    StatusBar1.Text = "Number of units must be positive"
End If
```

The outer Else clause will only be reached if the input is valid. It covers two possibilities: the student either is a resident or is not. Therefore, an If...Else statement is nested within the Else clause:

```
Else
    If chkResident.Checked Then
        lblTuition.Text = Format(CInt(txtUnits.Text) * RESIDENT, "c")
    Else
        lblTuition.Text = Format(CInt(txtUnits.Text) * NONRESIDENT, "c")
    End If
    StatusBar1.Text = "Calculation successful"
End If
```

Before multiplying the number of units by the cost per units, the number of units, obtained from the Text property of a TextBox control, must be converted from a string to a numeric data type. This is a narrowing conversion, and therefore (if Option Strict is on) requires a type conversion to a numeric data type. This type conversion is accomplished by the CInt type conversion keyword.

The Format function returns a string, formatted as specified in the parameters in the function. Here, the formatting is as currency, but there are other predefined formats such as date and time. Additionally, you can create user-defined formats, such as changing a string of nine digits ("123456789") into a Social Security number ("123-45-6789").

The syntax of the Format function is:

```
Format([Expression to be formatted, [symbol specifying type of formatting])
```

The Format function often is on the right side of an assignment statement, since it returns a formatted string, which then is assigned to a string variable on the left side of the assignment statement.

Note

The Format function also has two additional optional parameters that are used only when the formatting is to specify a date and time.

The first parameter of the Format function is the result of the multiplication of the number of units by the cost per units. The second parameter specifies the type of formatting (currency in this case). Table 7-1 lists the predefined numeric formats that can be specified in the second parameter (the symbol that specifies the type of formatting):

Format Name	Description
General Number, G, or g	Displays number with no thousand separator.
Currency, C, or c	Displays number with thousand separator, if appropriate; displays two digits to the right of the decimal separator. Output is based on system locale settings.
Fixed, F, or f	Displays at least one digit to the left and two digits to the right of the decimal separator.
Standard, N, or n	Displays number with thousand separator, at least one digit to the left and two digits to the right of the decimal separator.
Percent, P, or p	Displays number multiplied by 100 with a percent sign (%) appended to the right. Always displays two digits to the right of the decimal separator.

Table 7-1   Predefined Numeric Formats

Format Name	Description
Scientific, E, or e	Uses standard scientific notation.
D or d	Displays number as a string that contains the value of the number in decimal (base 10) format. This option is supported for integral types (Byte, Short, Integer, Long) only.
X or x	Displays number as a string that contains the value of the number in hexadecimal (base 16) format. This option is supported for integral types (Byte, Short, Integer, Long) only.
Yes/No	Displays No if number is 0; otherwise, displays Yes.
True/False	Displays False if number is 0; otherwise, displays True.
On/Off	Displays Off if number is 0; otherwise, displays On.

Table 7-1   Predefined Numeric Formats (*continued*)

Setting the Text property of the StatusBar control to "Calculation successful" is done outside of the inner If...Then...Else statement because it is independent of that statement. The output is the same whether the residency check box is checked or not.

1-Minute Drill

● Would you use the CheckBox or RadioButton control for an If...ElseIf...Else statement?

● What control enables you to have more than one group of radio buttons on a form?

7

● RadioButton control.
● The GroupBox control.

The Select Case Statement

The Select Case statement is quite similar to the If...ElseIf statement, but they are not the same. The primary difference is that in the If...ElseIf statement, the If and ElseIf clauses each may evaluate completely different expressions, whereas a Select Case statement may evaluate only one expression, which then must be used for every comparison.

For example, the condition of an If clause could be whether Night > Day, the condition of the following ElseIf clause whether Citizenship = U.S., the condition of the next ElseIf clause whether NumberOfClasses >= 4, and so on. Usually the conditions evaluated by the If and ElseIf clauses are related, but they can be completely independent of each other.

By contrast, the Select Case statement evaluates one test expression, and that test expression is used for all of the following comparisons.

The syntax of a Select Case statement is:

```
Select [test expression]
   Case [expression or expression list]
      [code]
   ' More Case statements optional
   Case Else    'also optional
      [code]
End Select
```

The test expression may be any literal, constant, variable, readable property, or expression that evaluates to one of the following data types: Boolean, Byte, Char, Date, Double, Decimal, Integer, Long, Object, Short, Single, and String.

The expression or expression list following the Case clause is compared to the expression or expression list, and may be one of the following:

- An expression, such as Case 80. This means that the condition is whether the test expression equals the expression—in this example, whether the test expression equals 80. The setting of Option Compare can affect string comparisons. Under Option Compare Text, the strings "Apples" and "apples" compare as equal, but under Option Compare Binary, they do not.

- An expression list, such as Case 80 To 90. This means that the condition is whether the test expression equals a value within the expression list—here 80 through 90. If the values are not consecutive, commas can delimit them.

For example, Case 1 To 4, 7 To 9, 11 means that the condition is whether the test expression equals 1 through 4, or 7 through 9, or 11.

- The Is keyword (not the same as the Is operator used for comparing objects) combined with a comparison operator. For example, Case Is > 8 means that the condition is whether the test expression is greater than 8.

These alternatives can be combined. For example, Case 1 To 3, 5, Is > 8 means that the condition is whether the text expression is 1 through 3, 5, or greater than 8.

While the Select Case statement differs from the If...ElseIf...Else statement in that it may evaluate only one expression which then must be used for every comparison, it otherwise behaves quite similarly to the If...ElseIf...Else statement:

- If the condition following an If (or ElseIf) clause in an If...ElseIf...Else statement evaluates as True, the code following that clause executes, and none of the following ElseIf (or Else) clauses are evaluated. Similarly, if the expression or expression list following a Case clause matches the test expression, the code following the Case clause executes, and any remaining Case clauses are not evaluated.

- If the condition following an If (or ElseIf) clause in an If...ElseIf...Else statement instead evaluates as False, the code following that clause does not execute, and each of the following ElseIf (or Else) clauses is evaluated in order. Similarly, if the expression or expression list following a Case clause does not match the test expression, the code following that clause does not execute, and each of the following Case clauses is evaluated in order.

- If none of the conditions following the If and ElseIf clauses in an If...ElseIf...Else statement evaluates as True, the code following the Else clause executes if there is an Else clause. Similarly, if none of the conditions following the Case clauses in a Select...Case statement matches the test expression, the code following the Case Else clause executes if there is a Case Else clause. The Case Else statement is analogous to the Else clause, covering the "none of the above" circumstance.

7

- Once execution of the If...ElseIf...Else statement is completed, the program continues to the code following the End If statement. Similarly, once execution of the Select...Case statement is completed, the code program continues to the code following the End Select statement.

You also can nest a Select Case statement inside another Select Case statement, just as you can nest an If statement inside another If statement.

The following code illustration of the Select Case statement assumes that AverageOfScores previously was declared as an Integer variable and assigned a value. The Select Case statement evaluates the value of that variable and then outputs the grade based on that value:

```
Select AverageOfScores
    Case 90 to 100
        Debug.Write "Your grade is an A"
    Case 80 to 89
        Debug.Write "Your grade is an B"
    Case 70 to 79
        Debug.Write "Your grade is an C"
    Case 60 to 69
        Debug.Write "Your grade is an D"
    Case Else
        Debug.Write "Your grade is an F"
End Select
```

1-Minute Drill

What is the fundamental difference between a Select Case statement and an If...ElseIf statement?

- In an If...ElseIf statement, the If and ElseIf clauses each may evaluate completely different expressions. By contrast, a Select Case statement may evaluate only one expression, which then must be used for every comparison.

prj7-2.zip

Project 7-2: Arithmetic Calculator

This project performs basic arithmetic: addition, subtraction, multiplication, and division. The user inputs the two operands and chooses an operator by clicking a radio button corresponding to the operator. The application, before performing the arithmetic calculation, confirms that the user entered a number, and if not, notifies the user instead of making the calculation. In the case of division, the program also checks that division by zero is not being attempted. Figure 7-2 shows the project in action.

Step-by-Step

1. Create a Windows application.

2. From the Toolbox, add to the default form (the only one used in this project) a GroupBox control. Here, the GroupBox control has the aesthetic purpose of framing other controls, specifically the radio buttons discussed in the next step.

3. Add inside the GroupBox control four RadioButton controls with the following values for their Name and Text properties:

- radAdd, +
- radSubtract, -
- radMultiply, *
- radDivide, /

These controls correspond to the four arithmetic operators to be used in this Calculator project. To have one radio button start out checked, set the Checked property of radAdd to True. The Checked property of the other radio buttons

7

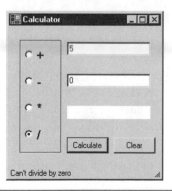

Figure 7-2   Arithmetic calculator

automatically will be False, since only one radio button per group can be chosen at a time.

4. Add two TextBox controls, named txtOperand1 and txtOperand2, and set their Text properties to an empty string (""). Set the MaxLength property (used in the Tuition project) of each TextBox control to 10. This is an arbitrary limit, but there should be some limit to avoid the input and resulting value overflowing the boundaries of the data type.

5. Below the two TextBox controls, add a Label control named lblResult, and set its Text property to an empty string (""). As in the Tuition project, set the label's BackColor property to HighlightText to give the label control a white background consistent with the text boxes above it.

6. As in the Tuition project, add a StatusBar control to the bottom of the form. Here too you can keep the default name of StatusBar1, since there will only be one status bar in the program, but set the Text property to an empty string.

7. Add two CommandButton controls, one named cmdCalculate and captioned Calculate, and the other named cmdClear and captioned Clear.

8. Declare the following module-level variable:

```
Private Op as Char
```

This variable will hold the operator currently selected. It is declared at module level since it will be accessed by several procedures.

9. Place the following code in the Load event procedure of the form:

```
Private Sub Form1_Load(ByVal sender As System.Object, _
    ByVal e As System.EventArgs) Handles MyBase.Load
        op = "+"c
End Sub
```

This code give the op variable an initial value of "+" since radAdd is the radio button selected by default when the application starts. The c following "+" is a literal type character. Its purpose is to indicate to the compiler that "+" is a Char rather than a String data type. The c literal type character is necessary if Option Strict is on because without it "+" would be treated as a String and, with Option Strict on, a String cannot be converted to a Char.

10. Place the following code in the Click event procedure of the four radio buttons:

```
Private Sub radAdd_Click(ByVal sender As Object, _
    ByVal e As System.EventArgs) Handles radAdd.Click
```

```
         If radAdd.Checked = True Then op = "+"c
End Sub

Private Sub radSubtract_Click(ByVal sender As Object, _
    ByVal e As System.EventArgs) Handles radSubtract.Click
        If radSubtract.Checked Then op = "-"c
End Sub

Private Sub radMultiply_Click(ByVal sender As Object, _
    ByVal e As System.EventArgs) Handles radMultiply.Click
        If radMultiply.Checked Then op = "*"c
End Sub

Private Sub radDivide_Click(ByVal sender As Object, _
    ByVal e As System.EventArgs) Handles radDivide.Click
         If radDivide.Checked Then op = "/"c
End Sub
```

This code sets the value of the op variable to the operator selected by the user clicking a radio button.

11. Place the following code in the Click event procedure of the cmdCalculate command button, which is used to perform the arithmetic calculation:

```
Private Sub cmdCalculate_Click(ByVal sender As Object, _
    ByVal e As System.EventArgs) Handles cmdCalculate.Click
      If IsNumeric(txtOp1.Text) And IsNumeric(txtOp2.Text) Then
          StatusBar1.Text = "Can't divide by zero"
          Select Case op
             Case "+"c
             lblResult.Text = CStr(CSng(txtOp1.Text) + CSng(txtOp2.Text))
              Case "-"c
             lblResult.Text = CStr(CSng(txtOp1.Text) - CSng(txtOp2.Text))
              Case "*"c
              lblResult.Text = CStr(CSng(txtOp1.Text) * CSng(txtOp2.Text))
              Case "/"c
              If Trim(txtOp2.Text) = "0" Then
                  StatusBar1.Text = "Can't divide by zero"
              Else
                  lblResult.Text = CStr(CSng(txtOp1.Text) / CSng(txtOp2.Text))
              End If
           End Select
        Else
           StatusBar1.Text = "Both operands must be numeric"
        End If
End Sub
```

This code first checks that both operands are numeric. If not, the status bar advises the user and no arithmetic calculation is performed. Otherwise, a Select Case statement executes a block of code based on the current value of the op variable. The CSng type conversion keyword first is used to convert the String to a Single data type (the number may be a floating point instead of a whole number so Single is a better choice than Integer) to perform the arithmetic calculation, and then the CStr type conversion keyword is used to convert the Single to a String data type before assigning it to the Text property of the Label control. Additionally, if division is requested, the code first checks that division by zero is not being attempted, and if it is, warns the user via the status bar instead of performing the division.

12. Place the following code in the Click event procedure of the cmdClear command button, which is used to clear the text boxes and label:

```
Private Sub cmdClear_Click(ByVal sender As Object,
    ByVal e As System.EventArgs) Handles cmdClear.Click
        txtOp1.Text = ""
        txtOp2.Text = ""
        lblResult.Text = ""
        StatusBar1.Text = ""
End Sub
```

Ask the Expert

Question: I understand that the difference between If…ElseIf and Select Case statements is that If and ElseIf clauses each may evaluate completely different expressions, while a Select Case statement may evaluate only one expression, which then must be used for every comparison. But how do I decide whether to use an If…ElseIf and Select Case statement?

Answer: First, you may not have a choice. While any code you write using a Select Case statement can also be written using an If statement, the reverse is not true. If you need to evaluate several different expressions in a block of code, you cannot use a Select Case statement, which may evaluate only one expression and then must be used for every comparison.

> If you do have a choice, the decision is one of personal preference, concerning which way is easier to write and easier to understand. Often your choice may be the Select Case statement. Its structure often is more readable of the two. Try writing the equivalent of Case 1 To 4, 7, 8 To 11, 14 in an If or ElseIf statement—you will have a very long list of comparisons joined by a number of And and Or operators.

Summary

Module 6 showed you how to use comparison and logical operators to evaluate expressions as True or False. This module showed you how to structure your code using control structures, an If statement or a Select Case statement, so that different blocks of code execute depending on whether an expression evaluates as True or False.

The application user interacts with your code, including If and Select Case statements, through the GUI of your application. This module showed you how to use two controls that are used with If and Select Case statements. The CheckBox control is used when there are only two choices, and the RadioButton control is used when there are more than two choices. Additionally, the GroupBox control enables you to have independent groups of RadioButton controls on a form.

7

✓ Mastery Check

1. The IIf function most closely resembles which of the If statements?

   A. If...Then

   B. If...Then...Else

   C. If...ElseIf

2. Which of the If statements may concern the most alternatives?

   A. If...Then

   B. If...Then...Else

☑ Mastery Check

C. IIf

D. If...ElseIf

3. Which statement may be done with a single line of code?

    A. If...Then

    B. If...Then...Else

    C. IIf

    D. If...ElseIf

4. Which can you have more than one of in an If statement?

    A. If

    B. Else

    C. IIf

    D. ElseIf

5. You would use the CheckBox instead of the RadioButton control for an If...ElseIf...Else statement.

    A. True

    B. False

6. What control enables you to have more than one group of radio buttons on a form?

    A. CommandButton

    B. GroupBox

    C. Label

    D. TextBox

☑ *Mastery Check*

7. What is the fundamental difference between a Select Case statement and an If...ElseIf...Else statement?

8. In an expression list for a Select Case statement, which of the following is how you would express a number between 1 and 10 or 13?

   A. 1 through 10 or 13

   B. 1 through 10, 13

   C. 1 To 10 or 13

   D. 1 To 10, 13

7

Module 8

Loops and Arrays

The Goals of this Module

- Understand loops
- Know how to create and resize arrays
- Use loops to initialize and access arrays

Loops are used to repeat the execution of code statements. This is useful in a variety of contexts. For example, if an application user enters invalid data, you may want to ask the user whether they want to retry or quit. If they retry and still enter invalid data, you again would ask the user whether they want to retry or quit. This process keeps repeating until the user either enters valid data or quits.

An array permits you to use a single variable to store many values. The values are stored at consecutive indexes, starting with zero and then incrementing by one for each additional element of the array. For example, to store sales for each day of the week, you can create one array with seven elements, rather than declaring seven separate variables. Not only is it easier to keep track of one variable than seven, but you can also use a loop to access each consecutive element in an array, whether to assign a value of that element or to display that value.

Loop Structures

Loop structures allow you to execute one or more lines of code repetitively. You can repeat the statements until a condition is true, false, repeat it a specified number of times, or just once for each object in an array. The loop structures supported by Visual Basic .NET are:

- For...Next

- While

- Do

- For Each...Next

The For Each...Next loop will be covered in the following section on arrays since it generally is used in conjunction with arrays.

The For...Next Statement

A For...Next statement generally is used to repeat the execution of a statement a fixed number of times. The syntax of a For...Next statement is:

```
For counter = start To end [ Step step ]
   [ statements ]
[ Exit For ]
   [ statements ]
Next [ counter ]
```

Table 8-1 lists and describes the parts of the For...Next statement.

The *step* argument can be either positive or negative. If the value of the *step* argument is positive, the loop executes as long as *counter* <= *end*. If the value of the *step* argument is negative, the loop executes as long as *counter* >= *end*.

The *counter* variable is compared to *end* every time before the loop is entered. This includes the first time the For...Next statement is executed. Therefore, if the value of *start* is past the value of *end* when the loop is entered, the statements inside the loop are not executed, and execution passes immediately to the statement following the Next statement.

Part	Required or Optional	Description
counter	Required	Variable, usually of Integer data type, that evaluates to a whole number.
start	Required	Expression, usually a literal, which evaluates to a whole number value. Represents starting value of *counter*.
end	Required	Expression, usually a literal, which evaluates to a whole number value. Represents ending value of *counter*.
step	Optional	Expression, usually a literal, which evaluates to a whole number value. Represents the amount by which *counter* is incremented or decremented (if step is negative) each time through the loop. If not specified, *step* defaults to 1.
statements	Optional	Code that executes each iteration of the loop.
Exit For	Optional	Ends the loop prematurely, before *counter* reaches the value of *end*.

Table 8-1   Parts of the For...Next Statement

After the statements inside the loop have executed, *step* is added to *counter*. At this point, the For clause again compares *counter* to *end*. As a result of this comparison, either the statements in the loop execute again or the loop is terminated and execution continues with the statement following the Next statement.

For example, the following code will print the numbers 1 through 10 to the Debug window:

```
Dim I As Integer
For I = 1 To 10
   Debug.Write (I & " ")
Next I
```

Since there is no Step statement, Step 1 is implied. Therefore, the initial test is I <= 10. By contrast, the following code will not print anything to the Debug window because, since the Step statement is negative, the initial test is I >= 10, which evaluates to False:

```
Dim I As Integer
For I = 1 To 10 Step -1
   Debug.Write (I & " ")
Next I
```

The expressions *start*, *end*, and *step* are all evaluated only once, when the For clause is first reached. These expressions are not evaluated again, even if statements inside the loop change their values.

By contrast, *counter* is evaluated each iteration of the loop. Since *counter* increases (or decreases) by the positive (or negative) amount of the *step* statement, there is no need to add code to change the value of *counter*. Indeed, you should avoid using statements inside the loop to change the value of *counter*, as this can make it more difficult to read and debug your code.

The comparison of *counter* to *start*, and *counter* to *end*, must each be capable of evaluating to True or False. Therefore, these expressions should be of the same data type.

The Exit For statement transfers control immediately to the statement following the Next statement. While a For...Next loop may contain multiple Exit For statements, the loop ends upon reaching the first Exit For statement.

The Exit For statement often is used in combination with the evaluation of a condition by an If...Then...Else statement. For example, the following code will output only 1 through 7, not 1 through 10, since the loop ends prematurely when I equals 8:

```
Dim I As Integer
For I = 1 To 10
    If I > 7 Then
        Exit For
    End If
    Debug.Write(I & " ")
Next I
```

You can nest For...Next loops by placing one loop within another. Each loop must have a unique *counter* variable. The following construction is correct:

```
Dim I As Integer, X As Integer
For I = 1 To 3
    For X = 1 To 3
        Debug.Write("I = " & I & vbCrLf)
        Debug.Write("X = " & X & vbCrLf)
    Next X
Next I
```

The output is:

```
I = 1
X = 1
I = 1
X = 2
I = 1
X = 3
I = 2
X = 1
I = 2
X = 2
I = 2
X = 3
I = 3
X = 1
I = 3
X = 2
I = 3
X = 3
```

8

1-Minute Drill

● What is the data type to which the *condition* in a For...Next statement must evaluate?

● Will a For...Next statement compile if the condition never evaluates as True?

● Can the *counter* in a For...Next statement change by a value different than 1?

The While...End While Statement

The While...End While statement repeats the execution of a statement as long as a given condition is True. The syntax is:

```
While condition
    [ statements ]
[Exit While]
End While
```

Table 8-2 lists and describes the parts of this statement.

If *condition* is True, all of the *statements* are executed until the End While statement is encountered. Control then returns to the While statement and *condition* is again checked. If *condition* is still True, the process is repeated. If it is False, execution resumes with the statement following the End While statement.

Part	Required or Optional	Description
condition	Required	Expression, usually a comparison, which must evaluate to True or False.
statements	Optional	One or more statements following While that are executed while *condition* is True.
Exit While	Optional	Ends the loop prematurely, before *condition* becomes False.

Table 8-2 Parts of the While Statement

● Boolean.
● Yes. The statements inside the loop simply never execute.
● Yes. You simply use a Step statement with a value different than 1, such as 3, –4, and so on.

For example, the following While...End While statement outputs 1 through 9 to the Debug window:

```
Dim counter As Integer = 1
While counter < 10
   Debug.Write x
   counter += 1
End While
```

One significant difference between a While...End While statement and a For...Next statement is that in a While...End While loop you have to affirmatively change the value of the *counter*, whereas in a For...Next loop the Step statement, whether express or implied, takes care of that detail for you. Thus, you would have an infinite loop if you did not change the value of *counter* in the preceding While...End While statement.

Tip

Press CTRL-BREAK to stop an endless loop.

Another difference between a While...End While statement and a For...Next statement is that a For...Next statement generally is intended to run a fixed number of times, whereas a While...End While statement may run an indefinite number of times. For example, if you want a menu to display until the user chooses the option to quit, the While...End While statement would be a better choice than the For...Next statement since the programmer could not predict how many times the user would choose to continue before selecting to quit.

Although there are significant differences between a While...End While statement and a For...Next statement, there also are similarities. A While...End While statement, like a For...Next statement, may never execute the statements inside it if initially the condition is False. Nothing will be written to the Debug window in the following example because the condition initially is False:

```
Dim counter As Integer = 1
While counter > 10
   Debug.Write("This will never display")
End While
```

You also can nest a While...End While statement inside another While...End While statement, just as you can nest a For...Next statement inside another For...Next statement.

8

Additionally, the Exit While statement serves the same function in a While...
End While statement as the Exit For statement does in the For...Next statement,
ending the While...End While statement prematurely. The following code will only
output 1 through 5, not 1 through 9, to the Debug window:

```
Dim counter As Integer = 1
While counter < 10
    If counter = 6 Then
        Exit While
    End If
    Debug.Write(counter)
    counter += 1
End While
```

The Do Statement

The Do statement comes in two varieties, one testing a condition at the top of
the statement, the other at the bottom. When it tests the condition at the top
of the statement, the Do statement is quite similar to the While...End While
statement, the only difference being the syntax:

```
Do { While | Until } condition
    [ statements ]
[ Exit Do ]
    [ statements ]
Loop
```

Table 8-3 lists and describes the parts of this statement.

Part	Required or Optional	Description
While	Required unless Until is used	Repeat the loop until *condition* is False.
Until	Required unless While is used	Repeat the loop until *condition* is True.
condition	Required	Expression, usually a comparison that must evaluate to True or False.
statements	Optional	One or more statements following Do that are executed while *condition* is True.
Exit Do	Optional	Ends the loop prematurely, before *condition* becomes False.

Table 8-3 Parts of the Do Statement

The following code will output 1 through 9 to the Debug window using the While keyword:

```
Dim counter As Integer = 1
Do While counter < 10
   Debug.Write(counter)
   counter += 1
Loop
```

The same result could be achieved by using Until:

```
Dim counter As Integer = 1
Do Until counter = 10
   Debug.Write x
   counter += 1
Loop
```

Whether you use While or Until is a matter of choice, depending on which is more intuitive to you.

The other variation of the Do statement tests the condition at the end of the loop. Its syntax is:

```
Do
   [ statements ]
[ Exit Do ]
   [ statements ]
Loop { While | Until } condition
```

8

With this syntax, the statements inside the loop will always execute at least once, because the first test is at the bottom of the loop after the statements. A menu is one example of when you may want the statements inside the loop to execute at least once. Another example, which uses InputBox and IsNumeric functions as well as the MessageBox class discussed in prior modules, requires the user either to input a numeric value or quit by clicking the Cancel button, which returns an empty string:

```
Dim strInput As String
Dim intInput As Integer
Do
   strInput = InputBox("Enter a number or quit by clicking Cancel")
   If strInput = "" Then
```

```
      MessageBox.Show ("Nothing entered or Cancel selected.")
   ElseIf Not IsNumeric(strInput) Then
      MessageBox.Show("You need to enter a number")
   End If
Loop Until IsNumeric(strInput) Or strInput = ""
```

The test in this example should be at the bottom rather than at the top of the loop since the user would have to enter a value before there would be a test.

1-Minute Drill

- Which loop statement may test the condition at the bottom instead of at the top?
- Which loop statement is designed to execute a fixed number of times?

Ask the Expert

Question: Why does Visual Basic .NET support both a While… End While statement and a Do statement with a test at the top of the loop if they both do the same thing?

Answer: Not being on a first name, or even last name, basis with Bill Gates, I have to make an educated guess. The Do statement also was used in prior versions of Visual Basic, so Visual Basic programmers making the transition to Visual Basic .NET should be familiar with it. The While…End While statement is new to Visual Basic, but is used in other programming languages, such as C++, so it is familiar to programmers who may not have used Visual Basic before.

- The Do statement.
- The For…Next statement.

Arrays

Module 4 demonstrated how to declare variables of different data types such as Integer or Single. The variables discussed in that module were *scalar* variables. They can store only one value at a time.

An array permits you to use a single variable to store many values. The values are stored at consecutive indexes, or subscripts. The index is a whole number that starts with zero, and then increments by one for each additional element of the array.

For example, to store sales for each day of the week, you can create one array named arrSalesPerDay with seven elements, rather than declaring seven separate variables. Each element in the array contains one value, which you access by specifying the element's index. The sales for the first day of the week would be accessed by arrSalesPerDay(0), the sales for the second day of the week would be accessed by arrSalesPerDay(1), and so on. You could use a loop to display the sales for each day of the week:

```
Dim intCounter as Integer
For intCounter = 0 to 6
   Debug.Write arrSalesPerDay(intCounter)
Next intCounter
```

You also could use a loop to obtain a running total of all sales for the week:

```
Dim intCounter as Integer
Dim intRunningTotal as Integer = 0
For intCounter = 0 to 6
   intRunningTotal += arrSalesPerDay(intCounter)
Next intCounter
Debug.Write ("Total Sales: " & intRunningTotal)
```

By contrast, you could not similarly use a loop if, instead of using an array, you had used seven different variables to store sales for each day of the week.

8

The array arrSalesPerDay used to store sales for each day of the week has one dimension. An array may have more than one dimension, however. For example, two-dimensional arrays are used so that one dimension concerns a row and another a column, or one an x coordinate and the other a y coordinate. You can specify up to 60 dimensions, although more than three is extremely rare.

Declaring an Array

Array variables are declared the same way as other variables, using the Dim, Public, Protected, or Private statement, and can be declared either at module level or inside a procedure. You include a pair of parentheses after the variable name to indicate that the variable is an array rather than a scalar variable.

The syntax for declaring an array variable is:

```
Dim | Public | Private | Protected variablename ([length]) _
    As Data Type [ = { values } ]
```

The *length* is not the number of elements in the array. Rather, it is the *upper bound*, or highest index or subscript, of the array. Since the number of the lowest index is always zero, the number of elements is always one more than the value of *length*.

Note

The length of every dimension of an array is limited only by the maximum value of a Long data type, which is $(2 \wedge 64) - 1$. However, Visual Basic allocates space for each array element up to the *length*. Therefore, to avoid using more memory than necessary, you should avoid declaring an array larger than necessary.

The *values* are the values assigned to each index in the array.

Note

Usually an array is declared with one of the built-in data types, such as Integer, String, and so on. If so, all of its elements must be of that data type. However, if the data type is Object, the individual elements can contain different kinds of data (objects, strings, numbers, and so on).

You can declare an array variable without length or values:

```
Dim arrSalesPerDay() As Integer
```

This declaration does not specify the number of elements in the array. Consequently, no memory has been allocated to store the elements of the array. Therefore, you cannot access an array element such as arrSalesPerDay(0) because it does not exist in memory. Attempting to do so will create a runtime error, an unhandled exception of type System.NullReferenceException.

You need to allocate memory to store array elements before you can access them. You have two alternatives to do so.

The first alternative is to declare the array variable with either *length* or *values*. The following array variable declaration supplies the length, but not the values:

```
Dim arrSalesPerDay(6) As Integer
```

In this event, each of the seven elements of the array has a default value. The specific value depends on the data type of the array. If, as here, the data type is Integer, each element of the array has a value of 0. Looping through the elements of the array as in the following code will output seven zeros to the Debug window:

```
Dim arrSalesPerDay(6) As Integer
Dim I As Integer
For I = 0 To 6
    Debug.Write(arrSalesPerDay(I))
Next I
```

You also can declare the array variable with values, but not the length:

```
Dim arrSalesPerDay() As Integer = {0, 0, 0, 0, 0, 0, 0}
```

In this event, the array implicitly has seven elements, or an upper bound of 6, based on the number of values supplied. Therefore, looping through the elements of the array as in the following code also will output seven zeros to the Debug window:

```
Dim arrSalesPerDay() As Integer={0, 0, 0, 0, 0, 0, 0}
Dim I As Integer
For I = 0 To 6
    Debug.Write(arrSalesPerDay(I))
Next I
```

You can supply either the length or the values of the array, but you cannot supply both. If you attempt to do so, as with the following code, the compiler will complain, "explicit initialization is not permitted for arrays declared with explicit bounds":

```
'compiler error if you supply both the length and the values
Dim arrSalesPerDay(6) As Integer = {0, 0, 0, 0, 0, 0, 0}
```

If you do not supply either the length or the values of the array when you declare it, you need to allocate memory for the array variable before you can store values in that array. You do so by assigning an array object to the array variable. The syntax is:

```
Variablename = New DataType ( [length] ) { [values] }
```

The *length* and the *values* have the same meaning when creating array objects as when declaring array variables. The *length* is the upper bound of the array, and the *values* are the values assigned to each index in the array.

The following code, which uses the *length* but not the *values* argument, will output seven zeros to the Debug window:

```
Dim arrSalesPerDay() As Integer
arrSalesPerDay = New Integer(6) {}
Dim I As Integer
For I = 0 To 6
    Debug.Write(arrSalesPerDay(I))
Next I
```

Similarly, the following code, which uses the *values* but not the *length* argument, also will output seven zeros to the Debug window:

```
Dim arrSalesPerDay() As Integer
arrSalesPerDay = New Integer() {0 ,0, 0, 0, 0, 0, 0}
Dim I As Integer
For I = 0 To 6
    Debug.Write(arrSalesPerDay(I))
Next I
```

As with declaring an array variable, using the *values* argument implicitly allocates memory for the number of values specified. However, unlike declaring an array variable, you also can use both the *length* and *values* arguments when creating an array object:

```
Dim arrSalesPerDay() As Integer
arrSalesPerDay = New Integer(6) {0 ,0, 0, 0, 0, 0, 0}
```

Note

While your code will compile and run even if you do not specify either the *length* or *values* argument, you should specify one in order to allocate storage space.

You also can combine the declaration of the array variable and the assignment of the array object in one statement, optionally supplying either the length or values of the array, both, or neither. All of the following alternatives will compile:

```
'does not supply either the length or values
Dim arrSalesPerDay () As Integer = New Integer() {}
'supply the values but not the length
Dim arrSalesPerDay() As Integer = New Integer() {0, 0, 0, 0, 0, 0, 0}
'supply the length but not the values
Dim arrSalesPerDay() As Integer = New Integer(6) {}
'supply both the length and the values
Dim arrSalesPerDay() As Integer = New Integer(6) {0, 0, 0, 0, 0, 0, 0}
```

If you do supply both initial lengths and element values in the New clause, the number of elements must match the length. The following declaration, declaring a length of seven but supplying only six element values, will cause the compiler error "Array initializer has one too few elements":

```
Dim arrSalesPerDay() As Integer = New Integer(6) {0, 0, 0, 0, 0, 0}
```

Note

You must follow a New clause with braces ({}) even if the braces are empty.

Useful Array Functions, Properties, and Methods

The UBound function returns the upper bound of the indicated dimension of an array. Its syntax is:

```
UBound(arrayname, [rank])
```

The *rank* argument is used in multidimensional arrays, where 1 indicates the first dimension, 2 the second dimension, and so on. If *rank* is not specified, the default is 1, which works fine for a one-dimensional array.

The UBound function can be used in the following loop:

```
Dim arrSalesPerDay(6) As Integer
Dim I As Integer
For I = 0 To UBound(arrSalesPerDay) 'Instead of For I = 0 To 6
   Debug.Write(arrSalesPerDay(I))
Next I
```

The UBound function permits you to loop through an array without having known the upper bound of the array when you wrote your code.

Note

Visual Basic .NET also supports an LBound function, which returns the lowest bound of the array. However, unlike prior versions of Visual Basic, in Visual Basic .NET, the lowest bound of an array is always zero, so the LBound function is not particularly useful.

An array is an object, specifically an Array object. The Array object, like other objects, has properties and methods. Table 8-4 lists and describes several properties and methods you may find useful in your programming.

Property or Method	Description
Clear	Method. Sets a range of elements in an array to default values for their data type, such as zero for numeric values and False for Boolean values.
Copy	Method. Copies a section of one array to another array.
CopyTo	Method. Copies all the elements of a one-dimensional array to another one-dimensional array starting at the specified destination array index.
GetLength	Method. Gets the number of elements in the specified dimension of an array.
GetLowerBound	Method. Gets the lower bound of the specified dimension in an array.

Table 8-4   Useful Properties and Methods of Array Objects

Property or Method	Description
GetUpperBound	Method. Gets the upper bound of the specified dimension in an array.
GetValue	Method. Gets the value of the specified element in an array.
IndexOf	Method. Returns the index of the first occurrence of a value in a one-dimensional array or in a portion of the array.
LastIndexOf	Method. Returns the index of the last occurrence of a value in a one-dimensional array or in a portion of an array.
Length	Property. Total number of elements in all the dimensions of the array.
Rank	Property. Returns number of dimensions in the array.
Reverse	Method. Reverses the order of the elements in a one-dimensional array or in a portion of the array.
SetValue	Method. Sets the specified element in an array to the specified value.
Sort	Method. Sorts the elements in a one-dimensional array, such as sorting strings alphabetically.

Table 8-4   Useful Properties and Methods of Array Objects (*continued*)

Resizing an Array

You need to specify the size of an array before you can use it so memory is allocated for all elements of the array. However, Visual Basic .NET permits you to resize the array as necessary. This helps you manage memory efficiently. For example, you can use a large array for a short time and then change it to a smaller size, freeing up memory you no longer need.

You have two alternative methods of resizing an array. The first is to assign a different array object to the same array variable using a standard assignment statement. For example, assume initially that an array variable is assigned to an array object with seven Integer elements:

```
Dim arrSalesPerDay() As Integer = New Integer(6) {0, 0, 0, 0, 0, 0, 0}
```

You could resize the array to six Integer elements by assigning another array object to it, with six Integer elements:

```
arrSalesPerDay = New Integer(5) {}
```

8

The other alternative is to use the ReDim statement. The syntax is:

```
ReDim [Preserve] name [(boundlist)]
```

Table 8-5 lists and describes the components of this statement.

The following code uses the ReDim statement to resize the array from seven to six Integer elements:

```
Dim arrSalesPerDay() As Integer = New Integer(6) {1, 2, 3, 4, 5, 6, 7}
ReDim arrSalesPerDay(5)
```

However, when you use ReDim to resize an array, the previous values in the array are lost. Thus, in the preceding code snippet, the values of the array would not be 1 through 6, but all zeros. To preserve the previous values in the array, you use, not surprisingly, the Preserve keyword. In the following code snippet, use of the Preserve keyword results in the new array having the values 1 through 6:

```
Dim arrSalesPerDay() As Integer = New Integer(6) {1, 2, 3, 4, 5, 6, 7}
ReDim Preserve arrSalesPerDay(5)
```

Name	Required or Optional	Described
ReDim	Required	Keyword to indicate resizing of array.
Preserve	Optional	Keyword used to preserve the data in the existing array when you change the size of only the last dimension.
name	Required	Name of the array variable. You can redimension multiple array variables in the same statement, separating them by commas and specifying the *name* and *boundlist* parts.
boundlist	Required	A positive integer representing the upper bound of the redefined array. If the array has more than one dimension, *boundlist* is a list of positive integers, separated by commas, each representing the upper bound of a dimension of the redefined array.

Table 8-5   Elements of the ReDim Statement

Ask the Expert

Question: How can the ReDim statement resize the array since the amount of memory, once allocated, is fixed?

Answer: The ReDim statement does not really resize the array. Instead, it allocates a new array, initializes its elements from the corresponding elements of the existing array if the Preserve keyword is used, and assigns the new array to the array variable.

Question: What happens to the old array?

Answer: It gets thrown out in the trash. Visual Basic .NET has a "garbage collection" mechanism that frees up memory allocated to objects that are no longer needed.

1-Minute Drill

- Can you change the lower bounds of an array?
- How do you change the upper bound of an array?

8

The For Each...Next Statement

You can use a For...Next statement to access each element of an array.

```
Dim arrSalesPerDay() As Integer = New Integer(6) {1, 2, 3, 4, 5, 6, 7}
Dim I As Integer
For I = 0 To UBound(arrSalesPerDay)
   Debug.Write(arrSalesPerDay(I))
Next I
```

You also can use a For Each...Next statement to access each element of an array. A For Each...Next loop is similar to the For...Next loop. Both execute a fixed number of times. The difference is that the number of times a For...Next

---

- No. You can only change the upper bound. The lower bound is always zero.
- With either the ReDim statement or an assignment statement using a new Array object.

loop executes depends on the values of the *start*, *end*, and *step* expressions, while the number of times a For Each...Next loop executes depends on the number of elements in an array or collection.

The syntax of a For Each...Next statement is:

```
For Each element In group
    [ statements ]
[ Exit For ]
    [ statements ]
Next [ element ]
```

Table 8-6 lists and describes the parts of this statement.

The following code uses a For Each...Next statement to output the value of each element of the array to the Debug window:

```
Dim arrSalesPerDay() As Integer = New Integer(6) {1, 2, 3, 4, 5, 6, 7}
Dim intElement As Integer
For Each intElement In arrSalesPerDay
    Debug.Write(intElement)
Next
```

Part	Required or Optional	Description
element	Required	Variable of the data type of *group*. Used to iterate through the elements of the array.
group	Required	Object variable that refers to an array. May also refer to a collection.
statements	Optional	Code that executes each iteration of the loop.
Exit for	Optional	Ends the loop prematurely, before all elements of the array have been accessed.

Table 8-6   Parts of the For Each...Next Statement

Ask the Expert

Question: Which is better to use with an array, a For Each...Next statement or a For...Next statement?

Answer: Either works fine to access the entire array. I prefer the For Each...Next statement simply because it relieves me from having to worry about the number of elements in the array. However, if the position of an element in the array is important, a For...Next statement may be preferable since code in it usually has the value of the index of the current array element.

You may have a For Each...Next statement even if there are no elements in the group. In this situation, the statements inside the loop simply will not execute.

Once the For Each...Next statement is reached in code, the *statements* are executed for the first element in the *group*, and then for the second element (if any), and so on until all of the elements of the *group* have been accessed. When there are no more elements to access, the loop is terminated and execution continues with the statement following the Next statement.

The Exit For statement serves the same function with a For Each...Next statement as it does with a For...Next statement. You also can nest For Each... Next statements just as you can For...Next statements.

8

1-Minute Drill

● Do you need to specify in a For Each...Next statement the number of elements in the array?

● No. This is what distinguishes a For Each...Next statement from a For...Next statement.

prj8-1.zip

Project 8-1: Day of Week Calculator

Surprisingly often I want to know the day of the week of an upcoming birthday or other particular date. This application will enable you to choose any date from 1990 through 2000 and determine the day of the week that date falls on. Figure 8-1 shows the project in action.

This project introduces the ComboBox control. This control lists choices from which the application user may pick. This project will have three ComboBox controls, from which the user may choose the month, day, and year respectively. Having the application user choose the date from the ComboBox controls eliminates the possibility of the application user choosing an invalid date. We will use arrays and loops to populate the ComboBox controls, and also use arrays to verify that the values in the "day" ComboBox control do not exceed the maximum number of days in the chosen month.

Once the user chooses a date using the three ComboBox controls, we will use a *DateTime* class, and the *DayOfWeek* property of that class, to determine the day of the week that the particular date falls on.

The code may appear somewhat complex, particularly in leap years, when February has 29 days instead of 28. However, the code appears more complex than it really is. Just be patient and go through the code step by step. Indeed, you may find a better way to write it!

Step-by-Step

1. Create a Windows application.

2. Name the default form *frmDayOfWeek*, and set its *Caption* property to "Day of Week Calculator."

3. Add a ComboBox component to the form from the Toolbox. This component will list the twelve months of the year and permit the application user to pick one. Set the following properties to the following values:

● *Name – cboMonths.*

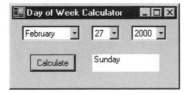

| **Figure 8-1** | Day of Week Calculator |

- *Text* – This property gets or sets the string shown in the text portion of the ComboBox. Set this property to a blank string. We will set through code the string shown in the text portion of the ComboBox.

- *DropDownStyle* – Set this property to *DropDownList*. The *DropDownStyle* property has three potential values: (a) *DropDownList*, where the text portion is not editable and you must select the arrow to view the drop-down, (b) *DropDown* (the default), the same as *DropDownList* except the text portion is editable, and (c) *Simple*, where the list always displays. *DropDownList* is preferred here to *DropDown* because the text portion should not be editable as the component lists the 12 months of the year, and also is preferred to *Simple* to save space on the form by not always displaying the list.

- *MaxDropDownItems* – This property gets or sets the maximum number of items to be shown in the drop-down portion of the ComboBox. Since there are 12 months, set this property to 12. Depending on the number of items in the list, you may not want the drop-down portion to show all of them at once, but here 12 items can be shown without the drop-down appearing unduly long.

4. Add another ComboBox component to the form from the Toolbox. This component will list from one to the maximum number of days of the month chosen in *cboMonths*, and will permit the application user to pick one. Set the following properties to the following values:

- *Name* – *cboDays*.

- *Text* –Set this property to a blank string. As with *cboMonths*, we will set through code the string shown in the text portion of *cboDays*.

- *DropDownStyle* – Set this property to *DropDownList*.

- *MaxDropDownItems* – Set this property to 10. Depending on the month, there will be 28 to 31 items in the list, too many to display all at once.

5. Add a third ComboBox component to the form from the Toolbox. This component will list years from 1990 to 2000, and permit the application user to pick one. Set the following properties to the following values:

- *Name* – *cboYears*.

- *Text* – Set this property to a blank string. As with the other ComboBox controls, we will set through code the string shown in the text portion of *cboYears*.

- *DropDownStyle* – Set this property to *DropDownList*.

- *MaxDropDownItems* – Set this property to 11. All 11 years can be shown without the drop-down appearing unduly long.

8

6. Add a *Label* component to the form from the Toolbox. Name it *lblDayOfWeek*, and set its *Text* property to blank and its *BackColor* property to *HighlightText*.

7. Add a *Button* component to the form from the Toolbox. Name it *btnCalculate*, and set its *Text* property to "Calculate."

8. Add the following module level variable and constant declarations. The code above these declarations also is included to assist you in knowing where these declarations should be placed:

```
Option Strict On
Public Class frmDayOfWeek
    Inherits System.Windows.Forms.Form
#Region " Windows Form Designer generated code"
'start of variable and constant declarations
Const arrMonths() As String = _
    {"January", "February", "March", "April", "May", _
    "June", "July", "August", "September", _
    "October", "November", "December"}
Const arrDaysInMonths() As Integer = _
    {31, 28, 31, 30, 31, 30, 31, 31, 30, 31, 30, 31}
Const BASEYEAR As Integer = 1990
```

The array variable *arrMonths* is an array of the names of all of the months of the year. This array will be used to fill the ComboBox *cboMonths*. The array variable *arrDaysInMonths* is an array of the highest day in order of each month of the year (January has 31 days, February 28, and so on). This array will be used to confirm that the days listed in cboDays do not exceed the highest day in the chosen month. The issue of February having 29 days in a leap year is dealt with in code explained in the following paragraphs. Finally, since the lowest year in this application is 1990, a constant is declared for that year. These variables and constants are declared at module-level since they will need to be accessed in more than one procedure.

9. Add the following event procedure for the *Load* event of *frmDayOfWeek*:

```
Private Sub frmDayOfWeek_Load(ByVal sender As Object, _
    ByVal e As System.EventArgs) Handles MyBase.Load
Dim intCounter As Integer
For intCounter = 0 To UBound(arrMonths)
    cboMonths.Items.Add(arrMonths(intCounter))
Next
For intCounter = 0 To UBound(arrDaysInMonths)
    cboDays.Items.Add(arrDaysInMonths(intCounter))
Next
```

```
For intCounter = 1990 To 2000
   cboYears.Items.Add(CStr(intCounter))
Next
cboMonths.SelectedIndex = 0
cboDays.SelectedIndex = 0
cboYears.SelectedIndex = 0
End Sub
```

The first *For* loop fills the ComboBox *cboMonths* with the elements of the array *arrMonths*. The second *For* loop fills the ComboBox *cboYears* with values from 1990 to 2000. The ComboBox *cboDays* will be filled using code explained in the following paragraphs. Finally, the *SelectedIndex* property of each ComboBox is set to zero. The *SelectedIndex* property is a zero-based index of the currently selected item in the ComboBox. Setting the *SelectedIndex* property of a ComboBox to zero will cause the first item in the ComboBox to display in the text portion.

10. Add the following event procedure for the *SelectedIndexChanged* event of *cboMonths*:

```
Private Sub cboMonths_SelectedIndexChanged(ByVal sender As Object, _
   ByVal e As System.EventArgs) Handles cboMonths.SelectedIndexChanged
Dim intCurrDay As Integer = cboDays.SelectedIndex + 1
cboDays.Items.Clear()
Dim intCounter, intMaxDay As Integer
If cboMonths.SelectedIndex = 1 And _
   (cboYears.SelectedIndex + BASEYEAR) Mod 4 = 0 Then
   intMaxDay = 29
Else
   intMaxDay = arrDaysInMonths(cboMonths.SelectedIndex)
End If
For intCounter = 1 To intMaxDay
   cboDays.Items.Add(intCounter)
Next
If intCurrDay > intMaxDay Then
   cboDays.SelectedIndex = intMaxDay - 1
Else
   cboDays.SelectedIndex = intCurrDay - 1
End If
End Sub
```

The *SelectedIndexChanged* event of a ComboBox class occurs when the *SelectedIndex* property has changed. The *SelectedIndex* property of *cboMonths* changes when the user chooses a different month. When that happens, the number of days to be listed in *cboDays* may change also. For example, if the user changes the month from January to April, the number of days listed in *cboDays* must change from 1 through 31 to 1 through 30. The ComboBox

8

class has an *Items* collection, which contains all of the items in the ComboBox. This collection has a *Clear* method, which empties out the ComboBox before we fill it. The *For* loop fills *cboDays* with 1 through the maximum number of days in that month based on the corresponding value in *arrDaysInMonths*. Each item is added using the *Add* method of the *Items* collection of the ComboBox class. The first If block concerns the possibility that the month is February and the year is a leap year, in which case the number of days is 29, not 28. The second and final If block adjusts the day displayed in *cboDays* if it is too high for the newly chosen month. For example, if the previous selected day was January 31, and the month was changed from January to April, since April has only 30 days, not 31, the code changes the day of the month from 31 to 30.

11. Add the following event procedure for the *SelectedIndexChanged* event of *cboYears*:

```
Private Sub cboYears_SelectedIndexChanged(ByVal sender As Object, _
    ByVal e As System.EventArgs) Handles cboYears.SelectedIndexChanged
Dim intCounter As Integer
If cboMonths.SelectedIndex = 1 Then
    Dim intCurrDay As Integer = cboDays.SelectedIndex + 1
    If CBool((cboYears.SelectedIndex + BASEYEAR) Mod 4) Then
        If cboDays.Items.Count = 29 Then
            cboDays.Items.Clear()
            For intCounter = 1 To 28
                cboDays.Items.Add(intCounter)
            Next
            If intCurrDay = 29 Then
                cboDays.SelectedIndex = 27
            End If
        End If
    Else
        If cboDays.Items.Count = 28 Then
            cboDays.Items.Clear()
            For intCounter = 1 To 29
                cboDays.Items.Add(intCounter)
            Next
            cboDays.SelectedIndex = intCurrDay - 1
        End If
    End If
End If
End Sub
```

While the code is lengthy, the concept is fairly straightforward. A change in the year will affect the number of days displayed in *cboDays* only if the month chosen is February and the year has been changed from a leap year to a non leap year, or vice versa. The remainder of the code is similar to that of the corresponding event procedure in *cboMonths*.

12. Add the following event procedure for the Click event of *btnCalculate*:

```
Private Sub btnCalculate_Click(ByVal sender As Object, _
    ByVal e As System.EventArgs) Handles btnCalculate.Click
Dim dtChosenDay As New DateTime _
    (cboYears.SelectedIndex + BASEYEAR, _
    cboMonths.SelectedIndex + 1, _
    cboDays.SelectedIndex + 1)
Select Case dtChosenDay.DayOfWeek
    Case DayOfWeek.Sunday
        lblDayOfWeek.Text = "Sunday"
    Case DayOfWeek.Monday
        lblDayOfWeek.Text = "Monday"
    Case DayOfWeek.Tuesday
        lblDayOfWeek.Text = "Tuesday"
    Case DayOfWeek.Wednesday
        lblDayOfWeek.Text = "Wednesday"
    Case DayOfWeek.Thursday
        lblDayOfWeek.Text = "Thursday"
    Case DayOfWeek.Friday
        lblDayOfWeek.Text = "Friday"
    Case DayOfWeek.Saturday
        lblDayOfWeek.Text = "Saturday"
End Select
End Sub
```

8

This code creates a *DateTime* variable using three arguments, which are the year, month and day respectively. The values for these arguments are based on the index of the selected items in the ComboBox controls. The *DayOfWeek* property returns an enumerated value based on the day of the week that date falls on. A Select Case statement is used to set the Text property of *lblDayOfWeek* to a string corresponding to the enumerated value.

Summary

Loops are used to repeat the execution of code statements. The For…Next statement is used to repeat code execution a specified number of times. By contrast, the While…End While and Do statements are used to repeat code execution an indefinite number of times. Additionally, the Do statement can test the condition at the end of the loop instead of at the beginning.

An array permits you to use a single variable to store many values. The values are stored at consecutive indexes, starting with zero and then incrementing by one for each additional element of the array. You can use the ReDim statement to resize an array, and the Preserve keyword to retain the values of the original array.

The array is an object, and has useful properties and methods. For example, the Length property returns the number of elements in the array and the GetUpperBound method returns the upper bound of an array.

Loops and arrays work well together. You can use a loop to access each consecutive element in an array, whether to assign a value of that element or to display that value. The For Each…Next statement is designed to work with arrays, and does not require code concerning the number of elements in the array.

☑ *Mastery Check*

1. The condition in a loop is of which data type?

   A. Boolean

   B. Byte

   C. Integer

   D. String

2. Which loop may test the condition at the bottom instead of at the top?

   A. Do

   B. For…Next

   C. For Each…Next

   D. While…End While

3. Which loop statement is designed to execute a fixed number of times?

   A. Do

   B. For…Next

   C. For Each…Next

   D. While…End While

4. Statements inside a For Each…Next loop must be executed at least once.

   A. True

   B. False

5. You can use the _____ statement to change by code the upper bound of an existing array.

6. You can change the lower bound of an array.

   A. True

   B. False

8

☑ *Mastery Check*

7. Which statement do you use to retain the values of the original array when you resize it?

A. Next

B. Preserve

C. ReDim

D. Step

8. Which of the following statements is true about a difference between a For Each...Next statement and a For...Next statement?

A. Only a For Each...Next statement can be used to access arrays.

B. Only a For...Next statement can be used to access arrays.

C. In a For Each...Next statement, you need to specify the number of elements in the array.

D. In a *For...Next* statement, you need to specify the number of elements in the array.

Module 9

Procedures

The Goals of this Module

- Understand what a procedure is
- Know the different types of procedures and the differences among them
- Understand how to call a procedure
- Know the different ways of passing arguments
- Know how to use the return values of functions

A *procedure* is a block of one or more code statements. All Visual Basic .NET code is written within procedures. Visual Basic .NET has many built-in procedures. Additionally, you can write your own procedures.

This module will explain the different types of procedures and how to write them. It also will explain how you call a procedure so the code within it will execute, how you can pass information to the procedures, and how the procedures return information to the code that called them.

Types of Procedures

Visual Basic .NET supports three types of procedures:

- A *subroutine*, which contains code that performs actions, but does not return a value to the code that calls the subroutine. Event procedures are subroutines.

- A *function* is the same as a subroutine except that a function returns a value to the code that calls the function. The InputBox function is an example of a function.

- A *property procedure* returns or assigns the value of a property of an object.

This module will cover subroutines and functions. Property procedures are covered in Module 10.

Since all Visual Basic .NET code must be written within procedures, we necessarily have been working with procedures, specifically subroutines and functions, since the early modules.

In Module 3, we started working with event procedures. Event procedures contain a block of code that executes when an event happens to an object. In the following example from Module 3, when the form is clicked, the code statement Me.Text = "Clicked" within the Click event procedure executes, causing the title of the form to change to "Clicked":

```
Private Sub Form1_Click(ByVal sender As Object, _
    ByVal e As System.EventArgs) Handles MyBase.Click
        Me.Text = "Clicked"
End Sub
```

Event procedures are subroutines. While the code within them executes, they do not return a value as a function does.

A procedure we discussed in Module 5 that does return a value is the InputBox function, which returns the value of text input by the application user. In the following example, the InputBox function assigns the application user's input to the variable strName:

```
Dim strName As String
strName = InputBox("Enter your name")
```

Built-in vs. Programmer-defined Procedures

Event procedures and the InputBox function have in common that they are built into Visual Basic .NET. The code inside the event procedure executes, seemingly automatically, when the specified event happens to the specified object. You need not write any code to cause the event procedure to execute when the specified event happens. Similarly, you do not need to write any code for the InputBox function to do what it does, display an input box and return the value typed by the application user in the input box.

Built-in procedures simplify your programming tasks. For example, you could write a procedure that duplicates what the InputBox function does. However, Visual Basic .NET saves you the trouble by providing the InputBox function for you. Visual Basic .NET has many other built-in procedures that simplify your programming tasks.

While Visual Basic .NET has numerous useful built-in procedures, not even the creators of Visual Basic .NET could anticipate every conceivable programming task and supply a built-in procedure to perform that task. Indeed, even if they could, the Visual Basic .NET language might become too large and unwieldy. Thus, there are many times when you need to create your own procedures. Visual Basic .NET enables you to do so, and this module will show you how.

Methods Contrasted

We also have been using methods since the early modules. For example, in Module 3, the Write method of the Debug object outputs to the Debug window the coordinates of the mouse as the mouse moves across the form:

```
Private Sub Form1_MouseMove(ByVal sender As Object, _
   ByVal e As System.Windows.Forms.MouseEventArgs) _
   Handles MyBase.MouseMove
      Debug.Write(e.X & "," & e.Y & " ")
End Sub
```

9

Methods are procedures, but not all procedures are methods. The primary difference between a method and a procedure is that a method may only be called from a specific object, whereas a procedure may be called independently from an object.

For example, the Write method belongs to the Debug object. You could not call the Write method from a Form object, or independently of any object. That is why the Debug object and the Dot (.) operator precede the Write method. By contrast, the InputBox function is not preceded by any object name.

1-Minute Drill

● What is the difference between a subroutine and a function?

● Are you limited to the procedures built into Visual Basic .NET?

● What is the difference between a procedure and a method?

Ask the Expert

Question: Do programmers have to create their own procedures?

Answer: No, they don't have to. You could write inside an event procedure the same code that you would place a procedure you create. However, writing your own procedures has several advantages. Your code is more readable if divided up among several smaller procedures than if it is all put in to one procedure that contains pages of code. Additionally, if you are performing essentially the same task from several places in the program, you can avoid duplication of code by putting the code that performs that task in one place, as opposed to repeating that code in each place in the program that may call for the performance of that task. Having the code in one place doesn't just mean less initial typing. If you later have to fix a bug in how you perform that task, or simply find a better way to perform the task, you only have to change the code in one place rather than many.

● A function returns a value whereas a subroutine does not.
● No. Visual Basic .NET enables you to create your own procedures.
● The primary difference between methods and procedures is that a method may only be called from a specific object, whereas a procedure may be called independently from an object.

Subroutines

There are two steps to using subroutines. The first step is to create them, by declaring the subroutine, much as you create a variable by declaring it. The second step is to call the subroutine so the code within it executes. Additionally, you can pass information to the subroutine by using arguments.

Declaring a Subroutine

Event procedures are built into Visual Basic .NET. Therefore, you do not need to tell Visual Basic .NET what these procedures are or what they do.

However, if you write your own procedures, you do need to tell Visual Basic .NET what they are or what they do. Otherwise, the compiler will not be able to recognize, much less execute, the procedure, and the result will be a compiler error.

As you tell Visual Basic .NET what a variable is by declaring it, you similarly tell Visual Basic .NET what a procedure is and does by declaring the procedure.

The syntax for declaring a Sub procedure is:

```
[accessibility] Sub name[(argumentlist)]
    Statements
    [Return | Exit Sub]
End Sub
```

Table 9-1 lists and describes the elements of the Sub procedure.

Element	Required or Optional	Description
accessibility	Optional	Determines where the subroutine may be called from.
Sub	Required	Keyword indicating procedure is a subroutine.
name	Required	Name of subroutine.
argumentlist	Optional	Information passed to the subroutine.
Statements	Required	Code that executes each time the subroutine is called.
Return	Optional	Ends execution of the subroutine before *End Sub* statement. Alternative to *Exit Sub*.
Exit Sub	Optional	Ends execution of subroutine before the End Sub statement. Alternative to Return.
End Sub	Required	Ends execution of the subroutine.

Table 9-1   Elements of a Subroutine

The following programmer-defined subroutine, named PrintInput, illustrates this syntax. This subroutine outputs to the Debug window what the user types in an input box, unless the user either did not type anything or chose the Cancel button of the input box:

```
Private Sub PrintInput ()
Dim strInput As String
strInput = InputBox("Enter something")
If strInput = "" Then
   Return ' or Exit Sub
End If
Debug.Write strInput
End Sub
```

The accessibility specifier is Private. The name of the subroutine is PrintInput. This subroutine has no arguments, so the parentheses are empty. If strInput is an empty string, because either the user did not input anything or chose the Cancel button of the input box, then the Return statement, or alternatively an Exit Sub statement, ends the execution of the subroutine, so the Debug.Write strInput statement does not execute. Otherwise, that statement does execute.

Adding the Subroutine to the Code of a Form

You have two choices regarding where to add the PrintInput subroutine to your project (so you can run the code yourself).

You can add the subroutine to the code of the default form. As shown in Figure 9-1, place the subroutine after the Region directive "Windows Form Designer generated code." It does not matter where after the Region directive you place the subroutine, as long as you do not place it inside another procedure.

Once you have included the subroutine in the form's code, the subroutine will be included in the list of the procedures belonging to the form, as shown in Figure 9-2.

Alternatively, you can add the subroutine to a module. A module, like a form, contains code, but unlike a form, has no graphical user interface.

When you create a Windows application, Visual Basic .NET automatically adds a form to your project. However, you have to add the module. Choose Add Module from the Project menu. This displays the Add New Item – Procedure dialog box shown in Figure 9-3.

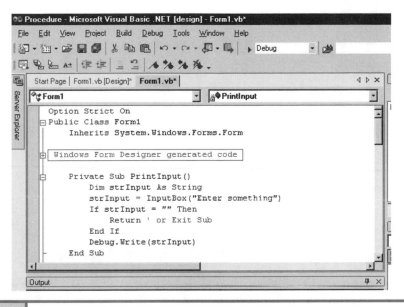

Figure 9-1   The subroutine in the code view of the form

Choose Module from the dialog box and click OK. This will add the module to your project and add the following code to the code window of that module:

```
Module Module1

End Module
```

You then put the subroutine between the two lines.

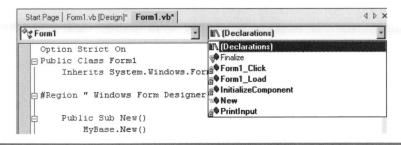

Figure 9-2   PrintInput in the list of procedures belonging to the form

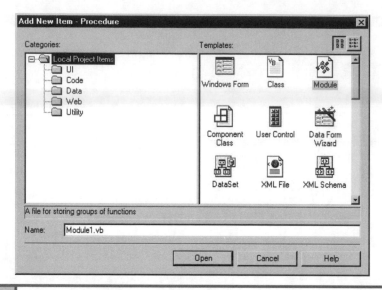

Figure 9-3   Adding a module to your project

Accessibility

The accessibility specifiers for the first procedures you will write will be either Private or Public. The accessibility specifier is optional. If omitted, the subroutine is Public.

These accessibility specifiers have essentially the same function with procedures as they do with module-level variables. A procedure declared with the Private accessibility specifier only can be called within the class in which it is declared, whereas a procedure declared with the Public accessibility specifier may be called outside the class in which it is declared. Thus, if you declare the procedure within a form and will only access the procedure from that form, you can declare the procedure as Private. However, if you declare the procedure in a module, and plan to access it from forms in your project, you should declare the procedure as Public.

Tip

As with module-level variables, declare procedures as Private unless you really need to be able to access them outside the class.

Naming the Procedure

You have relative freedom in naming a procedure as you do in naming variables. There are only a few limitations, such as no embedded spaces within the procedure name—for example, Print Input.

While Visual Basic .NET imposes few limitations on how you name a procedure, as with naming variables, you should name procedures so that what they do is reasonably clear to you and other programmers who may have to review your code. Procedure names such as Sub1, Sub2, Sub3, and so on are not very helpful. You, and even more so your fellow programmers, will have trouble remembering which of them does what. By contrast, descriptive procedure names such as PrintName, PrintAddress, PrintCity, and so on are quite helpful in describing what each procedure does.

I agree with Microsoft's recommendation in MSDN that you use the *NounVerb* or *VerbNoun* style to create a name that clearly identifies what the procedure does. For example, the procedure name PrintName is a concatenation of the verb Print, which indicates the action the procedure takes, and the noun Name, which indicates the information printed. You might have more than one noun, such as PrintCustomerName. In any event, the first letter of each noun and verb is capitalized.

Tip

When you store related procedures in the same module, the Procedures box in the Code window will display those procedures alphabetically, as shown in Figure 9-2. If you use the *NounVerb* naming style, related procedures are listed together. For example, if you have several procedures concerning customers, by using the *NounVerb* naming style, procedures such as CustomerAdd, CustomerDelete, and CustomerUpdate would all be displayed together in the Procedures dialog box.

9

Argument List

The PrintInput subroutine has no arguments. The subject of arguments—information given to a procedure that helps it perform its task—will be covered in this module as soon as we have covered the subject of calling the subroutine. This order will make the concept of arguments easier to understand. Accordingly, for now, the procedures we will use have no arguments.

Return and Exit Sub Statements

The Return statement ends execution of subroutine before the End Sub statement. In the example PrintInput subroutine, the Return statement ends the execution of the subroutine, so the Debug.Write strInput statement does not execute. Usually the Return statement is coupled with an If statement so that whether the Return statement executes depends on a condition that evaluates to True or False.

The Exit Sub statement accomplishes the same result as the Return statement. The two are interchangeable in subroutines.

Calling the Subroutine

Firefighters put out fires. However, they generally do not drive around looking for fires. Instead, they go out to a fire when called upon to do so.

In the same way, a subroutine does not just execute by itself. The statements within a subroutine do not execute until and unless the subroutine is called.

A subroutine may be called by user action or by code. Event procedures usually are called by user action. In the preceding example, in which the caption of a form was changed to "Clicked", the code inside the event procedure executed because of the user action of clicking a form.

By contrast, you could call the PrintInput subroutine from code—for example, from an event procedure such as the Click event of the form:

```
Private Sub Form1_Click(ByVal sender As Object, _
   ByVal e As System.EventArgs) Handles MyBase.Click
   PrintInput()
End Sub
```

Note

According to MSDN, if there are no arguments, the parentheses are optional. However, you may find that the Visual Basic .NET IDE insists on putting the parentheses after the name of the called subroutine.

Optionally, you can use the Call statement to call the PrintInput subroutine:

```
Call PrintInput()
```

Tip

The Call statement is a holdover from prior versions of Visual Basic. There really is no need to use it with subroutines.

Continuing the firefighter analogy, when firefighters arrive at the scene of the fire, they take control and maintain that control until they put out the fire. Similarly, once the subroutine is called, whether by user action or code, it takes control of the application, and no other code executes without being called by the subroutine, until the subroutine is finished.

Completing the analogy, when the firefighters successfully put out the fire, they pack up their equipment and go back to the fire station, relinquishing control of the fire scene. Similarly, when the subroutine finishes executing, it relinquishes control of the application, and whatever code (or user action) follows the call of the subroutine determines the further flow of the application.

Arguments

Returning to our firefighter analogy, when they are called to a fire, they need to know the location of the fire, the type of fire (house fire, chemical fire, and so on) so they know what equipment to bring, and other pertinent information. The particular location and type of fire may well vary from call to call, but in each case this information is necessary in order for the firemen to do their job.

Similarly, a procedure often needs information in order to perform its task. For example, a subroutine that outputs the square of a number to the Debug window needs to know the number to be squared. The value of that number may vary from call to call, but in each case the procedure will need to know the particular number to be squared. This information is called an argument, or its synonym, a parameter.

Declaring an Argument

If a procedure has no arguments, the parentheses following the procedure name are empty. However, if a procedure has one or more arguments, each argument must be declared within the parentheses.

The syntax for each argument in the argument list is as follows:

```
[Optional] [ByVal|ByRef] [ParamArray] argumentname As datatype
```

9

---Note -------

The As *datatype* clause is required for all procedure arguments unless Option Strict is off (which it should not be), in which case the As *datatype* clause is optional, except that if any one argument uses it, all arguments must use it. Additionally, if an argument is optional, you must also supply a default value in its declaration, as will be covered later in this section in the discussion on optional arguments.

The keywords Optional, ByVal, ByRef, and ParamArray will be discussed later in this section. The *argumentname* is a name, similar to a variable name, which will be used to refer to the argument inside the body of the procedure. The *datatype* is, as the word suggests, the data type of the argument.

The following example outputs the square of the argument to the Debug window. The *argumentname* is num, and the *datatype* is an Integer:

```
Private Sub Power(ByVal num As Integer)
Debug.Write(num & " to the 2nd power = " & num ^ 2)
End Sub
```

Passing an Argument to a Procedure

When you call the Power procedure, for example, in the Click event of the form

```
Power(5)
```

the output would be:

```
5 to the 2nd power = 25
```

The statement Power(5) has the effect of assigning the value 5 to the argument *num* in Power. Thus, the statement in Power

```
Debug.Write(num & " to the 2nd power = " & num ^ 2)
```

executes as follows when the value passed is 5:

```
Debug.Write(5 & " to the 2nd power = " & 5 ^ 2)
```

When you call a procedure, you must pass the exact number of arguments specified in the procedure's declaration. For example, if you tried to call the Power procedure with no arguments

```
Power()
```

the compiler would complain: "Argument not specified for the parameter 'num' of 'Private Sub Power(num As Integer)'."

Similarly, if you tried to call the Power procedure with more than one argument

```
Power(5, 3)
```

the compiler would complain: "Too many arguments to 'Private Sub Power(num As Integer)'."

The argument passed also must be the same data type specified in the procedure's declaration or converted to that data type with a widening conversion. For example, if you tried to call the Power subroutine as follows

```
Dim strInput As String
strInput = InputBox("Enter a number")
Power(strInput)
```

the compiler would complain: "Option Strict On disallows implicit conversions from 'String' to 'Integer'."

Tip

You could solve that problem by using the type conversion keyword CInt in the last line: Power(CInt(strInput)).

9

Multiple Arguments

A subroutine may require more than one argument in order to do its job. For example, the Power subroutine previously is limited to raising its argument to the power of 2. We can expand the functionality of this subroutine so it can raise the first argument to a different power than 2 by including a second argument, which is the power to which the first argument will be raised. The Power subroutine may be rewritten as follows:

```
Private Sub Power(ByVal num As Integer, _
  ByVal exponent As Integer)
   Debug.Write(num & " to the power of " & _
     exponent & " = " & num ^ exponent)
End Sub
```

As this example illustrates, the only difference between declaring a procedure with a single argument and declaring a procedure with more than one argument is that a comma separates the arguments. Similarly, when you call the procedure, a comma separates the arguments:

```
Power(5, 3)
```

The output with this call is 5 to the power of 3 = 125.

Argument Passing by Position and by Name

The two-argument example of the Power subroutine passed the two arguments by position. The first value passed, 5, was assigned to the first argument, num, and the second value passed, 3, was assigned to the second argument, exponent. Thus, had the call of the subroutine been Power(3, 5) instead of Power(5, 3), the result would have been 3^5 instead of 5^3.

You also can pass arguments by name, without regard to position. When you pass an argument by name, you specify the argument's declared name followed by a colon and an equal sign (:=), followed by the argument value. You can supply named arguments in any order. For example, if you call Power as follows

```
Power(exponent:=3, num:=5)
```

the resulting output ("5 to the power of 3 = 125") is the same as if you had called Power(5, 3).

Tip

You can supply arguments both by position and by name in a single procedure call. However, as my mother told me when I was a child, "Just because you can do something doesn't mean you should do it." My advice is not to mix supplying arguments by position and by name in a single procedure call because it makes your code more difficult to read.

1-Minute Drill

● Do arguments have to be passed in the order in which they are declared?

● Does the data type of the argument passed have to be identical to the data type of the argument declared?

● No, if they are passed by name.
● No, you can pass a data type that can be converted to the data type declared through a widening conversion.

Ask the Expert

Question: Which is better, passing arguments by position or by name?

Answer: As discussed later in this module, passing by name is advantageous when using optional arguments, and not possible when using a ParamArray. Leaving these particular instances aside, there is a tradeoff between passing arguments by name and passing arguments by position. Passing arguments by name involves less typing. However, passing arguments by name may make your code clearer, particularly if the argument names are self-describing. In other words, passing arguments by name will not make your code clearer if the argument names are num1, num2, and so on, but might if the argument names are exponent, birthday, and so on.

Functions

As with subroutines, functions need to be created by declaring them, and then invoked by calling them. Also, as with subroutines, you can pass information to functions by using arguments. However, unlike subroutines, functions present an additional consideration, the value they return.

Declaring Functions

The syntax for declaring a function is quite similar to that for declaring a subroutine:

```
[accessibility] Function name[(argumentlist)] As Type
   Statements
   [Exit Function]
   Return [ or functionname = ] return value
End Function
```

Table 9-2 lists and describes the elements of a function.

Element	Required or Optional	Description
accessibility	Optional	Determines where the function may be called from.
Function	Required	Keyword indicating procedure is a function.
name	Required	Name of the function.
argumentlist	Optional	Same as in subroutine, the information passed to the function.
As Type	Required if Option Strict on, otherwise Optional	Data type of the return value.
Statements	Required	Code that executes each time the function is called.
Return (or name =) return value	Optional	Returns value of the function. The Return statement also ends execution of the function before the End Function statement, whereas name = return value does not.
Exit Function	Optional	Ends execution of the function before the End Function statement.

Table 9-2   Elements of a Function

The following programmer-defined function, named ReturnInput, illustrates this syntax. This function returns what the user input in the input box, unless the user did not input anything or chose the Cancel button of the input box, in which case the function returns the string "Nothing entered":

```
Private Function ReturnInput() As String
Dim strInput As String
strInput = InputBox("Enter something")
If strInput = "" Then
   Return "Nothing entered"
End If
ReturnInput = strInput
End Function
```

There is a significant overlap between the syntax for declaring a function and the syntax for declaring a subroutine. The discussion in subroutines regarding accessibility, naming, argument list, and statements applies equally to functions. With respect to naming, unlike naming variables (when the prefix of the name indicates the variable's data type), when naming functions, it is not necessary to use a prefix or suffix to specify the data type of the return value.

Additionally, the Exit Function and End Function statements are to functions as the Exit Sub and End Sub statements are to subroutines. The sole difference is the substitution of the Function keyword for the Sub keyword.

The substantive differences in syntax between subroutines and functions relate to the fundamental difference between a subroutine and a function; the function, unlike a subroutine, returns a value.

First, if Option Strict is on, as it should be, then the As Type statement must follow the argument list to indicate the data type of the value being returned. In the ReturnInput example, the As Type statement indicates that the return value is a String. The data type being returned can be any built-in data type as well as programmer-defined data types.

Second, while the Exit Sub and Return statements are synonymous in subroutines, Exit Function and Return statements are not the same in functions. The Exit Function and Return statements are similar in that each ends the execution of the function before the End Function statement is reached. However, the Return statement also returns the value following it. In the ReturnInput example, the Return statement "Nothing entered" returns the literal string "Nothing entered".

Note

No Exit Function statement is required after the Return statement, as the Return statement, like the Exit Function statement, immediately ends the execution of the function.

Third, the Return statement is not the only way in which a function can return a value. The other alternative is to assign to the function name the value to be returned. In the ReturnInput example, the statement ReturnInput = strInput returns the value stored in the string variable strInput.

The function also could return the value stored in the string variable strInput with the statement Return strInput. The difference is that the syntax of returning a value by assigning it to the function name (such as ReturnInput = strInput) does not end the execution of the function, as is the case when using the Return statement. The function continues executing until an Exit Function or End Function statement is reached, and the return value assigned to the function name will remain the function's return value unless changed, either by assigning a different return value to the function name, or by using the Return statement.

Tip

As Microsoft points out in MSDN, you can use to your advantage that assigning a return value to the function name does not end the execution of the function by assigning a preliminary return value and adjusting it later in the function if necessary.

Technically, a function does not have to explicitly return a value. If the function ends, either by an Exit Function or End Function statement, without previously returning a value by either the Return statement or assigning a value to the function name, then the function returns the default value appropriate to the data type of the return value. This is 0 for Byte, Char, Decimal, Double, Integer, Long, Short, and Single; Nothing for Object, String, and all arrays; False for Boolean; and #1/1/0001 12:00 AM# for Date. However, it is good practice for functions to return a value.

Calling Functions

Calling a function is similar to calling a subroutine in that you refer to the function by name, followed by the arguments of the function in parentheses, or empty parentheses if the function has no arguments. The difference between calling a function and calling a subroutine concerns, once again, the return value of the function.

The most common scenario is to call the function on the right side of an assignment statement, with the left side of the assignment statement containing a variable or writable property of the same data type as the return value of the function. For example, converting the Power subroutine discussed earlier into a function, the Power function declared as follows will return the result of raising its first argument to the value of its second argument:

```
Private Function Power(ByVal num As Integer, _
    ByVal exponent As Integer) As Double
        Return num ^ exponent
End Function
```

You could call this function, such as in the Click event of the form, as follows, with the output being 125:

```
Dim dblResult As Double
dblResult = Power(5, 3)
Debug.Write(dblResult)
```

The steps are to declare a variable of the same data type as the return value of the function, then assign the return value of the function to that variable.

—⊦*Note:* ————————————————

The variable to which the return value of the function will be assigned does not have to be the same data type as the function return value. However, assuming Option Strict is on, any implicit conversion must be widening.

You also can call the function in an expression, such as:

```
Debug.Write(Power(5, 3))
```

The difference between calling the function on the right side of an assignment statement and calling the function in an expression is that when you call a function on the right side of an assignment statement, its return value is saved in a variable or writable property for later use. By contrast, when you call a function in an expression, its return value is not available for later use. Of course, this is not a problem unless you will need the return value later, which you may not.

Functions that return a Boolean value often are called in an expression in an If…Then control structure. For example, the following function, IsEmptyString, returns True if the string that is its argument is an empty string, and otherwise returns False:

```
Private Function IsEmptyString (ByVal str As String) As Boolean
If strInput = "" Then
    Return True
Else
    Return False
End If
End Function
```

The function may then be called following an If clause, and passed a string input by the user in an input box. If the user did not enter anything in the input box or chose the Cancel button, the function will return True, and the output

9

will be: "You didn't enter anything." If instead the user entered something in the input box, and chose the OK button, the function will return False, and the output will be: "You entered something."

```
Dim strInput As String
strInput = InputBox("Enter something")
If IsEmptyString(strInput) Then
    Debug.Write("You didn't enter anything")
Else
    Debug.Write("You entered something")
End If
```

Finally, you do not have to use the return value of the function. You can call the function as you would call a subroutine, such as:

```
IsEmptyString(strInput)
```

In that event, the return value simply would not be used. However, whatever code was in the function body still would execute.

Similarly, you also can call the function with the Call keyword:

```
Call IsEmptyString(strInput)
```

Here too the function's return value will be discarded. The difference is that you cannot use the Call keyword to call the function on the right side of an assignment statement or in an expression.

1-Minute Drill

- In returning the value of a function, what is the difference between using the Return statement and assigning the return value to the function name?

- How do you call a function to use its return value?

- What is the consequence of using the Call keyword to call a function?

- The difference between using the Return statement and assigning the return value to the function name when returning the value of a function is that the Return statement immediately ends execution of the function, whereas assigning the return value to the function name does not.
- To use a function's return value, you must call it either on the right side of an assignment statement or in an expression.
- The consequence of using the Call keyword to call a function is that the return value is discarded.

More on Arguments

So far, the examples of arguments have been relatively straightforward. However, there is far more to the subject of arguments. We first will explore the distinction between passing arguments ByVal and ByRef. We then will discuss optional arguments and parameter arrays.

Passing Arguments ByVal and ByRef

Previously, we have declared procedure arguments with the ByVal keyword, and have not used the alternative ByRef keyword. Now it is time to discuss the difference between the two keywords.

Difference Between ByVal and ByRef on Scalar Variables

Passing an argument by value (with the ByVal keyword) means the called procedure cannot modify the contents of a scalar variable (such as an Integer or Double) passed in the calling code as an argument. By contrast, passing by reference (with the ByRef keyword) means the called procedure can modify the contents of a variable passed in the calling code as an argument.

The following subroutine, named Swap, illustrates this difference. Swap takes two arguments and switches their values, so that when it finishes, the first argument has the value of the second, and the second argument has the value of the first. In this implementation of Swap, the arguments are passed ByVal.

```
Private Sub Swap(ByVal first As Integer, _
    ByVal second As Integer)
Dim temp As Integer
Debug.Write("Entering swap, first = " & _
    first & " and second = " & second & vbCrLf)
temp = first
first = second
second = temp
Debug.Write("Leaving Swap, first = " & _
    first & " and second = " & second & vbCrLf)
End Sub
```

Swap then is called from an event of the Form. This example uses the Load event, but another event, such as Click, also would work:

```
Private Sub Form1_Load(ByVal sender As System.Object, _
    ByVal e As System.EventArgs) Handles MyBase.Load
```

9

```
Dim intFirst, intSecond As Integer
intFirst = 1
intSecond = 2
Debug.Write("Before calling Swap, intFirst = " & _
   intFirst & " and intSecond = " & intSecond & vbCrLf)
Swap(intFirst, intSecond)
Debug.Write("After calling Swap, intFirst = " & _
   intFirst & " and intSecond = " & intSecond & vbCrLf)
End Sub
```

The output shows that the variables within Swap were changed, but intFirst and intSecond, the variables passed to Swap in the event procedure that called Swap, were not changed:

```
Before calling Swap, intFirst = 1 and intSecond = 2
Entering Swap, first = 1 and second = 2
Leaving Swap, first = 2 and second = 1
After calling Swap, intFirst = 1 and intSecond = 2
```

The reason why the variables passed to *Swap* were not changed is that they were passed by value by virtue of the *ByVal* keyword before the arguments in the declaration of *Swap*.

Now change the declaration of Swap so its arguments are declared with the ByRef keyword instead of the ByVal keyword. Otherwise, the declaration of Swap is unchanged.

```
Private Sub Swap(ByRef first As Integer, _
   ByRef second As Integer)
```

The output shows that intFirst and intSecond, the variables passed to Swap in the event procedure that called Swap, were changed:

```
Before calling Swap, intFirst = 1 and intSecond = 2
Entering Swap, first = 1 and second = 2
Leaving Swap, first = 2 and second = 1
After calling Swap, intFirst = 2 and intSecond = 1
```

Swap was able to change the value of variables passed to it ByRef because the value of variables can be changed. If a value that cannot be changed is passed as an argument, the called procedure can never modify its value, regardless of whether the value is passed ByVal or ByRef. For example, if instead of the call

```
Swap(intFirst, intSecond)
```

the call was

```
Swap(3, 5)
```

the passed values would not change, since they are literal values. The number 3 cannot have any value other than 3.

Difference Between ByVal and ByRef on Array Variables

The effect of ByVal and ByRef on arrays is slightly different than their effect on scalar variables such as Integer and Double.

As discussed in Module 8, an array variable points to the address in memory of an Array object. If an array is passed ByVal, the called procedure cannot change the array object to which the array variable points. However, it can change the values of the individual members of the array. If an array is passed ByRef, the called procedure can change either the array object to which the variable points or the values of the individual members of the array.

For example, the following subroutine, IncreaseByOne, increases by 1 the value of each element in the array passed to it by value:

```
Public Sub IncreaseByOne(ByVal A() As Long)
Dim J As Integer
For J - 0 To UBound(A)
   A(J) = A(J) + 1
Next J
End Sub
```

If IncreaseByOne is passed by an array, the value of each element of that array in the called code will be increased by 1:

```
Dim N() As Long = {10, 20, 30, 40}
IncreaseByOne(N)
```

Thus after IncreaseByOne is called, the element values of the array N are now 11, 21, 31, and 41. The same result would occur if the arguments were passed ByRef.

Next, the following subroutine, ReplaceArray, assigns a new array to its argument, and then adds 1 to each element of that new array:

```
Public Sub ReplaceArray(ByVal A() As Long)
Dim J As Integer
Dim K() As Long = {100, 200, 300}
A = K
```

9

```
For J = 0 To UBound(A)
   A(J) = A(J) + 1
Next J
End Sub
```

If ReplaceArray is passed by an array, the value of each element of that array in the called code will not be increased by 1:

```
Dim N() As Long = {10, 20, 30, 40}
ReplaceArray(N)
```

Instead, after ReplaceArray is called, the element values of the array N remain 10, 20, 30, and 40.

Because N was passed ByVal, ReplaceArray could not modify N by assigning a new array to it. When ReplaceArray created the new array instance K and assigned it to the argument A, then A, which had pointed to the array N in the calling code, instead pointed to the local array K. Consequently, A no longer pointed to the array N in the calling code. Thus, when the members of the array pointed to by A were changed, only the local array K, and not the array N in the calling code, was affected.

A different result would occur if in ReplaceArray the argument were declared ByRef. After ReplaceArray was called, the element values of the array N now would be 11, 21, 31, and 41. Since N was passed ByRef, ReplaceArray could modify N by assigning a new array to it. When ReplaceArray created the new array instance K and assigned it to the argument A, this also had the effect of assigning K to the array variable N in the calling code. Thus, when the members of the array pointed to by A were changed, the array N in the calling code was affected as well as the local array K.

Table 9-3 summarizes the effect of passing variables ByVal and ByRef.

Variable Type	Passed ByVal	Passed ByRef
Scalar (Integer, Double, and so on.)	The procedure cannot change the variable.	The procedure can change the variable.
Array (contains a pointer to a class or structure instance)	The procedure can change the values of the individual members of the array to which the variable points, but not the array object to which the variable points.	The procedure can change either the array object to which the variable points or the values of the individual members of the array.

Table 9-3   Effect of Passing Variables *ByVal* and *ByRef*

Overriding a ByRef Declaration

While the declaration of the arguments in the procedure determines whether arguments are passed ByVal or ByRef, the calling code can override a declaration that an argument is passed ByRef by enclosing the argument name in parentheses. The following example illustrates this:

```
Sub DoSomething(ByRef SomeNum As Integer)
SomeNum *= 2 'doubles SomeNum
End Sub
...
'Calling code
Dim intNum as Integer

intNum = 4
Call DoSomething((intNum))    ' Passes intNum ByVal even though declared ByRef
Debug.Write(intNum)       ' outputs 4, not 8
```

The reverse is not true. The calling code cannot override a declaration that an argument is passed ByVal by enclosing the argument name in parentheses.

Tip

The default in Visual Basic is to pass arguments by value. However, not everyone remembers defaults. Accordingly, your code will be easier to read if you include either the ByVal or ByRef keyword with every declared argument.

1-Minute Drill

● What is the difference between passing a scalar variable ByVal or ByRef as a procedure argument?

● What is the difference between passing an array variable ByVal or ByRef as a procedure argument?

Optional Arguments

You can specify that a procedure argument is optional by using the Optional keyword before ByVal or ByRef in the declaration of the argument, and

---

● The called procedure may modify the value of a scalar variable if it is passed ByRef, but not if it is passed ByVal.
● The called procedure may modify the values of the individual members of an array whether it is passed ByVal or ByRef, but may change the array object to which the array variable points only if it is passed ByRef.

Ask the Expert

Question: What should determine whether I pass an argument ByVal or ByRef?

Answer: The most important factor is whether you want to change the value of a variable passed as an argument in the calling code. If you do, the advantage of passing an argument ByRef is that the procedure can return a value to the calling code through that argument. You can only return one value, but you can pass multiple variables ByRef.

If you do not want to change the value of the variable passed as an argument in the calling code, the advantage of passing an argument ByVal is that it protects a variable from being changed by the called procedure.

However, when in more advanced programming you are passing large objects, such as an instance of a structure or a class, if you pass the object ByVal, the entire object is copied and passed, whereas if you pass the object ByRef, only the address of the object is passed, which could make your application run faster.

supplying the argument with a default value. An optional argument does not have to be passed when the procedure is called. In that event, its default value is passed automatically. However, if the argument is passed when the procedure is called, the value passed is used instead of the default value, and the procedure executes as if no optional argument was declared.

For example, you can modify the Power function previously discussed to make the *exponent* argument optional:

```
Private Function Power(ByVal num As Integer, _
    Optional ByVal exponent As Integer = 2) As Double
Return num ^ exponent
End Function
```

If the second argument is not passed

```
Debug.Write(Power(3))
```

then the default value of the *exponent* argument, 2, is used, and the output will be 9. However, if a value is passed for the *exponent* argument, that value is used instead of the default value. Thus, the following call to the Power function would output 27:

```
Debug.Write(Power(3, 3))
```

The rules for using optional arguments are:

- Every optional argument in the procedure definition must specify a default value.

- The default value for an optional argument must be a constant expression.

- Every argument following an optional argument in the procedure definition must also be optional.

In the example using the Power function, there was only one optional argument. However, sometimes you have several optional arguments, and you may want to supply values for some of them but not for others preceding them. For example, a procedure may have four arguments, for name, title, office, and bonus. Only the name argument is mandatory, the other three being optional, and you want to pass values for the name and bonus arguments, but not title and office arguments.

If you pass the values by position, you use successive commas to mark the positions of the omitted values. The following call supplies the mandatory name argument and the fourth, and optional, bonus argument, but not the optional title and office arguments:

```
Call HirePerson("Fred", , , 0)
```

Passing arguments by name is especially useful here, as you can avoid having to use consecutive commas to denote missing positional arguments:

```
Call HirePerson(name = "Fred", bonus = 0)
```

Passing arguments by name also makes it easier to keep track of which arguments you are passing and which ones you are omitting.

1-Minute Drill

● Do you have to specify a value for an optional argument?

● Can optional arguments be declared to the left or to the right of mandatory arguments?

Parameter Arrays

As a general rule, you must call a procedure with the same number of arguments specified in the declaration of the procedure. Optional arguments are one exception to this rule. However, even with optional arguments, you cannot call the procedure with more arguments than specified in the declaration of the procedure, only with less.

You may encounter circumstances in your programming when you do not know the exact number of arguments you will need. One example, given next, is when you are passing the scores that a student has earned on assignments he or she has submitted in the class. The number of such assignments will vary from class to class and is also based on whether it is early or late in the semester.

You use a parameter array when you need an indefinite number of arguments. The parameter array is always the last argument in the procedure, and is signified by the ParamArray keyword. The parameter array enables a procedure to accept an array of values for an argument. You do not have to know the number of elements in the parameter array when you define the procedure. The array size is determined individually by each call to the procedure.

The following subroutine StudentScores has two parameters. The first parameter, which is required, is the name of the student whose scores are being output. The second parameter is the parameter array, which contains the student's scores.

```
Sub StudentScores(ByVal Name As String, _
    ByVal ParamArray Scores() As String)
Dim I As Integer
Debug.WriteLine("Scores for " & Name & ":")
For I = 0 To UBound(Scores)
    Debug.WriteLine("Score " & I & ": " & Scores(I))
Next I
End Sub
```

● Yes.

● Every argument following an optional argument in the procedure definition must also be optional. Therefore, optional arguments can only be declared to the right of mandatory arguments.

Note

The StudentScores subroutine uses the WriteLine method of the Debug object. The WriteLine method, like the Write method we have been using, outputs to the Debug window. The difference is that the WriteLine method terminates output with a carriage return and line feed, so the next output to the Debug window will be on a different line.

The following rules apply in declaring a procedure with a parameter array:

- A procedure can have only one parameter array, and it must be the last argument in the procedure definition.

- The parameter array must be passed by value. It is good programming practice to explicitly include the ByVal keyword in the procedure definition.

- The code within the procedure must treat the parameter array as a one-dimensional array, each element of which is the same data type as the ParamArray data type.

- The parameter array is automatically optional. Its default value is an empty one-dimensional array of the parameter array's element type.

- All arguments preceding the parameter array must be required. The parameter array must be the only optional argument.

You then could call StudentScores passing six scores:

```
StudentScores("Anne", "10", "26", "32", "15", "22", "24")
```

The output would be:

```
Scores for Anne:
Score 0: 10
Score 1: 26
Score 2: 32
Score 3: 15
Score 4: 22
Score 5: 24
```

Next, you could call StudentScores with only four scores:

```
StudentScores("Mary", "High", "Low", "Average", "High")
```

The output would be:

```
Scores for Mary:
Score 0: High
Score 1: Low
Score 2: Average
Score 3: High
```

Instead of passing each score separately, you could declare an array, and pass that array as the parameter array:

```
Dim JohnScores() As String = {"35", "Absent", "21", "30"}
StudentScores("John", JohnScores)
```

The output would be:

```
Scores for John:
Score 0: 35
Score 1: Absent
Score 2: 21
Score 3: 30
```

When you call a procedure with a parameter array argument, you can pass any of the following for the parameter array:

- A list of an indefinite number of arguments, separated by commas. The data type of each argument must be implicitly convertible to the ParamArray element type. That is how the scores for Anne and Mary were passed in the preceding example.

- An array with the same element type as the parameter array. That is how the scores for John were passed in the preceding example.

- Nothing—that is, you can omit the ParamArray argument. In this case, an empty array is passed to the procedure. You can also pass the Nothing keyword, with the same effect.

One other restriction is that you can pass a parameter array only by position. You cannot pass a parameter array by name. The reason is that when you call the procedure, you supply an indefinite number of comma-separated arguments for the parameter array, and the compiler cannot associate more than one argument with a single name.

1-Minute Drill

● Can you use more than one parameter array in a procedure?

● Do you have to pass a value for a parameter array argument?

● Can a procedure have both a parameter array argument and another optional argument?

Procedure Overloading

You cannot declare two variables of the same name within the same procedure or at the level of the same module. You refer to variables by name, and with two variables of the same name and scope, the compiler would not be able to determine which of the two variables you intended to refer.

Similarly, you normally cannot declare two procedures with the same name within a module. You call procedures by name, and with two procedures with the same name, the compiler would not be able to determine which of the two procedures you intended to call.

However, having to use different names for closely related versions of a procedure can make your program needlessly complex for you and other programmers to read. For example, the following is a variant of the Power function used in previous examples, which raises an integer to a specified power:

```
Private Function Power(ByVal num As Integer, _
   ByVal exponent As Integer) As Double
Return num ^ exponent
End Function
```

Tip

The return value should be a Double and not an Integer because raising an integer to a negative exponent will result in a floating-point number. The compiler will object to the return value being an Integer if Option Strict is on since it expects a Double return value (for the reasons explained in the preceding sentence), and converting a Double to an Integer is a narrowing conversion prohibited by Option Strict.

● No. A procedure may not have more than one parameter array argument.
● No. The parameter array argument is optional. If you do not pass a value for the parameter array argument, an empty array of the specified data type is passed to the procedure.
● No. The parameter array argument must be the only optional argument in the procedure.

If you wanted to write a variant of the Power function that raises a Double (as opposed to an Integer) to a specified power, the only change would be that the first argument would be a Double instead of an Integer. Otherwise, the two variations of Power would be exactly the same.

```
Private Function Power(ByVal num As Double, _
    ByVal exponent As Integer) As Double
Return num ^ exponent
End Function
```

You could declare two differently named functions, such as PowerInteger and PowerDouble. However, since both functions essentially carry out the same task, it would be desirable simply to call Power, and pass it an Integer if you wanted to use the variant in which the first argument is an Integer, or pass it a Double if you wanted to use the variant in which the first argument is a Double. Thus, if you called

```
Debug.WriteLine(Power(5, 3))
```

the implementation of Power with the Integer being the first argument would be invoked, and the output would be 125. If instead the call of Power was

```
Debug.WriteLine(Power(5.5, 3))
```

the implementation of Power with the Double being the first argument would be invoked, and the output would be 166.375.

Visual Basic .NET enables you to overload a procedure by creating several different implementations of the procedure, all with the same name. You signify that a procedure is overloaded with the Overloads keyword, which goes after the access specifier (Private or Public) and before the Function or Sub keyword. The title of the Power function would be changed to make it an overloaded function as follows:

```
Private Overloads Function Power(ByVal num As Integer, _
    ByVal exponent As Integer) As Double
```

You overload procedures by naming them the same but varying their argument lists in at least one of the following respects:

- Number of arguments

- Order of the arguments

- Data types of the arguments (which is the case with the Power example)

You cannot overload a procedure without varying the argument list. In particular, you cannot overload a procedure by varying only one or more of the following items:

- Procedure modifier keywords, such as Public

- Argument names

- Argument modifier keywords, such as ByRef and Optional

- The data type of the return value, since the return value can be ignored

Using optional arguments limits your ability to use overloaded procedures. A procedure with an optional argument is equivalent to two overloaded procedures, one with the optional argument and one without it. Because of this, you cannot overload such a procedure with an argument list corresponding to either of these.

For example, the procedure definition:

```
Overloads Sub Q(ByVal B As Byte, Optional ByVal J As Long = 6)
```

is equivalent to the following two procedure definitions:

```
Overloads Sub Q(ByVal B As Byte)
Overloads Sub Q(ByVal B As Byte, ByVal J As Long)
```

Therefore, the following overload is not valid:

```
Overloads Sub Q(ByVal C As Byte, ByVal K As Long)    ' Not allowed.
```

However, the following overload uses a different argument list and is valid:

```
Overloads Sub Q(ByVal B As Byte, ByVal J As Long, ByVal S As Single)
```

The compiler considers a procedure with a ParamArray argument to have an infinite number of overloads, differing from each other in what is passed to the ParamArray argument. The possibilities include:

- One overload passing a one-dimensional array of the ParamArray element type

- One overload passing no argument to the ParamArray

- An overload passing one argument of the ParamArray element type, an overload passing two arguments of the ParamArray element type, an overload passing three arguments of the ParamArray element type, and so on

1-Minute Drill

- Overloaded procedures must differ from each other in what respect?

prj9-1.zip

Project 9-1: Calculator, Version 2

In Module 7 we wrote a Calculator application. That project performs basic arithmetic: addition, subtraction, multiplication, and division. The user inputs the two operands and chooses an operator by clicking a radio button corresponding to the operator. The application, before performing the arithmetic calculation, confirms that the user entered a number, and if not, notifies the user instead of making the calculation. In the case of division, the program also checks that division by zero is not being attempted. Figure 9-4 shows the project in action.

We will not change the GUI of the Calculator application we wrote in Module 7. However, we will change the code to make use of procedures.

- Overloaded procedures must differ from each other in respect to their argument list.

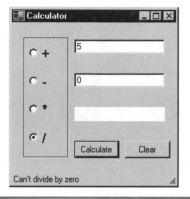

| **Figure 9-4** | The Calculator project |

Step-by-Step

1. Follow steps 1 through 7 of the Calculator project in Module 7.

2. Create the following function:

```
Private Function isValidInput() As Boolean
If IsNumeric(txtOp1.Text) And IsNumeric(txtOp2.Text) Then
    Return True
Else
    Return False
End If
End Function
```

This function returns True if both operands are numeric, and False otherwise. Actually, the body of the function could be condensed to one statement:

```
Return IsNumeric(txtOp1.Text) And IsNumeric(txtOp2.Text)
```

This code is more compact but probably less readable.

3. Create the following function:

```
Private Function DivideByZero() As Boolean
    Return radDivide.Checked And txtOp2.Text = "0"
End Function
```

This function returns True if the user has attempted division by zero, that is, has chosen the Division radio button and the second operand is the string representation of zero.

4. Create the following subroutine:

```
Private Sub Calculate()
If radAdd.Checked Then
   lblResult.Text = CStr(CSng(txtOp1.Text) + CSng(txtOp2.Text))
ElseIf radSubtract.Checked Then
   lblResult.Text = CStr(CSng(txtOp1.Text) - CSng(txtOp2.Text))
ElseIf radMultiply.Checked Then
   lblResult.Text = CStr(CSng(txtOp1.Text) * CSng(txtOp2.Text))
ElseIf radDivide.Checked Then
   lblResult.Text = CStr(CSng(txtOp1.Text) / CSng(txtOp2.Text))
End If
End Sub
```

This subroutine performs the arithmetic calcuation indicated by the selected radio button and displays the result in *lblResult*. The CSng type conversion keyword first is used to convert the String to a Single data type (the number may be a floating point instead of a whole number so Single is a better choice than Integer) to perform the arithmetic calculation, and then the CStr type conversion keyword is used to convert the Single to a String data type before assigning it to the Text property of the Label control.

5. Place the following code in the Click event procedure of the cmdCalculate command button, which is used to initiate the arithmetic calculation:

```
Private Sub cmdCalculate_Click(ByVal sender As Object, _
    ByVal e As System.EventArgs) Handles cmdCalculate.Click
If Not isValidInput() Then
   StatusBar1.Text = "Both operands must be numeric"
ElseIf DivideByZero() Then
   StatusBar1.Text = "Can't divide by zero"
Else
   StatusBar1.Text = ""
   Calculate()
End If
End Sub
```

This function first calls the *isValidInput* function to determine if both operands are numeric. If not, the status bar warns the user and no arithmetic calculation is made. Otherwise, the function next calls the *DivisionByZero* function to see if the user is attempting division by zero. If so, once again the status bar warns the user and no arithmetic calculation is made. If both the valid input and division by zero tests are passed, then this event procedure calls the Calculate subroutine.

6. Place the following code in the *Click* event procedure of the *cmdClear* command button, which is used to clear the text boxes and label:

```
Private Sub cmdClear_Click(ByVal sender As Object,
    ByVal e As System.EventArgs) Handles cmdClear.Click
        txtOp1.Text = ""
        txtOp2.Text = ""
        lblResult.Text = ""
        StatusBar1.Text = ""
End Sub
```

Compare this code to the code for the Calculator project in Module 7. Both do the same thing. However, the code here is more compact and understandable.

Summary

A procedure is a block of one or more code statements. All Visual Basic .NET code is written within procedures.

This module discussed two types of procedures, subroutines and functions. The difference between them is that functions return a value, whereas subroutines do not.

Visual Basic .NET has many built-in procedures. Some, such as event procedures, are subroutines. Others, such as the InputBox function, are functions.

Visual Basic .NET also enables you to create your own procedures. There are several reasons why you might want to create your own procedures. Your code is more readable if divided up among several smaller procedures than if it is all put in to one procedure that contains pages of code. Additionally, if you are performing essentially the same task from several places in the program, you can avoid duplication of code by putting the code that performs that task in one place, as opposed to repeating that code in each place in the program that may call for the performance of that task. Further, if you later have to fix a bug in how you perform that task, or simply find a better way to perform the task, you only have to change the code in one place rather than many.

9

Procedures don't execute by themselves. They need to be called. Subroutines are called by name, with any arguments in parentheses. Functions usually are called either on the right side of an assignment statement or in an expression, often with an If...Then control structure.

You use arguments to pass information to procedures. The arguments may be passed by value, using the ByVal keyword, or by reference, using the ByRef keyword. This module explained the difference between these two methods of passing arguments. Additionally, you can use optional arguments and the ParamArray argument. Finally, this module showed you how to overload procedures so closely related procedures can share the same name, differing only by their argument list.

Mastery Check

1. Which can only be called from a specific object, and cannot be called independently from an object?

    A. Function

    B. Method

    C. Subroutine

2. Arguments have to be passed in the same order in which they are declared.

    A. True

    B. False

3. The data type of an argument passed has to be identical to the data type of the argument declared.

    A. Always

    B. Never

☑ *Mastery Check*

    C. No, if the data type passed can be converted to the data type declared through a narrowing conversion

    D. No, if the data type passed can be converted to the data type declared through a widening conversion

4. What is the difference, if any, when returning the value of a function, between using the Return statement and assigning the return value to the function name?

    A. Assigning the return value to the function name immediately ends execution of the function, whereas the Return statement does not.

    B. The Return statement immediately ends execution of the function, whereas assigning the return value to the function name does not.

    C. No difference.

5. Which way of calling a function will *not* enable you to use the function's return value?

    A. Using the Call keyword

    B. Calling the function on the right side of an assignment statement or in an expression

    C. Calling the function in an expression

6. What is the effect, if any, that passing a scalar variable ByVal or ByRef as a procedure argument has on the called procedure's ability to modify the value of the variable passed as an argument in the calling code?

    A. The called procedure may modify the value of a scalar variable if it is passed ByRef, but not if it is passed ByVal.

    B. The called procedure may modify the value of a scalar variable if it is passed ByVal, but not if it is passed ByRef.

    C. There is no effect.

9

☑ *Mastery Check*

7. What is the effect, if any, that passing an array variable ByVal or ByRef as a procedure argument has on the called procedure's ability to modify the value of the individual elements of the array passed as an argument in the calling code?

   A. The called procedure may modify the individual elements of the array if the array is passed ByRef, but not if it is passed ByVal.

   B. The called procedure may modify the individual elements of the array if the array is passed ByVal, but not if it is passed ByRef.

   C. There is no effect.

8. What is the effect, if any, that passing an array variable ByVal or ByRef as a procedure argument has on the called procedure's ability to change the array object pointed to by the array passed as an argument in the calling code?

   A. The called procedure may change the array object pointed to by the array if the array is passed ByRef, but not if it is passed ByVal.

   B. The called procedure may change the array object pointed to by the array if the array is passed ByVal, but not if it is passed ByRef.

   C. There is no effect.

9. Which of the following statements is true?

   A. Optional arguments may be declared with mandatory arguments in any order.

   B. Optional arguments may be declared only before mandatory arguments.

   C. Optional arguments may be declared only after mandatory arguments.

   D. Optional arguments may not be declared with mandatory arguments.

✓ Mastery Check

10. You have to specify a value for an optional argument.

   A. True

   B. False

11. Which of the following statements is true?

   A. A procedure must have a parameter array argument.

   B. A procedure can have no more than one parameter array argument.

   C. A procedure may have more than one parameter array argument.

   D. A procedure may have both a parameter array argument and another optional argument.

12. Overloaded procedures must differ from each other in respect to _____.

   A. Their access specifier

   B. Their argument list

   C. Their return value

   D. Whether arguments are passed ByVal or ByRef

9

Part 4

The User Interface

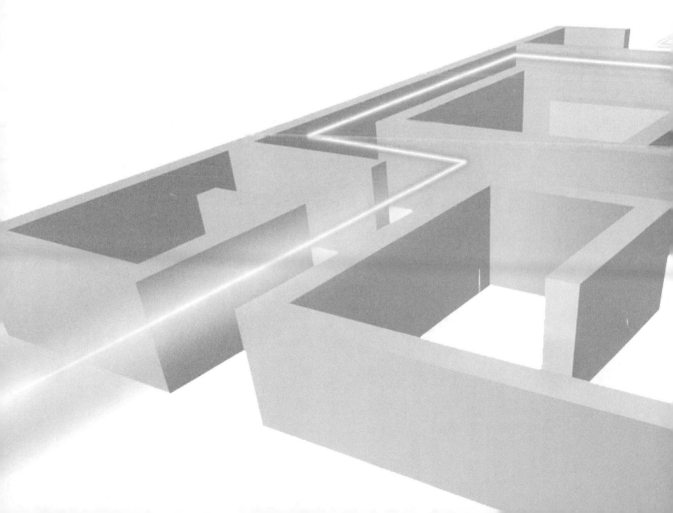

Module 10

Helper Forms

The Goals of this Module

- Create and use message and dialog boxes and owned forms
- Understand how forms can communicate with each other
- Use property procedures to retrieve and assign property values
- Understand how property procedures further the object-oriented principle of encapsulation

Forms are the most common user interface element in Visual Basic applications. Indeed, it is difficult to conceptualize a Windows application without at least one form. Forms are the windows, literally, through which application users view information and interact with the application.

Visual Basic .NET's automated creation of a new Windows application project includes a form that serves as the main application window. However, while the main application window may be the star of the show, that form needs a supporting cast of helper forms because Windows applications generally are far too complex for the main application window form to perform all the tasks required by the application. These helper forms are:

- **Message box**   Includes text that is either informative or a question, and buttons such as OK, Yes, No, Cancel, and so on for the application user's response and to close the message box. The message box is *modal*; the application user cannot return to the main form without closing the message box. An example of a message box is if you make changes to a document in Microsoft Word and then try to close the document without saving the changes, you are presented with a message box asking if you want to save the file before closing, with buttons for Yes, No, or Cancel.

- **Dialog box**   Similar to a message box, it also is modal, but may contain text boxes, check boxes, drop-down lists, and other controls. The Print dialog box displayed with the File | Print menu command is an example of a dialog box.

- **Owned form**   Similar to a dialog box, it also may contain controls, but unlike a dialog box, an owned form is *modeless*; the application user can return to the main form without having to close the owned form. The Find and Replace form in Microsoft Word, displayed with the Edit | Find menu command, is an example of an owned form.

Helper forms may simply be informational. For example, most Windows applications have an About dialog box, summoned by the main form's Help | About menu command, that displays information about the application, and then is dismissed by clicking its OK button.

However, helper forms are not limited to the role of passive purveyors of information and typically are interactive. The helper form usually asks the application user a question and obtains an answer based on the button the application user clicks. This presents you with two programming challenges:

- You need to communicate between two forms. The main form needs to know which button was clicked on the helper form.

- The main form should execute different code depending on which button was clicked. The main form should not execute the same code if the user clicked the No button as it would if the user clicked the Yes button.

This module will show you how to solve these challenges. Additionally, a dialog box or owned form may contain controls, including ones with which the application user may interact by typing text, checking a check box, selecting an item from a list, and so on. This presents you with the further programming challenge of writing code to enable one form to know (and take actions based on) what the application user typed, checked, or selected in the controls in the other form. This module will show you how to solve this challenge, using property procedures.

Message Boxes

Since the actions of the application user cause a Windows application to receive messages from the operating system, it seems only fair that a Windows application can send a message to the application user. Windows applications often use message boxes to inform and obtain a response from the application user.

Message boxes are valuable tools to use in applications. For example, one late evening, while working bleary-eyed to finish this module under pressure from my heartless editor, I forgetfully closed the document without first saving about an hour's worth of changes. Mercifully, up popped the message box shown in the following illustration, asking if I wanted to save my unsaved changes before the document was closed.

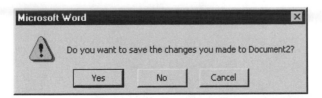

This message box, in addition to conveying valuable information, is also able to obtain and process my response. If I choose the Yes button, the unsaved changes are saved before the document is closed. If I choose the No button (bad choice), the unsaved changes are discarded and the document is closed. If I choose the Cancel button, the state just before I attempted to close the document is restored; the document is kept open, but the unsaved changes remain unsaved.

prj10-1.zip

Project 10-1: Message Boxes

In this project, you will create the message box shown in Figure 10-1, which asks the user if they want to quit the application. If the user chooses Yes, the application closes. If the user chooses No, the application will not close.

Step-by-Step

1. Create a Windows application.

2. Using the Toolbox, add a button to the form.

3. Use the Properties window to change the values of the following properties of the button:

● **Name**   Change from Button1 to btnClose to give the control a more logical name.

● **Text**   Change from Button1 to Close to give the application user a visual cue as to the purpose of the button.

The following shows the first form in design mode after you have added the button.

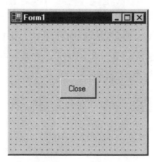

4. You do not need to add any other forms or controls. The message box is a form built into Visual Basic .NET. Therefore, you do not need to create or design the message box. All you need to do to create and show a message box, together with its buttons, icon, text, and title, is to call the aptly named

Show method of the MessageBox class. Accordingly, add this code to the Click event of btnClose:

```
Private Sub btnClose_Click(ByVal sender As System.Object, _
    ByVal e As System.EventArgs) Handles btnClose.Click
        Dim drQuit As DialogResult
        drQuit = MessageBox.Show_("Do you really want to quit?", _
            "Exit Confirmation", _
            MessageBoxButtons.YesNo, _
            MessageBoxIcon.Warning, _
            MessageBoxDefaultButton.Button2)
        If drQuit = DialogResult.Yes Then
            Me.Close()
        End If
End Sub
End Sub
```

Run the project and click Close to display the message box shown previously in Figure 10-1. This type of message box is common in Windows applications, providing the application user a last chance to decide whether they really want to quit the application. If the application user chooses the Yes button, the application will end. If instead the application user chooses the No button, just the message box will close and the application user will be returned to the main form. Thus, the clicking of the No button will restore the application to its state just before the application user chose the close button.

The code involves three logical steps:

1. Display the message box using the Show method.

2. Obtain the application user's choice, Yes or No, by the return value of the Show method.

3. If the choice is Yes, close the application.

10

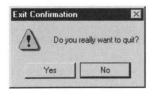

| **Figure 10-1** | The Message Box application running |

The Show Method

The Show method both creates and displays the message box. Visual Basic .NET also takes care of closing the message box. When you click a button, the message box closes, automatically.

The Show method is overloaded. This means that you can call it several different ways, depending on the number of parameters you include. The parameters of the Show method are listed in Table 10-1.

You can call the Show method with only the Text and Title parameters. In that case, the message box only will have one button, OK, which closes the message box when clicked. This may be sufficient if the message box simply provides information to the application user. For example, when filling out a form on a web site, a message box may have popped up telling you that you forgot to fill out a required field, or that the field only takes numbers, or the password must be at least six characters, and so on.

However, the objective of this project is to give the application user a choice of Yes or No concerning whether they really want to quit. You use buttons—here, Yes and No buttons—to give the application user this choice. The MessageBoxButtons enumeration contains the available button combinations, which are listed in Table 10-2.

Parameter	Description
Text	The prompt inside the message box to convey a question or information to the application user, in this case "Do you really want to quit?"
Title	The title of the message box, in this case "Exit application," to provide a visual cue to the application user of the purpose of the message box.
MessageBoxButtons	The buttons inside the message box, in this case Yes and No. The choices are listed in Table 10-2.
MessageBoxIcon	The graphic inside the message box, such as the exclamation mark in Figure 10-1. The choices are listed in Table 10-3.
MessageBoxDefaultButton	The button outlined as a cue that pressing ENTER is the same as clicking the button, in this case the Cancel button. The choices are listed in Table 10-4.

Table 10-1   Parameters of the Show Method

Name	Buttons Contained in Message Box
AbortRetryIgnore	Abort, Retry, and Ignore.
OK	OK. This is the default.
OKCancel	OK and Cancel.
RetryCancel	Retry and Cancel.
YesNo	Yes and No.
YesNoCancel	Yes, No, and Cancel.

Table 10-2   MessageBoxButtons Enumeration

The term *enumeration* means a list of related choices, which in this case represent the various available button combinations. The syntax of an enumeration is:

```
[Enumeration Name].[Choice Name]
```

For example, if the selected button combination is Yes and No, the syntax is:

```
MessageBoxButtons.YesNo
```

MessageBoxButtons is the name of the enumeration, and YesNo is the choice from the enumerated list.

The icon in the message box provides the application user with a visual cue of the nature and importance of the message, ranging from informational to warning or error. Similar to the buttons, the MessageBoxIcon enumeration contains the available icon choices, which are listed in Table 10-3.

10

Name	Icon in Message Box
Asterisk	White lowercase letter i in a circle with a blue background.
Error	White X in a circle with a red background.
Exclamation	Black exclamation point in a triangle with a yellow background.
Hand	White X in a circle with a red background.
Information	White lowercase letter i in a circle with a blue background.
None	None.
Question	Blue question mark in a circle with a white background.
Stop	White X in a circle with a red background.
Warning	Black exclamation point in a triangle with a yellow background.

Table 10-3   MessageBoxIcon Enumeration

Finally, you can designate a default button, which means that the user pressing the ENTER key is the same as the user clicking that button. The MessageBoxDefaultButton enumeration contains the available button choices, which are listed in Table 10-4.

Usually you choose as the default button the one whose choice would have the least drastic effect, if for no other reason than if the application user absentmindedly presses the ENTER key, nothing horrible will happen. Here the button with the least drastic effect is the No button, which will simply restore the status quo.

Assigning the Return Value of the Show Method to a Variable

The next step is to write code so the main form knows if the application user clicked the Yes or No button in the message box. The programming task is that one form needs to know an action taken in another form.

You solve this problem by using the return value of the Show method. The Show method is called from the main form, specifically the Click event of btnClose. The Show method returns a value that represents the button that the application user clicked in the message box.

Tip

The Show method returns a value, but not all methods do.

While it is not strictly necessary, it is usually a good idea to save the return value in a variable for later use in your application. A property of an object in scope can be accessed any time during the running of the program because the

Member Name	Description
Button1	The first button on the message box is the default button.
Button2	The second button on the message box is the default button.
Button3	The third button on the message box is the default button.

Table 10-4   MessageBoxDefaultButton Enumeration

object will always be there. By contrast, an unsaved return value is lost once your running application moves to the next line of code. By way of analogy, assume you have been asked a question you have to think about before answering. By the time you are ready to answer the question, the questioner is no longer present to hear your answer. If you then just answer the question verbally, the answer would be lost as a practical matter. Instead, you could save the answer by writing it down, and when the questioner returned they could review what you wrote.

You should use the DialogResult data type for the variable in which you will save the return value of the Show method because the Show method returns a value that is one of the DialogResult enumerations listed in Table 10-5.

The DialogResult enumerations correspond to the buttons in the MessageBoxButtons enumeration listed previously in Table 10-2, and will be returned if the corresponding button is chosen. Thus, if the application user chooses the Yes button, the Show method returns the value DialogResult.Yes.

Member Name	Description
Abort	The dialog box's return value is Abort, usually sent from a button labeled Abort.
Cancel	The dialog box's return value is Cancel, usually sent from a button labeled Cancel.
Ignore	The dialog box's return value is Ignore, usually sent from a button labeled Ignore.
No	The dialog box's return value is No, usually sent from a button labeled No.
None	Nothing is returned from the dialog box. This means that the modal dialog continues running.
OK	The dialog box's return value is OK, usually sent from a button labeled OK.
Retry	The dialog box's return value is Retry, usually sent from a button labeled Retry.
Yes	The dialog box's return value is Yes, usually sent from a button labeled Yes.

Table 10-5   DialogResult Enumerations

10

You could declare the variable that will store the return value of the Show method as follows:

```
Dim drQuit As DialogResult
```

Once you have declared the variable, the next step is to use it to store the return value of the Show method. The variable drQuit should be on the left side of the assignment operator, so it will receive the return value of the Show method that is called on the right side of the assignment operator:

```
drQuit = MessageBox.Show("Do you really want to quit?", _
         "Exit Confirmation", _
         MessageBoxButtons.YesNo, _
         MessageBoxIcon.Warning, _
         MessageBoxDefaultButton.Button2)
```

When this code statement executes, and the application user clicks a button in the message box, closing the message box, the value of the variable drQuit will be either DialogResult.Yes or DialogResult.No, depending on whether the application user clicked the Yes or No button.

Using the If Statement to Determine Whether to Close the Application

The form object has a Close method that, as its name indicates, closes the form. Since this is the only form in the project (other than the message box which will close when the user chooses the Yes or No button), closing the form ends the application as well. However, we only want to close the form if the application user chose Yes, not if the application user chose No.

The following code closes the form if, and only if, the application user's choice was Yes:

```
If drQuit = DialogResult.Yes Then
   Me.Close()
End If
```

This code statement first compares the value of drQuit and DialogResult.Yes using the If keyword. If the user chose Yes, the value of drQuit is DialogResult.Yes, so the comparison drQuit = DialogResult.Yes will be true and the Me.Close() statement is executed. However, if the user chose No, the value of drQuit is DialogResult.No, so the comparison drQuit = DialogResult.Yes will be false and the Me.Close() statement will not be executed.

1-Minute Drill

- What does it mean if a form is modal?
- How do you create and display a message box?
- How do you determine which button the user clicked in the message box?

Dialog Boxes

While the message box is a valuable tool, it is limited in that it only can contain text, buttons, an icon, and a title. The information you may need to obtain from the application user may be too complex for the simplicity of the message box. For example, the Print dialog box, shown by the File | Print menu command, contains text boxes, labels, radio buttons, check boxes, and drop-down lists. In these circumstances, you can create a custom and more complex version of a message box, the dialog box.

prj10-2.zip

Project 10-2: Dialog Box

In this project, you will create the dialog box shown in the following illustration, which enables the user to change the title of the calling form. If the user chooses the OK button, the title of the calling form will be changed to the text the user typed into the text box. If instead the user chooses the Cancel button, the dialog box simply will close, with no change made to the title of the calling form.

10

- The application user must close the modal form to return to the main form.
- You create and display a message box by using the Show method of the MessageBox class.
- You use the return value of the Show method to determine which button the user clicked in the message box.

Step-by-Step

1. Create a Windows application.

2. Using the Properties window, change the StartPosition property of the form from the default (WindowsDefaultLocation) to CenterScreen to center the form on the screen. The start position is one of the FormStartPosition enumerations listed in Table 10-6.

3. Using the Toolbox, add a button to the form.

4. Use the Properties window to change the values of the following properties of the button:

- **Name**   Change from Button1 to btnNewCaption.
- **Text**   Change from Button1 to New Caption.

5. You need to add a second form to the project to serve as the dialog box. While the MessageBox object is built into Visual Basic .NET, the dialog box is a custom form—that is, you have to create it. Use the Project | Add Windows Form menu command to display the Add New Item dialog box shown in Figure 10-2. You can keep the default name form2.vb for the new form. Click the Open button. The following illustration shows the Solution Explorer, in which the second form now appears.

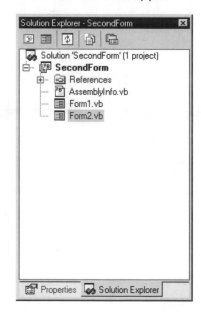

Member Name	Description
CenterParent	The form is centered within the bounds of its parent form.
CenterScreen	The form is centered on the current display and has the dimensions specified in the form's size.
Manual	The location and size of the form will determine its starting position.
WindowsDefaultBounds	The form is positioned at the Windows default location and has the bounds determined by the Windows default.
WindowsDefaultLocation	The form is positioned at the Windows default location and has the dimensions specified in the form's size.

Table 10-6   FormStartPosition Enumeration

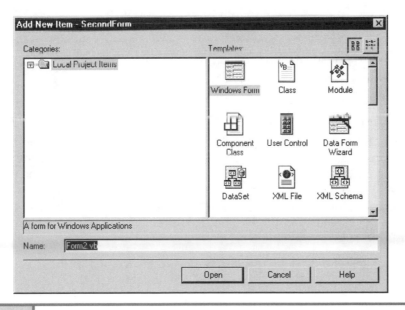

Figure 10-2   The Add New Item dialog box

10

6. Using the Properties window, change the values of the following properties of Form2:

- **Text**   Change from Form2 to Dialog so you have a visual cue that you are looking at the dialog box.

- **ControlBox**   Change from the default (True) to False. This eliminates the close, minimize, and maximize buttons in the top-right corner of the window and the system menu, which also has close, minimize, and maximize commands, in the top-left corner of the window. The purpose is so Form2 cannot be resized and can be closed only by clicking one of the buttons that you will be adding next to the form.

- **StartPosition**   Change from the default (WindowsDefaultLocation) to CenterParent so the dialog box is centered on the main form.

- **FormBorderStyle**   Change from the default (Sizable) to FixedDialog. This change is not required for the program to function, but does give the form a more dialog-like appearance. The available border styles are in the FormBorderStyle enumeration and are listed in Table 10-7.

7. Using the Toolbox, add a button to the second form.

8. Use the Properties window to change the values of the following properties of the button:

- **Name**   Change from Button1 to btnOK.

- **Text**   Change to OK.

- **DialogResult**   Choose OK from the drop-down list.

Since the message box is a built-in Visual Basic .NET form, clicking the OK button automatically returns OK as the DialogResult value. By contrast, the dialog box is not a built-in Visual Basic .NET form, but instead one that you create, so you need to correlate the clicking of the OK button with OK as the DialogResult value. You do so by setting the button's DialogResult property to one of the buttons listed in the DialogResult enumeration listed previously in Table 10-5, in this case OK.

9. Using the Toolbox, add a second button to the second form.

10. Use the Properties window to change the values of the following properties of the second button:

- **Name**   Change from Button1 to btnCancel.

- **Text**   Change to Cancel.
- **DialogResult**   Choose Cancel from the drop-down list.

The DialogResult property was explained previously in connection with the OK button.

11. Use the Properties window to change the values of the following properties of the second form, using the drop-down list:

- **AcceptButton**   btnOK
- **CancelButton**   btnCancel

This is similar to the MessageBoxDefaultButton enumeration shown previously in Table 10-4. Pressing the ENTER key is the equivalent of clicking the button designated in the AcceptButton property. Similarly, pressing the ESCAPE key is the equivalent of clicking the button designated in the CancelButton property.

12. Using the Toolbox, add a TextBox to the second form.

13. Use the Properties window to change the values of the following properties of the TextBox:

- **Name**   Change to txtNewCaption.
- **Text**   Delete the default so it is blank so no text shows in the text box when you run the application.

14. Add the following code to the second form after the #End Region statement:

```
Public Property Caption() As String
```

When you type this code and press the ENTER key, the Visual Basic .NET IDE finishes the code for you so it appears as follows:

```
Public Property Caption() As String
        Get
        End Get
        Set(ByVal Value As String)
        End Set
End Property
```

15. Insert the following code between the Get and End Get statements:

```
Caption = txtNewCaption.Text
```

10

Now the property procedure should appear as follows:

```
Public Property Caption() As String
    Get
        Caption = txtNewCaption.Text
    End Get
    Set(ByVal Value As String)
    End Set
End Property
```

The TextBox has a Text property whose value is the text, if any, typed in the TextBox. This code will enable you to retrieve the value of that text from another form (the main one).

16. Add the following code to the Click event of btnNewCaption in the first form:

```
Private Sub btnNewCaption_Click(ByVal sender As System.Object, _
    ByVal e As System.EventArgs) _
    Handles btnNewCaption.Click
        Dim frmCaption As New Form2()
        frmCaption.ShowDialog()
        If frmCaption.DialogResult = DialogResult.OK Then
            Me.Text = frmCaption.Caption
        End If
End Sub
```

Run the project. Click the New Caption button in the first form, and type some text in the second form. If you then click OK, the second form will close, and the first form will have a new title, the text you typed in the second form. If you instead click Cancel, the second form will still close, but the title of the first form will not change.

Member Name	Description
Fixed3D	A fixed, three-dimensional border.
FixedDialog	A thick, fixed dialog-style border.
FixedSingle	A fixed, single line border.
FixedToolWindow	A tool window border that is not resizable.
None	No border.
Sizable	A resizable border.
SizableToolWindow	A resizable tool window border.

Table 10-7   FormBorderStyle Enumeration

The ShowDialog Method

The ShowDialog method of the Form object is similar to the Show method of the MessageBox class in that it will show the form that is invoking the method. However, there are several important differences. The primary difference is that while the Show method of the MessageBox class shows a built-in form, the ShowDialog method of the Form object shows a form that you have created, here Form2. Therefore, unlike the MessageBox example, here you need to explicitly declare and create an instance of Form2 before you show it using the ShowDialog method:

```
Dim frmCaption As New Form2()
frmCaption.ShowDialog()
```

As discussed in Module 2, you use a class to instantiate (create) an object that is an instance of that class. The class we are using is Form2. As also discussed in Module 2, the New keyword is used to instantiate the object. The object is represented by a variable, here frmCaption. The object (represented by the variable frmCaption) then calls the ShowDialog method.

The second form, like the message box, is modal—that is, the application user cannot return to the main form until they have dismissed the second form by clicking one of its buttons. However, while the Show method of the MessageBox class indicates the button the user clicked by returning a DialogResult value, the ShowDialog method of the Form object indicates the button the user clicked by assigning that value to the dialog form's DialogResult property. Thus the comparison is:

```
If frmCaption.DialogResult = DialogResult.OK Then
```

10

Tip

You do not need to write code to show the form that the Visual Basic .NET IDE creates by default to serve as your main application window. However, you do need to write code to show any additional forms you may create. You can change the form that starts up by default to one of those additional forms. In Solution Explorer, right-click the project and choose Properties. The Project property page opens with the General properties displayed. Choose the form you want as the startup form from the Startup Object drop-down list.

Public, Private, and Scope

If the value of the second form's DialogResult property is OK, all that is left to do is to change the title of the first form to the text you typed in the second form. The following code in the Click event procedure of btnNewCaption therefore is indicated:

```
Me.Text = frmCaption.txtNewCaption.Text
```

There is one minor problem. This code will not work. When you attempt to build this solution, the IDE will give you an error message that txtNewCaption "is Private, and is not accessible in this context."

Prior examples have used the keyword Private and its counterpart, Public, usually in starting procedure definitions such as Private Sub btnNewCaption_Click or Public Sub New. If an object, variable, or procedure is declared as Private, it can be accessed only within the code module of the form that contains it. By contrast, if an object, variable, or procedure is declared as Public, it can be accessed outside of the code module of the form that contains it.

For example, in the Label example in Module 3, you were able to directly access and change the Text property of the Label control in an event procedure:

```
lblX.Text = e.X
```

However, in that example the event procedure was in the same form that contained the label. By contrast, in this example, you are accessing the Text property of the TextBox control txtNewCaption in Form2 from an event procedure of btnNewCaption, which is contained in a different form, Form1.

The "Ask the Expert" following this section answers why you would ever declare anything as Private when it is easier to access an object, variable, or procedure that is declared as Public. In the meantime, however, we have to solve the problem of how to access from an event procedure within one form a property of an object in a different form. The answer is through another type of procedure, a property procedure.

Property Procedures

While you cannot directly access from one form the properties of objects in a different form, you can do so through property procedures.

A property procedure, like an event procedure, is a procedure—that is, code that executes when it is called. There are two significant differences between a property procedure and an event procedure:

- An event procedure is called by the occurrence of an event, usually generated by an action of the application user. By contrast, a property procedure is called explicitly by code.

- The code inside an event procedure may take any action the programmer deems appropriate. By contrast, the code inside a property procedure has one of two specialized purposes, either to change or to return the value of a property.

Similar to an event procedure, the first line of a property procedure defines it, including its scope, name, and parameters. The first line of the property procedure in this example

```
Public Property Caption() As String
```

consists of the following elements:

- **Public**   This keyword means that this property procedure can be accessed throughout the application, even by code in a different form.

- **Property**   This keyword designates this procedure as a property procedure.

- **Caption**   This is the name given by the programmer to refer to the property procedure. Another name could be used. Consistent with previous advice, the name of the property procedure should be logical to make your code readable. Additionally, it should not duplicate a keyword such as Text, which is the name of the property being accessed by the property procedure.

- **()**   The parentheses enclose parameters, consistent with an event procedure. Here there are no parameters.

- **As String**   This designates the data type that is the subject of the property procedure. The data type of the Text property is String.

10

Just as the Property statement begins the property procedure, the End Property statement ends it.

A property procedure may implement between the Property and End Property statements:

- A Get procedure, which returns the value of a property

- A Set procedure, which assigns a value to a property

By implementing both the Get and Set procedures within a property procedure, you can both read and write to a property. However, a property procedure may have only a Get procedure, making the property read-only outside its form, or only a Set procedure, making the property write-only outside its form.

The property procedure used in this example implements only the Get procedure, making the Text property of the TextBox control txtNewCaption read-only outside Form2, simply because this example does not require the ability to write to the Text property of txtNewCaption outside Form2. The next project, on owned forms, will use the Set procedure.

The Get and Set procedures each appear as an internal block. The Get procedure begins with the Get statement and ends with the End Get statement, with any code appearing in between. Similarly, the Set procedure begins with the Set statement and ends with the End Set statement, with any code appearing in between.

Similar to a method that returns a value, the Get procedure returns a value, namely the value of a property. The syntax is:

```
[Property Procedure Name] = [Object Name].[Property Name]
```

In this example, the Get procedure of the Caption property procedure returns the Text property of the TextBox control txtNewCaption:

```
Get
      Caption = txtNewCaption.Text
End Get
```

Also similar to a method that returns a value, the Get procedure is called typically on the right side of the assignment operator, with its return value assigned to the expression on the left side of the assignment operator. The syntax is:

```
[Value being changed] = [Object Name].[Property Procedure Name]
```

Finally, in the following code in the btnNewCaption event procedure in Form1, the value returned by the Caption property procedure, the Text property of the TextBox control txtNewCaption in Form2 is assigned to the Text property of Form1:

```
Me.Text = frmCaption.Caption
```

The object name used to call the Caption property procedure is frmCaption, not Form2. The following code would not work:

```
Me.Text = Form2.Caption
```

The compiler will complain: "This reference to a non-shared member requires an object reference, and none is supplied."

The compiler's explanation, while technically accurate, is also technically complex, so a plain(er) English translation is warranted. As you may recall from prior modules, Form2 is a class, a blueprint or template for an object. However, it is not an object itself. Instead, you created an instance of the Form2 class with the following code:

```
Dim frmCaption As New Form2()
```

It is frmCaption that is the instance of Form2 object running in your application. You need to call the Get procedure from that instance instead of from the generic class Form2 blueprint.

1-Minute Drill

- What is the basic difference between a message box and a dialog box?
- How do you create a dialog box?
- How do you display a dialog box?
- How do you determine which button the user clicked in the dialog box?

- A message box is built in to Visual Basic, whereas a dialog box is programmer-created, and therefore the programmer may add additional controls to the dialog box, such as a text box.
- You create a dialog box by creating another Windows form.
- You display a dialog box by using the ShowDialog method.
- You use the DialogResult property of the dialog form to determine which button the user clicked in the dialog box.

Ask the Expert

Question: Why would you ever declare anything as Private when it is easier to access objects, procedures, and variables that are declared as Public?

Answer: While the good news about the Public keyword is that it makes it easier to access objects, procedures, and variables, that also is the bad news. One of your major concerns in programming is to make sure the application user cannot enter invalid data, such as "Jeff" for a Social Security number. The more ways your code can access, for example, the Text property of a TextBox control, the more ways you can miss guarding against the entry of invalid data. If the Text property can be accessed only one way, through a property procedure, then you can put the data validation logic in that one place. The principle of making objects, procedures, and variables Private is known in object-oriented programming as encapsulation, and will be discussed throughout the upcoming modules.

Question: Both the Get and Set procedures of the Caption property procedure are called in the same way, frmCaption.Caption. How does the compiler know whether you are calling the Get or Set procedure of the property procedure?

Answer: If the property procedure is called from the left side of the assignment operator, the code is calling the Set procedure, because the property will be assigned the value on the right side of the assignment operator. If the property procedure is called from the right side of the assignment operator, the code is calling the Get procedure, because the return value will be assigned to the expression on the left side of the assignment operator.

Owned Forms

Both the message box and dialog box are modal, which means you cannot return to the form that called the message or dialog box until you have closed the box by clicking one of its buttons. This makes sense if the subject of the message or dialog box is of the nature that it needs to be resolved before the main application continues. For example, the question posed by the message box in Microsoft Word when you make changes to a document and then try to close the document without saving the changes—"Do you want to save the file before closing?"—needs to be answered before the application continues.

However, there are occasions when you want the application user to be able to return to the main application window without closing the dialog box. One example is the spell checker in Microsoft Word. The application user should be able to return to the application window to make a correction without having to close the spell checker dialog box.

Dialog boxes that do not have to be closed for the application user to return to the main application window often are referred to as modeless, as opposed to modal. In Visual Basic .NET, they also are referred to as owned forms. Owned forms have their own unique behavior. They are never displayed behind their owner form, and are minimized and closed with the owner form.

prj10-3.zip

Project 10-3: Owned Form

In this project, text selected in a TextBox control on the main form is replaced by text entered in a TextBox control on the owned form. If no text is selected in the TextBox control on the main form, or no text is entered in the TextBox control on the owned form, the user is warned and the status quo is restored. Figure 10-3 shows the project after the owned form is displayed by clicking the Replace Selected button on the main form.

Step-by-Step

1. Create a Windows application.

2. Using the Properties window, change the Text property of the form from Form1 to Text Editor.

3. Using the Toolbox, add a button to the form.

4. Use the Properties window to change the values of the following properties of the button:

- **Name** Change from Button1 to btnReplace.
- **Text** Change from Button1 to Replace Selected.

5. Using the Toolbox, add a TextBox control to the form.

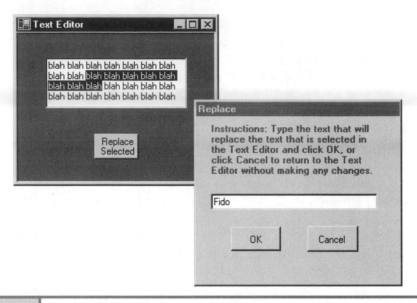

Figure 10-3 Owned form project running

6. Use the Properties window to change the values of the following properties of the TextBox:

- **Name**   Change to txtNewCaption.
- **Text**   Delete the default so it is blank so no text shows in the text box when you run the application.
- **Multiline**   Change from the default (False) to True so that more than one line of text may be entered and displayed.

The following illustration shows the first form in design mode after you have added the button.

7. Add a second form to the project. You can keep the default name form2.vb for the new form.

8. Using the Properties window, change the values of the following properties of Form2:

- **Text**   Change from Form2 to Replace so you have a visual cue that you are looking at the owned form.
- **ControlBox**   Change from the default (True) to False so Form2 can be closed only by clicking btnCancel or closing Form1, or minimized only by minimizing Form1.
- **FormBorderStyle**   Change from the default (Sizable) to FixedSingle.

9. Using the Toolbox, add a button to the second form.

10. Use the Properties window to change the values of the following properties of the button:

- **Name**   Change from Button1 to btnOK.
- **Text**   Change to OK.
- **DialogResult**   Choose OK from the drop-down list.

As in the dialog box example, you set OK as the DialogResult value to correlate the clicking of the OK button with OK as the DialogResult value.

11. Using the Toolbox, add a second button to the second form.

12. Use the Properties window to change the values of the following properties of the second button:

- **Name**   Change from Button1 to btnCancel.
- **Text**   Change to Cancel.
- **DialogResult**   Choose Cancel from the drop-down list.

As in the dialog box example, you set Cancel as the DialogResult value to correlate the clicking of the Cancel button with Cancel as the DialogResult value.

13. Use the Properties window to change the values of the following properties of the second form, using the drop-down list:

- **AcceptButton**   btnOK
- **CancelButton**   btnCancel

As in the dialog box example, pressing the ENTER key is the equivalent of clicking the button designated in the AcceptButton property, and pressing the ESCAPE key is the equivalent of clicking the button designated in the CancelButton property.

10

14. Using the Toolbox, add a TextBox control to the second form.

15. Use the Properties window to change the values of the following properties of the TextBox:

- **Multiline** Change from False to True as the text will require more than one line.

- **Text** Change to "Instructions: Type the text that will replace the text that is selected in the Text Editor and click OK, or click Cancel to return to the Text Editor without making any changes."

- **Enabled** Change from True to False as you do not want the application user to type in this text box. Instead, the purpose of the text box is to display instructions.

- **BackColor** Choose InactiveCaptionText from the drop-down list so the text box blends in with the surrounding form.

- **BorderStyle** Choose None from the drop-down list, again so the text box blends in with the surrounding form.

You do not need to change the Name property since you will not be referring to this TextBox in code.

16. Using the Toolbox, add another TextBox control to the second form.

17. Use the Properties window to change the values of the following properties of the TextBox:

- **Name** Change to txtReplace, as you will be referring to this text box in your code, so this control should have a logical name.

- **Text** Delete the default so it is blank so no text shows in the text box when you run the application.

The following illustration shows the second form in design mode after you have added the button control.

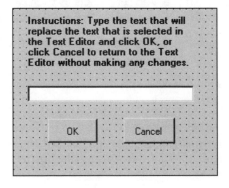

18. You're done designing the forms. Now it is time for you to write code. First, in the code view of Form1, add the following code to the Click event procedure of btnReplace:

```
Private Sub btnReplace_Click(ByVal sender As System.Object, _
    ByVal e As System.EventArgs) Handles btnReplace.Click
        If txtInput.SelectionLength > 0 Then
            Dim frmTwo As New Form2()
            Me.AddOwnedForm(frmTwo)
            frmTwo.Show()
        Else
MessageBox.Show("Nothing selected", "Notification")
        End If
End Sub
```

19. Add the following property procedure to the first form after the #End Region statement:

```
Public Property Selected() As String
        Get
            Selected = txtInput.SelectedText
        End Get
        Set(ByVal Value As String)
            If Value = "" Then
                MessageBox.Show("No replacement text",
"Notification")
            Else
                txtInput.SelectedText = Value
            End If
        End Set
    End Property
```

As discussed in the dialog box example, you only need to type the first line and then press the ENTER key. The Visual Basic .NET IDE finishes the skeleton of the code for you. You then can insert the code after the Get and Set statements.

20. In the code view of Form2, add the following code to the Click event procedure of btnOK:

```
Private Sub btnOK_Click(ByVal sender As System.Object, _
    ByVal e As System.EventArgs) Handles btnOK.Click
        Dim frm As Form1
        frm = Me.Owner
        frm.Selected = txtReplace.Text
        Me.Close()
End Sub
```

10

21. In the code view of Form2, add the following code to the Click event procedure of btnCancel:

```
Private Sub btnClose_Click(ByVal sender As System.Object, _
    ByVal e As System.EventArgs) Handles btnCancel.Click
        Me.Close()
End Sub
```

Run the project. If no text is selected when you click btnReplace on the Text Editor, the Replace form will not be displayed. Instead, a message box will appear, and there will be no changes to the Text Editor form. If text is selected, then the Replace form is displayed.

Once the Replace form is displayed, you can click either the Cancel or OK button. If you click the Cancel button, then the Replace form will close with no changes made to the selected text in the Text Editor. If instead you click the OK button, if no text is entered in the Replace form, a message box will appear, the Replace form will close, and the Text Editor will be restored with no changes to its selected text. Otherwise, the text in the Replace form will replace the text selected in the Text Editor and the Replace form will close.

Whether to Show the Replace Form

There is no purpose in showing the Replace form unless there is text selected in the Text Editor to be replaced. The TextBox control's SelectionLength property returns the number of characters selected in the text box. If nothing is selected, the value of the SelectionLength property is zero. If at least one character is selected, the value of the SelectionLength property will be greater than zero.

The following code in the Click event of btnReplace in the Text Editor uses the If...Else control structure, covered in Module 7, to show the Replace form if some text is selected, or a message box indicating "Nothing selected" if nothing is selected:

```
If txtInput.SelectionLength > 0 Then
    Dim frmTwo As New Form2()
    Me.AddOwnedForm(frmTwo)
    frmTwo.Show()
Else
MessageBox.Show("Nothing selected", "Notification")
    End If
```

Showing the Owned Form

If some text was selected, you need to show the Replace form as an owned form. This involves the following steps:

1. As with the dialog box, you need to explicitly declare and create an instance of the owned form, here with the statement:

```
Dim frmTwo As New Form2()
```

2. You may use the AddOwnedForm method to make the instance of Form2 an owned form of Form1. The syntax is:

```
[Owner Form].AddOwnedForm([Name of instance of owned form])
```

Thus, here the code is:

```
Me.AddOwnedForm(frmTwo)
```

3. Also as with the dialog box, you need to display the second form. Here you use the Show method instead of the ShowDialog method since you do not want to show the Replace form as a modal form:

```
frmTwo.Show()
```

Replacing the Selected Text

If the application user chooses the OK button in the Replace form, you want to replace the selected text in the Text Editor with the text in the Replace form.

As in the dialog box example, you will need to write a property procedure so code in the Replace form can access the property of an object in the Text Editor form. That property procedure, named Selected, will be analyzed next. First, however, you need to call the property procedure.

As discussed in the dialog box example, property procedures have Get and Set procedures. In this example, you will be using the Set procedure, as you will be using the property procedure to assign a value to a property of an object (txtInput) in the Text Editor form.

The syntax for calling a Set property procedure is:

```
[Object name].[Procedure name] = [value to be assigned]
```

10

The procedure name is Selected, and the value to be assigned is the Text property of txtReplace in the Replace form.

The object name is not so obvious since the property procedure belongs to Form1, but you are calling it from Form2. One possibility is Form1, so you would call the Set property procedure with the code:

```
Form1.Selected = txtReplace.Text
```

However, this will not work. The compiler will complain: "This reference to a non-shared member requires an object reference, and none is supplied." This will seem like "déjà vu all over again" because it is; the same issue came up in the dialog box example using the Get procedure. As you may recall, you need to call the property procedure from the currently running instance of the form, not the generic class blueprint.

In the dialog box example, obtaining the currently running instance was relatively easy because the dialog box had been created in the same event procedure that then accessed its property procedure. Here, however, there is no similarly available reference to the currently running instance of Form1.

In the Form1 code module, you can refer to the instance of Form1 with the Me keyword. However, you cannot do that here because you are in the Form2 code module, where the Me keyword refers to the current instance of Form2, not Form1.

The solution starts with using the owned form's Owner property. That property's value is the instance of the owned form that is its owner. Thus, the statement Me.Owner in Form2 will point to the current instance of the owner form, Form1.

You first declare a variable of the type Form1:

```
Dim frm As Form1
```

You then assign to that Form1 variable the value of the Owner property of Form2:

```
frm = Me.Owner
```

Finally, you use the Form1 variable to call the Selected property procedure:

```
frm.Selected = txtReplace.Text
```

The Set Property Procedure

Calling the Selected property procedure on the left side of an assignment statement involves the Set portion of the property procedure, with the value on the right side of the assignment operator (txtReplace.Text) held by the parameter Value:

```
Set(ByVal Value As String)
```

The next step is to check if there is any replacement text—that is, was any text typed into the text box in the Replace form? If not, instead of replacing text, you simply want an informational message box advising the application user that there is no replacement text.

Since there are only two possible choices—there either is replacement text or there isn't—the If...Else control structure is indicated:

```
If Value = "" Then
    MessageBox.Show("No replacement text", "Notification")
Else
    txtInput.SelectedText = Value
End If
```

If the Value is blank (""), which it will be if there is no replacement text, instead of replacing text, a message box informs the application user that there is no replacement text. This illustrates how a property procedure can be used to validate data before the data is used.

If there is replacement text, the code following the Else statement executes. The value of the text box's SelectedText property is the text that is selected in the text box. The effect of the assignment is to replace that text with the text in the parameter Value.

Closing the Owned Form

Unlike the dialog box example, it is necessary to close the Replace form when the application user chooses the OK or Cancel button in the Replace form, with the statement:

```
Me.Close()
```

A form shown as a dialog box with the ShowDialog method will close automatically when one of its buttons is selected. The reason is that the dialog

10

box is modal so, until it closes, the application user cannot return to the main form. By contrast, an owned form is modeless, so its being open would not prevent the application user from returning to the main form. Therefore, it is necessary to write code to close the owned form.

1-Minute Drill

● What does it mean that a form is modeless?

● Do you have to write code to close an owned form?

Summary

Visual Basic .NET's automated creation of a new Windows application project includes a form that serves as the main application window. The main application window often needs a supporting cast of helper forms, because Windows applications generally are far too complex for the main application window form to perform all the tasks required by the application.

This module showed you how to create and use three helper forms: the message box, dialog box, and owned form. All three include text that either is informative or a question, and buttons such as OK, Yes, No, Cancel, and so on for the application user's response. The message box is modal; the application user cannot return to the main form without closing the message box, which is accomplished by the user choosing one of its buttons. The dialog box is similar to the message box, but also may contain text boxes, check boxes, drop-down lists, and other controls. The owned form is similar to the dialog box, in that it also may contain controls, but it is modeless, which means the application user can have both the owned and main forms open at once.

When helper forms pose a question rather than simply being informational, you need to write code to enable the application to know which button the user clicked when they closed the message box. The MessageBox class has a Show method. The Show method's parameters specify not just the text, title, and icon

---

● The application user may return to the main form without closing the modeless form.

● Yes. Modal forms such as message and dialog boxes close automatically when a button is clicked, but owned forms, being modeless, do not have that automatic behavior.

of the message box, but also the buttons that will be displayed. The Show method has a return value that represents the button the user clicked. That return value is stored in a variable. The dialog box and owned form work slightly differently, with their DialogResult property representing the button the user clicked. Whether you are using a return value or the DialogResult property, you then use the If statement, either by itself or with the Else statement, to run different code depending on which button the user clicked.

Additionally, a dialog box or owned form may contain controls, including ones with which the application user may interact by typing text, checking a check box, selecting an item from a list, and so on. This presents you with the further programming challenge of writing code to enable the main form to know and take actions based on what the application user typed, checked, or selected in the controls in the helper form. You solve this challenge by using property procedures. A property procedure may contain a Get procedure and a Set procedure. A Get procedure is used to return the value of a property, whereas a Set procedure is used to assign a value to a property.

10

☑ *Mastery Check*

1. Which of the following helper forms do you not have to create in the Windows Forms Designer?

   A. Message box

   B. Dialog box

   C. Owned form

2. Which of the following helper forms is modeless?

   A. Message box

   B. Dialog box

   C. Owned form

3. In which of the following helper forms do you employ the return value of the method used to determine which button the user clicked?

   A. Message box

   B. Dialog box

   C. Owned form

4. What is the difference between showing a form using its ShowDialog method or its Show method?

5. Which of the following helper forms does not automatically close when one of its buttons is clicked?

   A. Message box

   B. Dialog box

   C. Owned form

6. Which of the following helper forms cannot contain a TextBox control?

   A. Message box

   B. Dialog box

   C. Owned form

☑ Mastery Check

7. The keyword Private means you cannot access the object, variable, or procedure in question.

A. True

B. False

8. You use a property procedure to access from one form the property of an object in another form.

A. True

B. False

9. Which part of a property procedure do you use to retrieve the value of the property of an object?

A. Get

B. Set

10. Which of the following statements is correct?

A. You can have an If without an Else.

B. You can have an Else without an If.

10

Module 11

Menus and Toolbars

The Goals of this Module

- Know how to create a menu both with the Menu Designer and programmatically
- Understand how to create context menus and link them to the main menu items
- Know how to create toolbars and handle their events

Application users need to give commands to the application, such as to open, save or close a file, print a document, cut, copy or paste text, and so on. Application users give such commands through the GUI of the application. The three most common GUI elements through which application users give commands to an application are the menu, shortcut or context menus, and toolbars.

Menus

It is a rare Windows application that does not have a menu. The menu provides a GUI through which the application user can issue commands to the application.

The menu is not the exclusive way through which the GUI may enable the application user to issue commands to the application. However, the menu has several advantages over alternatives. The menu enables the programmer to organize commands in a logical hierarchy. For example, commands related to file operations, such as Open and Save, are under the File menu, whereas commands related to editing, such as Cut, Copy, and Paste, are under the Edit menu. Additionally, menus save valuable screen space. Submenu items collapse unless the menu item above them is chosen. This enables your application to remain uncluttered, by not showing commands that are not immediately needed.

Everything in Visual Basic .NET is an object, and menus are no exception. A MainMenu object represents a menu on a Windows form. The MainMenu object contains a collection of MenuItem objects, each of which is an item on the menu. Each MenuItem can be a command for your application or a parent menu for other submenu items. Figure 11-1 shows submenu items under the File menu in Microsoft Word. The Open menu item performs a command, displaying the File Open dialog box. By contrast, the Send To submenu is a parent menu for other submenu items, such as Mail Recipient.

Creating a Menu

You can add a menu to a Windows form either at design time in the Windows Forms Designer or programmatically at runtime. Either way, creating a menu is a two-step process. You first add a MainMenu object to your form, and then you append MenuItem objects to it.

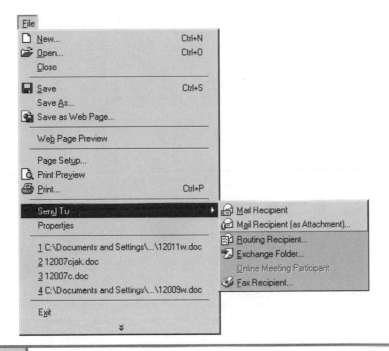

Figure 11-1 Submenu items

Creating a Menu at Design Time

You add a menu to a form similar to how you would add a control such as a CommandButton to the form. First, in the Windows Forms Designer, you open the form to which you wish to add the menu. Next, in the Toolbox, double-click the MainMenu component. As shown in Figure 11-2, this adds a rectangular area underneath the top left corner of the form displaying the text "Type Here," and the MainMenu component is added to the component tray.

Once you have added a MainMenu component to your Windows form, the next step is to add menu items to it. Click the text "Type Here" and type the name of the desired menu item to add it. If the text "Type Here" is not displayed as in Figure 11-2, you can display it by clicking the MainMenu component on the Windows form.

11

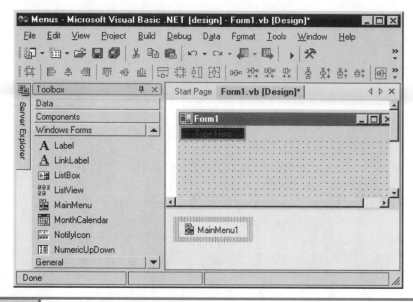

Figure 11-2 Adding a menu using the Windows Forms Designer

We will add a File menu item since that is the first top-level item in Windows applications. Most top-level menu items have an access shortcut so that the menu item can be accessed by the keyboard combination of the ALT key plus a letter in the menu item. The letter in the menu item that is part of the keyboard combination is underlined. The keyboard combination for the File menu item is ALT-F. To add a keyboard shortcut, simply type an ampersand (&) before the letter to be underlined. Figure 11-3 shows the result of typing "&File" for the initial menu item; the "F" in "File" is underlined.

As Figure 11-3 shows, you now have "Type Here" options both below and to the right of the File menu item. You would add items below the File menu item such as Open and Save. You might add an Edit menu item to the right of the File menu item to be consistent with other Windows applications.

Tip

If you forget a menu item, right-click the menu item before which the new one will be inserted, and choose Insert New from the context menu. If you decide you do not want to include a menu item, right-click it and choose Delete from the context menu.

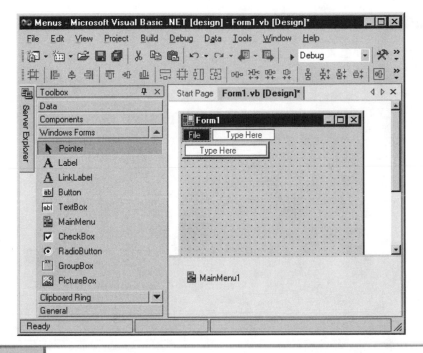

Figure 11-3   The Windows Forms Designer after adding first menu item

Figure 11-4 shows that a submenu item itself may have submenu items such as the Send To submenu item.

Creating a Menu at Runtime

You can add a menu programmatically to a Windows form in several steps:

1. Create a new public procedure, which in this example will be called AddMenuAndItems.

```
Public Sub AddMenuAndItems()
'code goes here
End Sub
```

2. Within that procedure, declare an instance of a MainMenu object. In this example, the instance will be named mnuFile.

```
Dim mnuFile as New MainMenu()
```

11

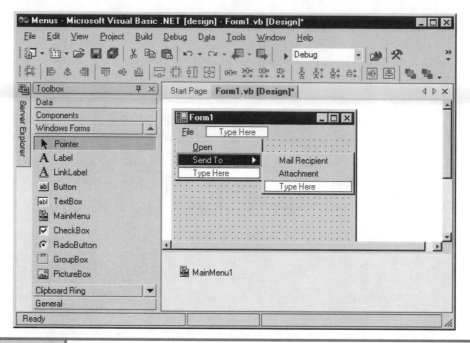

Figure 11-4 The submenu item with its own submenu items

3. Set the Menu property of the form to the MainMenu instance you just created. This associates mnuFile as the menu for the form:

```
Me.Menu = mnuFile
```

4. Within the procedure, create MenuItem objects to add to the MainMenu object's collection.

```
Dim mnuItemFile as New MenuItem("&File")
Dim mnuItemNew as New MenuItem("&New")
```

5. Since a MainMenu object starts with no menu items, the first menu item added becomes the menu heading. This is why the Text property of mnuItemFile is set to &File, and also why it is added to mnuFileMenu.

```
mnuFileMenu.MenuItems.Add(mnuItemFile)
```

6. The following menu item is added to mnuItemFile and not mnuFileMenu as it is not a top-level menu item, but instead subordinate to the File menu item:

```
mnuItemFile.MenuItems.Add(mnuItemNew)
```

The finished procedure should now read as follows:

```
Public Sub AddMenuAndItems()
Dim mnuFile as New MainMenu()
Me.Menu = mnuFile
Dim mnuItemFile As New MenuItem("&File")
Dim mnuItemNew As New MenuItem("&New")
mnuFile.MenuItems.Add(mnuItemFile)
mnuItemFile.MenuItems.Add(mnuItemNew)
End Sub
```

7. When you are finished programmatically creating the menu structure, you need to call the procedure you have created. A logical place to do so is the Load event of the form, so that the menu is created when the form loads:

```
Private Sub Form1_Load(ByVal sender As System.Object,
    ByVal e As System.EventArgs) Handles MyBase.Load
AddMenuAndItems()
End Sub
```

Figure 11-5 shows the resulting programmatically created menu.

Figure 11-5   The programmatically created menu

11

Note

In Figure 11-5, the "F" in File and the "N" in New are not underlined when you run the application until you press the ALT key. This is standard behavior in Windows applications.

You can add additional top-level items, such as Edit, the same way that you added File. First, declare a menu item whose text is Edit, and then add it to the MainMenu instance mnuFile:

```
Dim mnuItemEdit As New MenuItem()
mnuItemEdit.Text = "&Edit"
mnuFile.MenuItems.Add(mnuItemEdit)
```

Note that in this code snippet the menu item was declared without text, and then text was assigned to its Text property. The two lines could be combined as in the previous examples:

```
Dim mnuItemEdit As New MenuItem("&Edit")
```

You also can add menu items to other menu items and thereby create submenus. You do so by adding MenuItem objects to the MenuItems property of the parent MenuItem. From the preceding example, if you wanted to add a third menu item named mnuItemFolder as a submenu of the second menu item (mnuItemNew), you would include the following line of code:

```
Dim mnuItemFolder As New MenuItem("Folder")
mnuItemNew.MenuItems.Add(mnuItemFolder)
```

Add Functionality to the Menu Items

The purpose of a menu item is to do something when it is clicked, so you use the Click event procedure of the menu item to provide functionality for the menu item. The Click event does not occur only when the user clicks the menu item. The Click event also occurs if the user selects the menu item using the keyboard and presses the ENTER key, or if the user presses an access key or shortcut key that is associated with the menu item.

Note

If the MenuItems property for the MenuItem contains any items, this event is not raised. This event is not raised for parent menu items.

The following code outputs "New" to the Debug window when the menu item named mnuItemNew is clicked:

```
Private Sub mnuItemNew_Click(ByVal sender As System.Object, _
   ByVal e As System.EventArgs)
Debug.Write("New")
End Sub
```

If you added the menu item at design time, you can add the event procedure by choosing the menu item by name from the Class Name drop-down list and Click from the Method Name drop-down list. If instead you added the menu item programmatically, you need to type in the event procedure.

If you add the menu item at design time, Visual Basic .NET automatically adds the following code in the Windows Forms Designer generated code region so the menu item will handle events, in this case the Click event. In the following code, the menu item added at design time is named mnuEditCopy:

```
Friend WithEvents mnuEditCopy As System.Windows.Forms.MenuItem
```

However, if you added the menu item programmatically, you need to add an event handler of the Click event of the MenuItem. You can do so by adding the following line of code to the AddMenuAndItems procedure you already have written:

```
AddHandler mnuItemNew.Click, AddressOf Me.mnuItemNew_Click
```

AddHandler is a keyword that associates the event (Click) of the control (mnuItemNew) that follows it to the procedure that follows the AddressOf keyword. The procedure is the Click event procedure of mnuItemNew, which is found in the module of the current form (Me).

11

Enhancing the Menu

You can add four enhancements to a menu to convey information to users:

- Check marks can be used to designate whether a feature is turned on or off. In Microsoft Word, the Ruler menu item under the View menu is checked depending on whether a ruler is displayed along the margin of the window displaying the document.

- Shortcut keys are keyboard commands to access menu items within an application. In Microsoft Word, the New menu item under the File menu can be accessed with the shortcut key CTRL-N.

- Access keys allow keyboard navigation of menus by pressing a combination of the ALT key and the underlined access key. In Microsoft Word, the File menu is accessed by the combination ALT-F, and the New menu item under the File menu by the combination ALT-F-N.

- Separator bars are used to group related commands within a menu and make menus easier to read. In Microsoft Word, under the File menu, a separator bar separates the New, Open, and Close menu items from the following menu items.

Figure 11-6 shows these four enhancements.

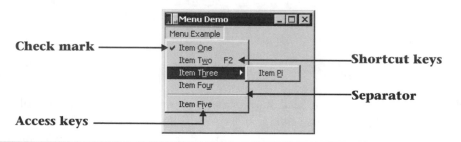

Figure 11-6 Menu enhancements

Adding a Check Mark

You can add a check mark both at design time and at runtime. You have two methods of adding a check mark to a menu item at design time. After selecting the menu item within the Menu Designer, you can set the Checked property to True in the Properties window. Alternatively, click the area to the left of the menu item. As shown in Figure 11-7, a check mark appears, indicating the Checked property has been set to True. Clicking the area again eliminates the check mark.

┤Note

The menu item's RadioCheck property customizes the appearance of the selected item. If the RadioCheck property is True, a radio button appears next to the item; if the RadioCheck property is False, a check mark instead appears next to the item.

You add a check mark to a menu item programmatically simply by setting the menu item's Checked property to True:

```
mnuItemNew.Checked = True
```

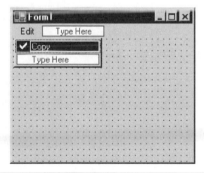

Figure 11-7 | Adding a check mark in the Menu Designer

11

Adding a Shortcut Key

You can add a shortcut key both at design time and at runtime. You add a shortcut key to a menu item at design time by selecting the menu item within the Menu Designer, selecting the Shortcut property from the Properties window, and choosing one of the values offered in the drop-down list as shown in Figure 11-8.

You add a shortcut key to a menu item programmatically simply by setting the menu item's Shortcut property to one of the available values. The following code sets the shortcut key of a menu item to F6:

```
mnuItemNew.Shortcut = System.Windows.Forms.Shortcut.F6
```

Adding an Access Key

You can add an access key both at design time and at runtime. The preceding section on "Creating a Menu" showed how to add an access key to the File menu. You add an access key to a menu item at design time or runtime. When setting the Text property in the Properties window, the Menu Designer, or in code, enter an ampersand (&) prior to the letter you want to be underlined as the access key.

Figure 11-8   Shortcut keys displayed in the Properties window

Adding a Separator Bar

You don't add a separator bar to a menu item as you do a shortcut key, access key, or check mark. Instead, you add a shortcut key as a menu item. This also can be done at design time or runtime. When setting the Text property in the Properties window, the Menu Designer, or in code, enter a hyphen to make that menu item a separator bar. Alternatively in the Menu Designer, right-click the location where you want a separator bar, and choose New Separator.

Disabling Items on Windows Forms Menus

Microsoft Word contains the menu items Cut and Copy under the Edit menu. Initially, Cut and Copy are grayed out (disabled). They are grayed out because no text is selected, therefore, there is nothing to cut or copy. However, once you select text, Cut and Copy are no longer grayed out, or in other words, are enabled.

A menu item should not be enabled when the command it represents should not be available. It would be frustrating for the application user to click Cut or Copy and see nothing happen. The application user might be misled into thinking there is something wrong with your application. When you gray out, or disable, the menu item, the application user is given a visual cue that the menu item is not available.

Disabling a menu item that should not be available has an additional advantage, error prevention. The code for cutting text may understandably assume there is selected text. If there is no selected text, executing the code for cutting text may cause an error. By disabling the menu item when no text is selected, the code for cutting text cannot be executed when no text is selected, thus avoiding the error.

Menu items are enabled by default when they are created. However, you can disable a menu item by setting its Enabled property to False. You can do this at design time, when the menu item is selected in the Menu Designer, and through the Properties window. You also can do this programmatically:

```
mnuItemNew.Enabled = False
```

11

Disabling the first or top-level menu item in a menu, such as the File menu item in a traditional File menu, disables all the menu items contained within the menu. Similarly, disabling a menu item that has submenu items disables the submenu items.

If all the commands on a given menu are unavailable to the user, you should hide as well as disable the entire menu. You hide the menu by setting the Visible property of the top-most menu item to False. This presents a cleaner user interface by not cluttering up your menu structure with disabled items.

Caution

Hiding the menu alone is not sufficient. You must also disable the menu, because hiding alone does not prevent access to a menu command via a shortcut key.

1-Minute Drill

● What class do you use to create a menu?

● How do you add a menu item to a menu programmatically?

● What enhancements can you add to a menu?

● Does hiding a menu disable it?

Context Menu

Many Windows applications have shortcut menus, which are displayed when the user clicks the right mouse button over the area of the form, or over a control on the form. Figure 11-9 shows a shortcut menu in Microsoft Word.

● You use the MainMenu class to create a menu.
● You add the menu item using the Add method of the MenuItems collection of a MainMenu or MenuItem object.
● Check marks, shortcut keys, access keys, and separator bars.
● No. You can still access the menu using a shortcut key.

Ask the Expert

Question: Should I create a menu using the Menu Designer or do it programmatically?

Answer: I recommend using the Menu Designer when you can, simply because it is faster and less prone to error than creating the menu by code.

Question: Why would I create a menu programmatically when using the Menu Designer is faster and less prone to error?

Answer: As you progress in Visual Basic .NET and deal with more complex applications, you may need to modify menus dynamically— that is, while the application is running. This is not possible using the Menu Designer; you can only do so programmatically.

Also, creating a menu by code teaches you much more about how a menu works than using the Menu Designer, which hides the details from you.

Shortcut menus also are called context menus, because the particular menu items displayed depend on the context, such as the application state, or where on the form or control the right mouse button was clicked. Indeed, in Visual Basic .NET, the ContextMenu class represents shortcut menus.

Context menus typically are used to combine different menu items from a MainMenu of a form that are useful for the user given the context of the application. For example, you can use a shortcut menu assigned to a TextBox control to provide immediate access to menu items also found in the MainMenu to cut, copy, and paste text, find text, change the text font, and so on. However, a context menu also may contain menu items not found in the form's MainMenu, such as to provide situation-specific commands that are not appropriate for the MainMenu to display.

11

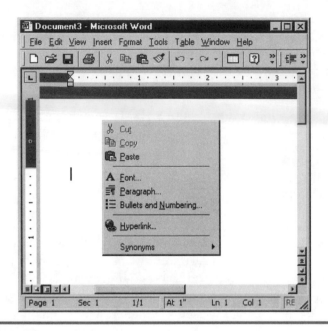

A shortcut menu

Creating a Context Menu

As with the MainMenu, you can add a context menu to a Windows form either at design time in the Windows Forms Designer or programmatically at runtime. Either way, creating a menu is a two-step process. You first add a ContextMenu object to your form, and then you append to it MenuItem objects.

Creating a Context Menu at Design Time

You add a context menu to a form similarly to how you add a MainMenu to the form.

1. In the Windows Forms Designer, open the form to which you wish to add the context menu.

2. Double-click the ContextMenu component in the Toolbox. As shown in Figure 11-10, this adds a context menu to the form, displaying the text "Type Here." The ContextMenu component is added to the component tray.

3. Associate the context menu with the form or a control on the form by choosing the ContextMenu object from the drop-down list in that form, or control's ContextMenu property in the Properties window.

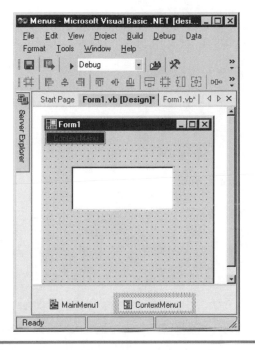

Figure 11-10   Adding a ContextMenu component to a form

┼*Note*

More than one control can use a ContextMenu. You can use the SourceControl property to determine which control last displayed the shortcut menu in order to perform tasks specific to the control or to modify the shortcut menu displayed for the control.

11

Creating a Context Menu at Runtime

You can add a context menu programmatically to a Windows form in several steps:

1. Create a new public procedure, which in this example will be called AddContextMenu:

```
Public Sub AddContextMenu()
'code goes here
End Sub
```

2. Within that procedure, declare an instance of a ContextMenu object. In this example, the instance will be named mnuContextMenu.

```
Dim mnuContextMenu as New ContextMenu()
```

3. Set the ContextMenu property of the form to the MainMenu instance you just created:

```
Me.ContextMenu = mnuContextMenu
```

The procedure now should read:

```
Public Sub AddContextMenu()
Dim mnuContextMenu as New ContextMenu()
Me.ContextMenu = mnuContextMenu
End Sub
```

Adding Items to the Context Menu

Once you have added a ContextMenu component to your Windows form, the next step is to add menu items to it. You can do this at design time, runtime, or by copying menu items from a MainMenu.

Adding Items to the Context Menu at Design Time

Adding menu items to a context menu at design time is essentially the same as adding menu items at design time to a MainMenu. You click the text "Type Here" and type the name of the desired menu item to add it. If the text "Type Here" is not displayed, you can display it by clicking the ContextMenu component on the Windows form. To add another menu item, click another "Type Here" area within the Menu Designer. You click the area below the current menu item to add another menu item, or click the area to the right of the current menu item to add submenu items.

One difference between a ContextMenu and a MainMenu is that a ContextMenu usually does not have a top-level item, such as File in the MainMenu.

Adding Items to the Context Menu at Runtime

Adding menu items to a context menu programmatically is essentially the same as adding menu items programmatically to a MainMenu. We'll start with the AddContextMenu procedure we created in the preceding section "Creating a Context Menu at Runtime":

```
Public Sub AddContextMenu()
Dim mnuContextMenu as New ContextMenu()
Me.ContextMenu = mnuContextMenu
End Sub
```

1. Within the procedure, create MenuItem objects to add to the ContextMenu object's collection:

```
Dim mnuItemNew as New MenuItem()
Dim mnuItemOpen as New MenuItem()
```

2. Within the procedure, set the Text property for each of these menu items:

```
mnuItemNew.Text = "&New"
mnuItemOpen.Text = "&Open"
```

3. Within the procedure, add the menu items to the MenuItems collection of the ContextMenu object:

```
mnuContextMenu.MenuItems.Add(mnuItemNew)
mnuContextMenu.MenuItems.Add(mnuItemOpen)
```

A context menu also may contain submenus. You create a submenu by adding add MenuItem objects to the MenuItems collection of the parent MenuItem. In the preceding example, if you wanted to add a third menu item (myMenuItemOpenWith) as a submenu of the second menu item (myMenuItemOpen), you would include the following lines of code:

```
Dim mnuItemOpenWith as new MenuItem()
mnuItemOpenWith.Text = "Open &With..."
mnuItemOpen.MenuItems.Add(mnuItemOpenWith)
```

Copying Menu Items from Menus to Context Menus

You may want the context menu to duplicate commands in the main menu. For example, the Cut, Copy, and Paste menu commands in Microsoft Word's Edit menu are often duplicated in a menu when you click the document.

You do not need to re-create the entire menu structure when you want to duplicate a given menu's functionality. You can use the Menu Designer at design time to copy menus, or the CloneMenu method at runtime to duplicate a given menu's functionality.

11

To copy menu items at design time:

1. Within the Menu Designer, choose the MainMenu component, select the menu item or items you would like to duplicate, right-click them, and choose Copy, as shown in the following illustration:

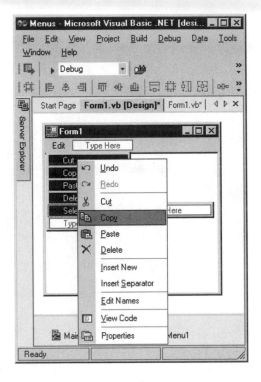

2. Choose the ContextMenu component, select the "Type Here" area where you would like the first menu item to appear, then right-click and choose Paste, as shown in the next illustration:

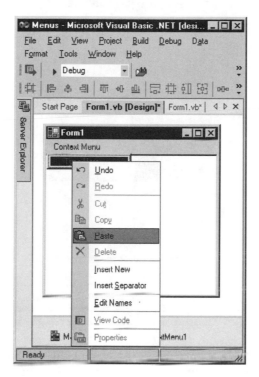

Here is the end result.

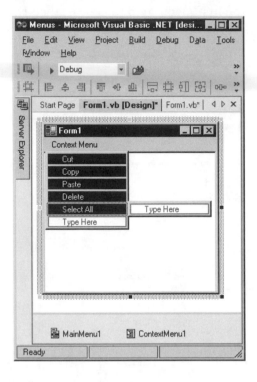

You use the CloneMenu method of the MenuItem class to copy menu items programmatically. In this example, an Edit menu with three commands, Cut, Copy and Paste, is copied to a ContextMenu component in the same form:

```
Private mmMainMenu As MainMenu
Private miEditMenu As MenuItem
Private cmEdit As ContextMenu

Private Sub CopyMenuItems()
'Create instances of global MainMenu and top-level MenuItem objects
mmMainMenu = New MainMenu
miEditMenu = New MenuItem("&Edit")
'Create three menu items as part of MainMenu menu structure
miEditMenu.MenuItems.Add("&Cut")
miEditMenu.MenuItems.Add("&Copy")
miEditMenu.MenuItems.Add("&Paste")
```

```
'Add top-level menu item to MainMenu component
mmMainMenu.MenuItems.Add(miEditMenu)
'Set MainMenu component to be form's menu
Form1.Menu = mmMainMenu
'Create instance of global Context Menu object
cmEdit = New ContextMenu
'Clone top-level MenuItem of MainMenu component
'Then add duplicated MenuItem to ContextMenu component
cmEdit.MenuItems.Add(miEditMenu.CloneMenu())
'Set ContextMenu component of form
Form1.ContextMenu = cmEdit
End Sub
```

Add Functionality to the Menu Items

You add functionality to a context menu the same way you add functionality to a MainMenu, by using the Click event procedure of the menu item. However, if you copied items from a MainMenu to the ContextMenu, then you would want the menu item in the context menu to use the event handler of the corresponding menu item in the main menu.

According to MSDN, copying menu items preserves property settings and event handlers you have established with the original menu items, so that the new menu items you have created use these same event handlers because the entire MenuItem object is cloned. However, based on my experimentation, this may only be true if you copy a menu item programmatically, and not if you do so at design time using copy and paste in the Menu Designer. Nevertheless, you have three alternatives of having the Click event procedure for the main menu item also handle the Click event for the corresponding context menu item.

One alternative is to use AddHandler, which was covered earlier in this module. The following code assumes the context menu item is cmnSelectAll and the corresponding main menu item is mnuEditSelectAll:

11

```
AddHandler cmnSelectAll.Click, AddressOf Me.mnuEditSelectAll_Click
```

This line of code logically could be placed in the load event of the form.

Another alternative is to expand the Handles clause of the Click event procedure of the main menu item (here mnuEditSelectAll). This event procedure already has the clause Handles mnuEditSelectAll.Click. You add cmnSelectAll.Click to the Handles clause, using a comma to separate it from mnuEditSelectAll.Click:

```
Private Sub mnuEditSelectAll_Click(ByVal sender As Object, _
   ByVal e As System.EventArgs) _
   Handles mnuEditSelectAll.Click, cmnSelectAll.Click
txtEdit.SelectAll()
End Sub
```

The third alternative is to call the Click event procedure of the main menu item from the Click event procedure of the context menu item:

```
Private Sub cmnSelectAll_Click(ByVal sender As System.Object, _
   ByVal e As System.EventArgs) Handles cmnSelectAll.Click
mnuEditSelectAll_Click(sender, e)
End Sub
```

Note

You must pass the parameters sender and e to the mnuEditSelectAll_Click call because the Click event procedure of that MainMenu item expects those arguments.

1-Minute Drill

● Does a context menu typically have a top-level menu item such as File in a MainMenu?

● Can the Click event procedure of a menu item in a context item call the event procedure of a menu item in a MainMenu?

● Can the Click event procedure of a menu item in a MainMenu also handle the Click event of a menu item in a context menu?

● No.
● Yes.
● Yes. The Click event procedure of a menu item in a MainMenu also may handle the Click event of a menu item in a context menu by expanding the Handles clause of the MainMenu menu item's event procedure.

Ask the Expert

Question: When should I use a context menu?

Answer: Context menus are useful as an alternate way to display commands whose immediate accessibility will enhance the application user's ability to effectively use the application. However, long context menus tend to clutter up the screen, which is unnecessary since they duplicate commands already available from the menu, if not a toolbar. Therefore, while I would recommend using context menus often, I equally recommend keeping them short.

Toolbars

The Windows Forms ToolBar control is used on forms as a control bar that displays a row of bitmapped buttons and drop-down menus that activate commands. Thus, clicking a toolbar button can be equivalent to choosing a menu command. Indeed, a toolbar button often duplicates the functionality of a menu item. "Ask the Expert" following this section discusses why toolbar buttons are used to duplicate the functionality of a menu item.

Adding the Toolbar and Buttons

You create a toolbar by dragging a ToolBar control from the Toolbox onto the form. However, unlike the MainMenu and ContextMenu components, the ToolBar control does not appear in the component tray. Instead, it appears as a large gray area under the menu.

The next step is to add buttons to the toolbar. You can add buttons to the toolbar at both design time and runtime.

Adding Buttons at Design Time

1. In the drop-down list at the top of the Properties window, select the ToolBar control you added to your form.

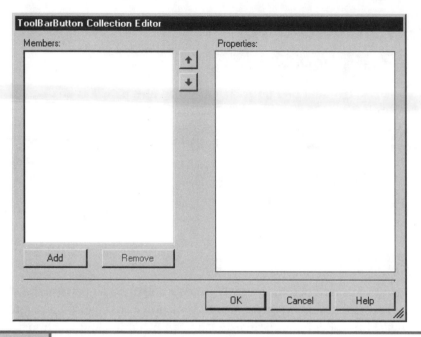

Figure 11-11 The ToolBarButton Collection Editor

2. Click the Buttons property to select it and click the ellipsis (...) button to open the ToolBarButton Collection Editor shown in Figure 11-11.

3. Use the Add and Remove buttons to add and remove buttons from the ToolBar control.

4. Configure the properties of the individual buttons in the Properties window that appears in the pane on the right side of the editor as shown in Figure 11-12.

   Table 11-1 lists important properties of the ToolBarButton and Table 11-2 lists important values of the ToolBarButtonStyle.

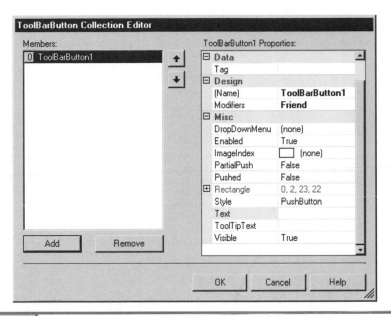

Figure 11-12 | Adding buttons in the ToolBarButton Collection Editor

Property	Description
DropDown Menu	Sets the menu to be displayed in the drop down toolbar button. The toolbar button's Style property must be set to DropDownButton. This property takes an instance of the ContextMenu class as a reference.
PartialPush	Sets whether a toggle-style toolbar button is partially pushed. The toolbar button's Style property must be set to ToggleButton.
Pushed	Sets whether a toggle-style toolbar button is currently in the pushed state. The toolbar button's Style property must be set to ToggleButton or PushButton.
Style	Sets the style of the toolbar button. Must be one of the values in the ToolBarButtonStyle enumeration in Table 11-2.
Text	The text string displayed by the button.
ToolTipText	The text that appears as a ToolTip for the button. To display ToolTips, the ShowToolTips property must be set to True.

Table 11-1 | Important Toolbar Properties

11

Member Name	Description
DropDownButton	A drop-down control that displays a menu or other window when clicked.
PushButton	A standard, three-dimensional button.
Separator	A space or line between toolbar buttons. The appearance depends on the value of the Appearance property.
ToggleButton	A toggle button that appears sunken when clicked and retains the sunken appearance until clicked again.

Table 11-2 ToolBarButtonStyle Enumeration

5. Click OK to close the dialog box and create the panels you specified. Figure 11-13 shows the toolbar area after adding several buttons.

Adding Buttons Programmatically

You add buttons programmatically to a toolbar by the following steps:

1. In a procedure, create toolbar buttons by adding them to the ToolBarButtons collection.

2. In the same procedure, specify property settings for the individual buttons by passing the button's index via the Buttons property.

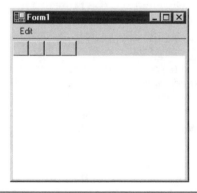

Figure 11-13 The toolbar area after adding several buttons

This example assumes that a ToolBar control named ToolBar1 already has been added to the form. The ToolBarButtons collection is a zero-based collection, so the index of the first button is 0, the index of the second button is 1, and so on.

```
Public Sub CreateToolBarButtons()
' Create buttons and set text property.
ToolBar1.Buttons.Add("One")
ToolBar1.Buttons.Add("Two")
ToolBar1.Buttons.Add("Three")
ToolBar1.Buttons.Add("Four")
' Set Style property
' Index is zero-based
ToolBar1.Buttons(0).Style = ToolBarButtonStyle.PushButton
ToolBar1.Buttons(1).Style = ToolBarButtonStyle.Separator
ToolBar1.Buttons(2).Style = ToolBarButtonStyle.ToggleButton
ToolBar1.Buttons(3).Style = ToolBarButtonStyle.DropDownButton
' Set the ToggleButton's PartialPush property.
ToolBar1.Buttons(2).PartialPush = True
' Instantiate a ContextMenu component and menu items.
' Set the DropDownButton's DropDownMenu property to the context menu.
Dim cm As New ContextMenu()
Dim miOne As New MenuItem("One")
Dim miTwo As New MenuItem("Two")
Dim miThree As New MenuItem("Three")
cm.MenuItems.Add(miOne)
cm.MenuItems.Add(miTwo)
cm.MenuItems.Add(miThree)
ToolBar1.Buttons(3).DropDownMenu = cm
' Set the PushButton's Pushed property.
ToolBar1.Buttons(0).Pushed = True
' Set the ToolTipText property of one of the buttons.
ToolBar1.Buttons(1).ToolTipText = "Button 2"
End Sub
```

11

Defining an Icon for a Toolbar Button

Toolbar buttons generally display icons for easy identification by users. You can display icons on toolbar buttons by adding images to the ImageList component and then associating the ImageList component with the ToolBar control. This can be done either at design time or programmatically.

Setting an Icon for a Toolbar Button at Design Time

1. Drag an ImageList component from the Toolbox to your form. The ImageList, like the MainMenu and ContextMenu components, will locate in the component tray.

2. In the Properties window of the ImageList control, click the Images property and add images to the ImageList control. In the Properties window, click the ellipsis button (…) next to the Images property. The Image Collection Editor appears as shown in Figure 11-14.

3. Use the Add and Remove buttons of the Image Collection Editor to add and remove images from the list. Figure 11-15 shows the result after using the Image Collection Editor to add buttons for Cut, Copy, Paste, and Undo.

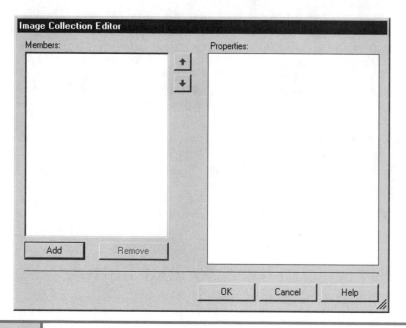

Figure 11-14 The Image Collection Editor

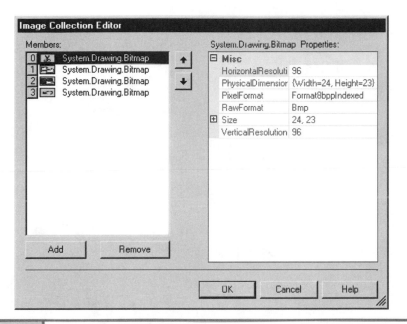

Figure 11-15 After adding buttons to the Image Collection Editor

4. In the Properties window, set the ToolBar control's ImageList property to the ImageList control you just added.

5. Click the ToolBar control's Buttons property to select it, and click the ellipsis (...) button to open the ToolBarButton Collection Editor.

6. In the Properties window that appears in the pane on the right side of the ToolBarButton Collection Editor, set the ImageIndex property of each toolbar button to one of the values in the list, which is drawn from the images you added to the ImageList component, as shown in Figure 11-16. The resulting form is shown in Figure 11-17.

11

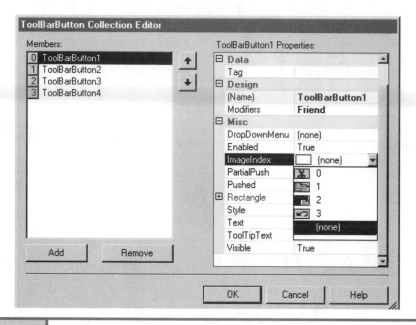

Figure 11-16 Associating an image with a toolbar button

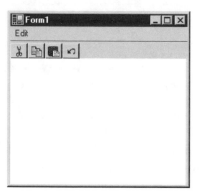

Figure 11-17 A form with a toolbar

Setting an Icon for a Toolbar Button Programmatically

You set an icon for a toolbar button programmatically by performing the following steps:

1. In a procedure, instantiate an ImageList component and a ToolBar control.

2. In the same procedure, assign an image to the ImageList component.

3. In the same procedure, assign the ImageList control to the ToolBar control and assign the ImageIndex property of the individual toolbar buttons.

The following code is derived from these steps:

```
Public Sub InitializeMyToolBar()
' Instantiate an ImageList component and a ToolBar control.
Dim ToolBar1 as New ToolBar
Dim ImageList1 as New ImageList
' Assign an image to the ImageList component.
' The image used below is for demonstration purposes only.
' Replace it with an image of your own choosing.
Dim myImage As System.Drawing.Image = Image.FromFile("C:\winnt\Sample.ico")
ImageList1.Images.Add(myImage)
' Create a ToolBarButton.
Dim ToolBarButton1 As New ToolBarButton()
' Add the ToolBarButton to the ToolBar.
ToolBar1.Buttons.Add(toolBarButton1)
' Assign an ImageList to the ToolBar.
ToolBar1.ImageList = ImageList1
' Assign the ImageIndex property of the ToolBarButton.
ToolBarButton1.ImageIndex = 0
End Sub
```

Adding Functionality to the Toolbar

11

You added functionality to both MainMenu and ContextMenu items by using their Click event procedure. The process for adding functionality to a toolbar is somewhat different.

You cannot create an event procedure for the individual toolbar buttons the same way you can for the individual menu items. Instead, you use the event procedure for the ToolBar itself, and the event is not the Click event, but the ButtonClick event.

The event procedure title for the toolbar's ButtonClick event is:

```
Private Sub ToolBar1_ButtonClick(ByVal sender As Object, _
    ByVal e As System.Windows.Forms.ToolBarButtonClickEventArgs)
```

The second argument is not System.EventArgs, as with the Click event procedure of the main and context menu items. Instead, the second argument type is System.Windows.Forms.ToolBarButtonClickEventArgs. Consequently, the event handlers for the main and context menu items cannot handle the ButtonClick event of the toolbar. The compiler will complain that the two event handlers do not have the same "signature," referring to the difference in the type of the second argument of the two event handlers.

Additionally, since the event procedure is for the toolbar and not for the individual toolbar buttons, you need to know which button the user clicked. The second argument, represented by the parameter *e*, gives you this information. Assuming the toolbar name is ToolBar1, the following statement will provide you with the index of the button that was clicked:

```
ToolBar1.Buttons.IndexOf(e.Button)
```

You can use this information in a Select Case statement to take action based on which button was clicked:

```
Private Sub ToolBar1_ButtonClick(ByVal sender As Object, _
    ByVal e As System.Windows.Forms.ToolBarButtonClickEventArgs) _
    Handles ToolBar1.ButtonClick
Select Case ToolBar1.Buttons.IndexOf(e.Button)
    Case 0
    'code for first button
    Case 1
    'code for second button
    Case 2
    'code for third button
End Select
End Sub
```

Assuming the first toolbar button performs a Cut of selected text, such as mnuEditCut, you can call the Click event of mnuEditCut as follows:

```
Case 0
    mnuEditCut_Click(sender, e)
```

Note

This call works even though the second argument of the ButtonClick event procedure of the toolbar is not the same as the second argument of the Click event procedure of the menu item. The reason is that the type of the second argument of the ButtonClick event procedure of the toolbar inherits from the type of the second argument of the Click event procedure of the menu item.

1-Minute Drill

● Do you use the Click or ButtonClick event procedure to handle when a toolbar button is clicked?

● Does the event procedure you use to handle when a toolbar button is clicked belong to the toolbar button or to the toolbar?

Ask the Expert

Question: Why are toolbar buttons used to duplicate the functionality of a menu item?

Answer: Toolbar buttons have two advantages over menu items. First, the toolbar buttons are immediately visible and accessible. By contrast, menu items may be nested several levels deep and can be accessed only by several mouse clicks or keystrokes. Second, toolbar buttons are visual, whereas menu items are text, and in general visual items are more attractive and apparent than text items to the application user. Therefore, the most commonly used menu items often have a corresponding toolbar button.

11

● ButtonClick.
● It belongs to the toolbar.

prj11-1.zip

Project 11-1: Text Editor

This project is a text editor. The application user can type and use the main menu, context menu, or toolbar to cut, copy, and paste. Figure 11-18 shows the text editor in action.

Step-by-Step

1. Create a Windows application.

2. Add a MainMenu component to the form from the Toolbox.

3. Using the Menu Designer, add a menu where the top-level menu is Edit and its menu items are Cut, Copy, Paste, Delete, and Select All. The menu is further described in the following table.

Name	Caption	Shortcut
mnuEdit	&Edit	None
mnuEditCut	Cu&t	CTRL-X
mnuEditCopy	&Copy	CRTL-C
mnuEditPaste	&Paste	CRTL-V

4. Using the Properties window, set the Menu property of the form to the name of your MainMenu component.

5. Add a ContextMenu component to the form from the Toolbox.

6. Copy the Cut, Copy, and Paste menu items from the MainMenu to the ContextMenu. Name these menu items in the context menu cmnuCut, cmnuCopy, and cmnuPaste.

7. Using the Properties window, set the ContextMenu property of the form to the name of your ContextMenu component.

Figure 11-18 An editing window

8. Add a ToolBar component to the form from the Toolbox.

9. Using the Properties window of the ToolBar control, click the ellipsis button (...) next to the Buttons property and add three buttons to the ToolBar using the Add button of the ToolBarButton Collection Editor.

10. Add an ImageList component to the form from the Toolbox.

11. Using the Properties window of the ImageList control, click the ellipsis button (...) next to the Images property and add images for Cut, Copy, and Paste to the ImageList control using the Add button of the Image Collection Editor.

12. In the Properties window, set the ToolBar control's ImageList property to the ImageList control you just added.

13. Using the Properties window of the ToolBar control, click the ellipsis button (...) next to the Buttons property to open the ToolBarButton Collection Editor.

14. In the ToolBarButton Collection Editor, set the ImageIndex property of each toolbar button to one of the values in the list, which is drawn from the images you added to the ImageList component. This assigns an image to each of the three buttons of the ToolBar.

15. From the Toolbox, add to the form a TextBox control named txtEdit whose Text property is blank (so there is nothing initially in the text box) and whose MultiLine property is True. By default, the TextBox control permits you to type only on one line. Setting the MultiLine property to True enables the application user to type on multiple lines.

16. In the Code editor, create Click event procedures for the three menu items of the MainMenu component:

```
Private Sub mnuEditCut_Click(ByVal sender As Object, _
    ByVal e As System.EventArgs) _
    Handles mnuEditCut.Click, cmnuCut.Click
txtEdit.Cut()
End Sub

Private Sub mnuEditCopy_Click(ByVal sender As Object, _
    ByVal e As System.EventArgs) _
    Handles mnuEditCopy.Click, cmnuCopy.Click
txtEdit.Copy()
End Sub

Private Sub mnuEditPaste_Click(ByVal sender As Object, _
    ByVal e As System.EventArgs) _
    Handles mnuEditPaste.Click, cmnuPaste.Click
txtEdit.Paste()
End Sub
```

11

The Handles clause of each menu item's Click event procedure has been expanded to include handling the Click event of the corresponding context menu item. Within the event procedure, the corresponding method of the TextBox control is called. The Cut method of the TextBox control cuts the text selected in the TextBox, the Copy method copies it, and the Paste method pastes the text in the Clipboard into the text box.

17. In the Code editor, create Click event procedures for the three menu items of the MainMenu component:

```
Private Sub ToolBar1_ButtonClick(ByVal sender As System.Object, _
    ByVal e As System.Windows.Forms.ToolBarButtonClickEventArgs) _
    Handles ToolBar1.ButtonClick
Select Case ToolBar1.Buttons.IndexOf(e.Button)
    Case 0
        mnuEditCut_Click(sender, e)
    Case 1
        mnuEditCopy_Click(sender, e)
    Case 2
        mnuEditPaste_Click(sender, e)
End Select
End Sub
```

This event procedure simply calls the event procedure of the corresponding menu item based on the index of the button that was clicked.

Run the application. Type some text in the text editor, select some text, and then cut, copy, and paste using the main menu, the context menu, and the toolbar buttons.

This text editor is certainly not ready for the commercial market. The Cut, Copy, and Paste items need to be disabled at the appropriate times. Additionally, further commands are needed, such as Undo, Select All, and so on. Nevertheless, the Text Editor project is useful in demonstrating how to tie together corresponding items on a main menu, context menu, and toolbar, as well as showing some methods of the TextBox control.

Summary

Application users need to give commands to the application, such as to open, save, or close a file, print a document, cut, copy, or paste text, and so on. Application users give such commands through the GUI of the application. The three most common GUI elements through which application users give commands to an application are the menu, shortcut or context menus, and toolbars. In this module, you learned how to create them and handle their events.

☑ Mastery Check

1. The Add method, which you use to add a menu item to a menu programmatically, is a method of a _____.

    A. ContextMenu object

    B. MainMenu object

    C. MenuItem object

    D. MenuItems collection

2. Which of the following typically appears when you right-click a form or control?

    A. ContextMenu

    B. MainMenu

    C. ToolBar

    D. ToolBarButton

3. You can use the Menu Designer to copy a menu item from a MainMenu component to a menu item in which of the following components?

    A. ContextMenu

    B. MainMenu

    C. ToolBar

    D. ToolBarButton

4. Which of the following typically has a bitmap image on it?

    A. ContextMenu

    B. MainMenu

    C. ToolBar

    D. ToolBarButton

11

☑ Mastery Check

5. Hiding a menu disables it.

    A. True

    B. False

6. For which control will you use the ButtonClick event procedure when it is clicked?

    A. ContextMenu

    B. MainMenu

    C. ToolBar

    D. ToolBarButton

7. For which object will you use the event procedure of another object when it is clicked?

    A. ContextMenu

    B. MainMenu

    C. ToolBar

    D. ToolBarButton

8. Which of the following statements is *not* correct?

    A. The Click event procedure of a menu item in a context item may call the event procedure of a menu item in a MainMenu.

    B. The Click event procedure of a menu item in a MainMenu also may handle the Click event of a menu item in a context menu.

    C. The Click event procedure of a menu item in a MainMenu also may handle the ButtonClick event of a ToolBar.

    D. The Click event procedure of a menu item in a context item may call the event procedure of a menu item in a MainMenu.

☑ *Mastery Check*

9. Which of the following statements is *not* correct?

A. A Click event for a menu item may occur if the user selects the menu item using the keyboard and presses the enter key.

B. A Click event may be raised for a menu item that has submenu items.

C. A Click event for a menu item may occur if the user presses an access key or shortcut key that is associated with the menu item.

Part 5

Error Handling
and Prevention

Module 12

Structured Exception Handling and Debugging

The Goals of this Module

- Understand what an exception is and the meaning of throwing and handling an exception

- Know how to create and use a structured exception handler

- Understand break mode and how to place your application in it

- Know how to navigate your program during debugging using step and run commands

- Understand how to use the debugging tools

The number of errors that potentially may occur in your Visual Basic .NET applications may seem almost infinite, especially late at night when you are trying to make your program work properly. Nevertheless, the following three categories cover virtually all errors:

- Syntax errors
- Runtime errors
- Logic errors

Syntax errors are the failure of your code to meet the requirements of the Visual Basic .NET programming language. Examples of syntax errors include misspelling a variable name, not calling a procedure with the right number of parameters, and so on. While syntax errors are quite common, they also are the easiest to correct. The compiler will flag syntax errors and output an error message in the Output window informing you of the location (filename and line number) and description of the syntax error. In fact, if you have Option Explicit or, even better, Option Strict turned on, often syntax errors will be highlighted in the code window even before you compile.

Runtime errors are those that appear while your application is running, often bringing your application to an inglorious termination, referred to as a "crash," with a cryptic message about an unhandled "exception"—a synonym for a runtime error and the term used in this module. Since the exception occurs while your application is running, your code necessarily could compile, so no syntax error is involved. The exception may be the result of faulty code, application user error such as not putting a floppy disk back in the floppy drive, or circumstances beyond the control of the programmer or the application user, such as the operating system running out of memory. Exceptions are harder to spot than syntax errors, since the compiler does not flag exceptions as it does syntax errors, but generally the programmer has a clue as to where in the code the problem occurred based on where your application crashed.

Logic errors do not cause your program not to compile or run. Instead, they cause weird results, such as 2 + 2 equaling 22 instead of 4. Logic errors are generally the most difficult type to fix, since it is not always clear where they originate.

This module will show you how to use structured exception handling to deal with exceptions, and how to use the debugger to resolve exceptions and logic errors.

Structured Exception Handling

Since structured exception handling is used to resolve exceptions, a good starting point is to discuss what an exception is and what happens when an exception occurs. Structured exception handling then is compared with an alternative, appropriately named unstructured exception handling. Finally, the syntax of implementing structured exception handling is covered, followed by a project to illustrate structured exception handling in action.

Exceptions

An exception may be defined as a problem that occurs while the program is executing that must be dealt with before the program can proceed. Examples of exceptions include the inability to open a file because it cannot be found, the application user did not insert the floppy disk that contains the file, the file is corrupt, the operating system does not have enough available memory remaining to open the file, and so on. The exception may be due to faulty code, application user error, or circumstances beyond the control of either the programmer or the application user, such as a crash of the operating system. Regardless of the cause, the program cannot proceed until the exception is resolved.

If an exception occurs, the Common Language Runtime (CLR) built into the .NET Framework throws an exception. The CLR does not know or care if the exception is the fault of the programmer, the application user, or beyond either's control. The exception is thrown regardless of its cause.

If an exception is thrown, the CLR looks for an exception handler. The exception handler's sole purpose is to catch and handle exceptions. The code within an exception handler does not execute in the absence of a thrown exception.

The result of the exception being handled depends on the exception and how the programmer chooses to handle it. You can easily handle some exceptions and have your application then continue. For example, an exception caused by a file not being found may be resolved by displaying a File | Open dialog box and having the application user locate and select the file from that dialog box. Other exceptions may prevent the application from continuing. For example, if the operating system runs too low on memory, the best that can be hoped for

12

may be that the application gracefully exits, such as by permitting the user to save all unsaved work.

However, there is no guarantee that the CLR will find an exception handler when an exception is thrown. If it does not, then during runtime the application user usually is presented with a dialog box providing a few choices, the chief one typically being program termination. In general, unhandled exceptions terminate, or put more colorfully, crash programs.

Thus, exceptions generally do not crash programs. *Unhandled* exceptions crash programs.

Structured vs. Unstructured Exception Handling

Whether the CLR will find an exception handler when an exception is thrown depends primarily on whether you, the programmer, wrote one.

Visual Basic .NET supports two ways of handling exceptions, *structured* and *unstructured* exception handling. Both permit your application to detect and recover from exceptions during execution of your application.

Unstructured exception handling is a carryover from prior versions of Visual Basic. Structured exception handling is new to Visual Basic in Visual Basic .NET, and is consistent with how exceptions are handled in other languages such as C++.

I recommend structured exception handling not because it is the new way to handle errors in Visual Basic, but because it is the better way. Structured exception handling encapsulates the error handling code with the code that may cause the error. By contrast, unstructured exception handling often results in so-called spaghetti code in which the error handling code appears loosely, if at all, connected with the code that may cause the error. Structured exception handling therefore makes your code easier to debug and maintain, and may also lead to better application performance than unstructured exception handling. Therefore, this module will focus on structured exception handling, not unstructured exception handling.

The Try...Catch...Finally Statement

The Try...Catch...Finally statement is used specifically for structured exception handling. The syntax of a Try...Catch...Finally statement is as follows:

```
Try
    ' code in "Try block"
Catch [optional exception parameter]
    ' code in "Catch block"
[Additional Catch blocks]
Finally
    ' code
End Try
```

The Try keyword starts a structured exception handler. The code between the Try keyword and the Catch keyword is referred to as the Try block. You place in a Try block code that might generate an exception. For example, code used to open a file might generate an exception because the file cannot be found, the file found is corrupt, and so on.

One or more Catch blocks immediately follow the Try block. Each Catch block starts with the Catch keyword and may specify an exception parameter representing the type of exception that the Catch block intended is designed to handle.

If an exception occurs in a Try block, the CLR throws an exception, and program control immediately shifts to the first Catch block. The CLR searches for the first Catch handler following the Try block that can process the type of exception that has occurred by comparing the thrown exception's type to each Catch handler's exception parameter type. A match occurs if the two types are identical or if the thrown exception's type is a derived class of the exception parameter type.

If the thrown exception's type is matched to a Catch handler's exception parameter type, the code in that Catch handler executes, and any remaining Catch handlers are ignored.

Alternatively, a Catch handler may not specify an exception parameter, in which case that Catch handler will handle all thrown exceptions, regardless of type.

If the procedure in which the exception was thrown has no Catch handler, or none whose exception parameter matches the type of the thrown exception, the CLR looks for a matching Catch handler in the procedure that called the procedure in which the exception was thrown, and then in the procedure that called that procedure, and so on. For example, if procedure A called procedure B, which called procedure C, in which an exception was thrown, the CLR would look for a matching Catch handler in the call stack, first in procedure C, then in procedure B, and finally in procedure A.

12

If the CLR cannot find a matching Catch handler in the call stack, an unhandled exception occurs, the usual consequences of which are program termination.

The code in the Finally section always executes last, just before the error handling block loses scope, regardless of whether the code in the Catch blocks has executed. The code in the Finally section usually contains so-called "cleanup" code, such as that for closing files and releasing objects.

1-Minute Drill

● Will an exception crash a program?

● Does the CLR look for Catch handlers only in the procedure in which the exception occurred?

● Must a Catch handler be followed by an exception parameter?

● Will the code in the Finally section execute regardless of whether any Catch handler catches the thrown exception?

prj12-1.zip

Project 12-1: Illegal Division

This project performs division. However, it uses exception handling for two potential exceptions. First, the user may type a non-numeric value in one or both of the text boxes that represent the numerator and divisor, respectively. Second, the user may attempt to divide by zero. Figure 12-1 shows the project in action if the application user enters valid values.

However, if the application user does not type anything in a text box, no division will occur, and the message box shown in Figure 12-2 will display instead.

Figure 12-1   Division

● Exceptions do not crash programs; unhandled exceptions do.
● No. The CLR will look for a matching Catch handler all the way up the call stack.
● No. The exception parameter is optional.
● Yes. The code in the Finally section will execute regardless of whether any Catch handler catches the thrown exception.

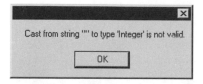

| **Figure 12-2** | An invalid cast message box |

Finally, if the application user types a number in the first text box and a zero in the second, attempting division by zero, again no division will occur, and instead the message box shown in Figure 12-3 will display.

Step-by-Step

1. Create a Windows application.

2. Add two TextBox components to the form from the Toolbox. Name these two text boxes txtNumerator and txtDenominator, respectively. The Text property of each is blank.

3. Add three Label components to the form from the Toolbox. Name the label between the two text boxes lblDiv and set its Text to "\". Name the label to the extreme right lblResult and set its BackColor property to HighlightText. Its Text property is blank. You need not rename the remaining label as it will not be involved in the code, but set its Text property to "=".

4. Write the following procedure:

```
Private Sub performDivision()
Dim numerator As Integer = CInt(txtNumerator.Text)
Dim denominator As Integer = CInt(txtDenominator.Text)
lblResult.Text = CStr(numerator \ denominator)
Catch zerodivide As DivideByZeroException
   MessageBox.Show (zerodivide.Message)
End Try
End Sub
```

| **Figure 12-3** | The divide by zero message box |

12

5. Place the following code in the Click event of lblDiv:

```
Private Sub lblDiv_Click(ByVal sender As Object, _
    ByVal e As System.EventArgs) Handles lblDiv.Click
Try
    performDivision()
Catch badcast As InvalidCastException
    MessageBox.Show (badcast.Message)
End Try
End Sub
```

Run the code. Type numbers in both text boxes and the application will perform division as in Figure 12-1. Type nothing in a text box and you will see the message box shown in Figure 12-2. Type a non-numeric value in a box and you will see the same message box as shown in Figure 12-2 except instead of "" you will see within the quotes the first non-numeric value you entered. Type a number in the first text box and a zero in the second and you will see the message box shown in Figure 12-3.

Exception Classes

Like seemingly everything else in Visual Basic .NET, exceptions are represented by a class with the highly original name of the Exception class. A number of more specialized classes derive from the Exception class. One of these is the InvalidCastException class. The InvalidCastException class represents the exception that is thrown for invalid attempts to explicitly convert an expression from one data type to another. For example, attempting to convert the string "Jeff" to an integer using the type conversion keyword CInt, such as CInt("Jeff"), would throw an exception of the type InvalidCastException.

Another specialized Exception class is the DivideByZeroException class. This class represents the exception that is thrown when there is an attempt to divide an integral or decimal value by zero.

The code in the subroutine performDivision first uses the CInt type conversion keyword to convert the string that the application user entered for the numerator and denominator into integers before performing the division.

```
Dim numerator As Integer = CInt(txtNumerator.Text)
Dim denominator As Integer = CInt(txtDenominator.Text)
```

If the application user did not enter a string representation of a number in the textbox, such as "Jeff", "3a", or nothing at all, the attempt to convert that non-numeric expression into an Integer using CInt will throw an InvalidCastException.

The CLR first will check for a Catch handler in the subroutine performDivision that handles exceptions of the type InvalidCastException. However, the only Catch handler in that subroutine handles exceptions of the type DivideByZeroException.

Since there is no Catch handler in the subroutine performDivision that handles exceptions of the type InvalidCastException, the CLR next will check for this Catch handler in the procedure that called performDivision, the Click event procedure of lblDiv. This event procedure does contain a Catch handler that handles exceptions of the type InvalidCastException, so that Catch handler in the calling procedure handles the error that originates in the called procedure.

The Catch handler for InvalidCastException displays the message box shown in Figure 12-2. The message box is displayed using the Show method, discussed in Module 10. The message displayed in the message box is not a literal string, however, but rather the Message property of the InvalidCastException instance that was thrown:

```
Catch badcast As InvalidCastException
    MessageBox.Show (badcast.Message)
```

The InvalidCastException class, like other classes, has properties. One of these properties is the Message property. This property displays an error message. The format of the error message for the InvalidCastException class is:

```
"Cast from string "[invalid value]" to type '[other data type]' is
not valid."
```

The [invalid value] is the string value that was input. The [other data type] is the data type to which the conversion was attempted. That data type here is an Integer, but also could be a Single or some other data type.

Each time an InvalidCastException is thrown, the Message property is assigned the string value that was input and the data type to which the conversion was attempted. Thus, if the string value input was "Jeff", the value of the Message property would be:

```
"Cast from string "Jeff" to type 'Integer' is not valid."
```

12

However, if no string value were input, the value of the Message property would be:

```
"Cast from string "" to type 'Integer' is not valid."
```

The DivideByZeroException will be thrown if the value of denominator in the following code from the performDivision subroutine is zero:

```
lblResult.Text = CStr(numerator \ denominator)
```

Note

The numerator and denominator are integers, and integer division (\) rather than floating point division (/) is the operation, because the CLR allows floating point division by zero.

Since there is a Catch handler in the subroutine performDivision that handles exceptions of the type DivideByZeroException, that Catch handler will execute, and the Message property of the DivideByZeroException instance thrown will be displayed in a message box:

```
Catch zerodivide As DivideByZeroException
    MessageBox.Show (zerodivide.Message)
```

If you type nothing or a non-numeric value in the first text box and a zero in the second text box, potentially both types of exceptions are involved. However, you will see the invalid cast message box, not the divide by zero message box, because given the code, the InvalidCastException will be thrown before the DivideByZeroException.

Debugging

Debugging is the art of identifying and ridding your application of programming errors, often referred to as bugs. While bugs may cause exceptions, not all bugs do. This is not necessarily good news. The cause of incorrect output often is far more difficult to spot than errors that cause exceptions. You generally know the point in your program where it came to a screeching halt. However, the cause of incorrect output at the end of your

?Ask the Expert

Question: What is the difference between structured exception handling and data validation?

Answer: Data validation, as its constituent words indicate, concerns whether data is valid, particularly data being input by the application user. For example, if test scores were being entered into an application, data validation would be used to ensure that each score entered was between 0 and 100. Input below 0 or above 100 would not create an exception. Rather, input below 0 or above 100 simply would be incorrect data. Thus, data validation is used to prevent invalid data, not exceptions.

Question: Can I use data validation to prevent exceptions?

Answer: Data validation techniques sometimes may be used to prevent exceptions. For example, in the Division project, instead of using structured exception handling for the InvalidCastException, you could check if the input was numeric before using the CInt keyword, and if it was not, warn the user and exit the subroutine:

```
If IsNumeric(txtNumerator.Text) Then
    CInt(txtNumerator.Text)
Else
    MessageBox.Show("Numerator must be numeric")
    Exit Sub
End If
```

Question: If data validation techniques may be used to prevent exceptions, what is the advantage in using structured exception handling instead?

Answer: The exceptions in the Division project were relatively simple, so data validation techniques as well as structured exception handling could be used to prevent exceptions. However, many exceptions cannot be caught easily or at all with data validation techniques. For example, if the application is attempting to open a file that is missing or corrupt, data validation techniques will not apply.

12

program could be far earlier in the program. Therefore, debugging logic errors is an important skill. While logic errors may be the most difficult to debug, debugging is also useful for exceptions.

Visual Basic .NET provides you with a number of debugging tools. These debugging tools, while quite sophisticated and useful, nevertheless are tools. Debugging fundamentally is detective work. The debugging tools make your detective work easier and faster. Therefore, this module will explain not only the Visual Basic debugging tools, but also strategies for using them.

Break Mode

Normally, you would be very happy that your computer is able to execute your Visual Basic .NET program seemingly at the speed of light. However, when you are trying to trace through your code to find a logic error, you need to slow down or even stop your program so you can take a careful look at its state at that point.

Visual Basic .NET enables you to suspend the execution of your program by placing your program in break mode. Entering break mode does not end the execution of your program; execution can be resumed when you choose.

The debugger automatically breaks execution of the program when an exception occurs. However, this does not help you if you are trying to debug a logic error rather than a runtime error.

Visual Basic .NET also enables you to place your program in break mode several ways, all of which are covered in this section:

- At the start of the program, using the Debug | Step Into or Debug | Start Over menu command.

- At a predetermined place in the program, using a breakpoint or run to cursor.

- While the program is running, using the menu command Debug | Break All.

Once you have placed your application in the programming equivalent of suspended animation, Visual Basic .NET provides you with a number of debugging tools that enable you to inspect and even change the values of variables, change the next statement to be executed, and perform other useful debugging tasks. These debugging tools generally are only available when your program is in break mode.

Starting Debugging

You can debug your program by stepping through your program one line at a time or by running your code to a specified point and then stopping. Which alternative you choose depends often on how far along you are in debugging your application. If you have just started debugging your application, you may want to start debugging from the beginning of your program. If you have done significant debugging of your program and have some idea of where the problem is or isn't, to save time you may want to bypass areas of the program you believe are problem-free and go straight to the area of the problem that is your concern.

If you want to start debugging from the beginning of your program, you may choose Step Into or Step Over from the Debug menu. Your application will start and then break on the first line. This first line often is in the New subroutine created by Visual Basic .NET in the Windows Form Designer generated code region.

Note

There are differences between Step Into or Step Over, but not in this context. The differences will be covered later in this section on "Stepping" Under "Controlling the Flow During Debugging."

Tip

In addition to the Debug menu, you also can access the Step and other debug commands through the Debug toolbar, which you can display with the menu command View | Toolbars | Debug. The Debug toolbar has ToolTips that explain the function of each button.

If instead you want to start debugging at a later point that you specify, you have two principal alternatives, setting a breakpoint or running to a cursor.

Setting a Breakpoint

You may set a breakpoint at a particular place of your choosing in your code. The breakpoint causes the debugger to place your program in break mode when the line of code marked by the breakpoint is reached in the execution of your program.

Breakpoints enable you to suspend execution where and when you need to, rather than having to wade line by line through your code until you get to the desired point. Breakpoints therefore greatly speed up the debugging process. This is especially important in large programs with thousands or tens of thousands of lines of code.

12

You set a breakpoint by clicking in the gray margin to the left of the line where you want execution to stop. When you have set a breakpoint, a red dot appears in the margin, and a red line highlights the line of code you have designated (see Figure 12-4).

Once you have set a breakpoint, you may run your project using the menu command Debug | Start. You may not reach the breakpoint right away. For example, in Figure 12-4, the breakpoint was set inside the Click event procedure of lblDiv in the Division project. Starting the project won't reach the code inside that Click event procedure. Instead, the code inside that Click event only will be reached when you click the label.

Once the breakpoint code is reached, a yellow arrow appears inside of the red dot (see Figure 12-5). The color of the line highlighting the line of code also changes to yellow.

You use the Breakpoints window, shown in Figure 12-6, to view and control all of your breakpoints at one glance. You display the Breakpoints window by the menu command Debug | Windows | Breakpoints. From the Breakpoints window, you can create new breakpoints, clear all breakpoints, or selectively remove, disable, or enable previously disabled breakpoints.

While a breakpoint normally stops execution every time it is reached, you can modify its properties so it behaves more flexibly. In particular, you can modify the breakpoint so it breaks only if a certain condition is true, or only after it has been reached a specified number of times.

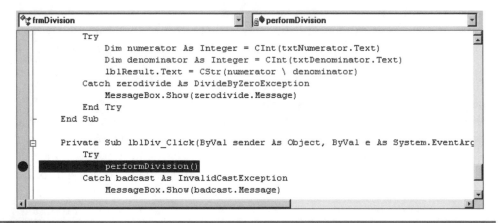

Figure 12-4 A breakpoint

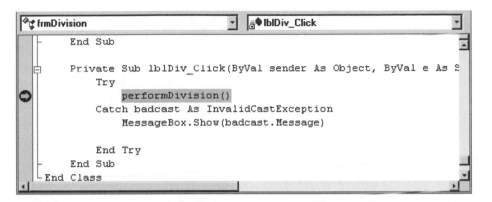

Figure 12-5   A breakpoint reached

You may access a breakpoint's properties by right-clicking it, either from its entry in the Breakpoints window or from the line in the source window on which the breakpoint was set, and choosing Properties from the context menu. This displays the Breakpoint Properties window shown in Figure 12-7.

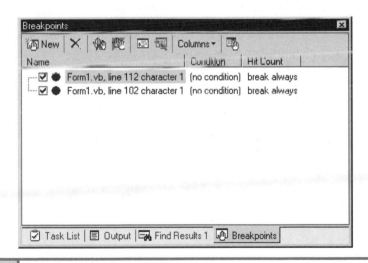

Figure 12-6   The Breakpoints window

12

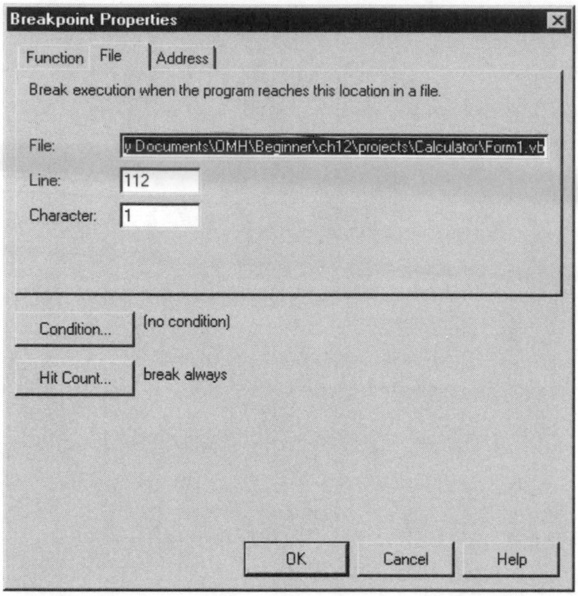

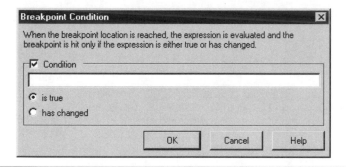

Figure 12-7 | The Breakpoint Properties window

The Breakpoints window has two command buttons, Condition and Hit Count. Choosing the Condition button displays the Breakpoint Condition dialog box shown in Figure 12-8.

As the dialog box states, the result of setting a condition is that when the breakpoint is reached, your application will go into break mode only if the

Figure 12-8 | The Breakpoint Condition dialog box

condition is True. The two types of conditions you can set are if an expression is true or if the value of an expression has changed.

For an example of setting a breakpoint to break when an expression is true, assume your program tracks students' grade point averages. No matter how badly a student is doing, the student's grade point average should never be less than 0.0. If a variable (hypothetically named sngGPA) representing the grade point average is less than 0.0, your program has a logic error. Therefore, you might want to set the breakpoint properties to break if sngGPA < 0.0.

Setting a breakpoint to break when an expression has changed also may be useful, especially in a loop to track if and when the value of a variable changes.

Choosing the Hit Count button displays the Breakpoint Hit Count dialog box shown in Figure 12-9.

The dialog box explains the meaning of hit count. A breakpoint is hit when the breakpoint location is reached and any condition is satisfied. The hit count is the number of times the breakpoint has been hit.

The Breakpoint Hit Count dialog box has a drop-down box providing choices concerning what happens when the breakpoint is hit. Figure 12-10 shows the choices in the drop-down box.

The choices are:

- Break always (the default)

- Break when the hit count is equal to

- Break when the hit count is a multiple of

- Break when the hit count is greater than or equal to

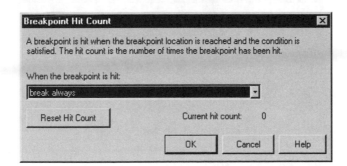

Figure 12-9   The Breakpoint Hit Count dialog box

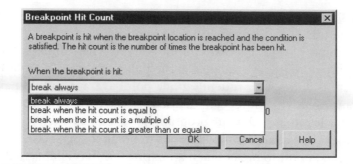

Figure 12-10 The Breakpoint Hit Count drop-down box

If your choice is other than break always, the dialog box provides an edit box for you to insert a number, as shown in Figure 12-11.

Hit counts are very useful in loops. You may find that a bug does not appear until the second or later iteration of a loop. Using the hit count permits you to bypass the breakpoint in the first iteration of the loop, speeding up your debugging.

Running to the Cursor

You also can right-click a line of code in the source window and choose Run To Cursor from the context menu shown in Figure 12-12. Your application starts up and runs until it reaches the cursor location (or an earlier breakpoint if there is one).

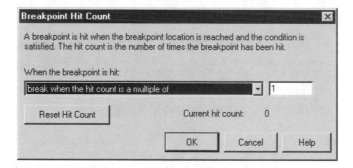

Figure 12-11 The Breakpoint Hit Count edit box

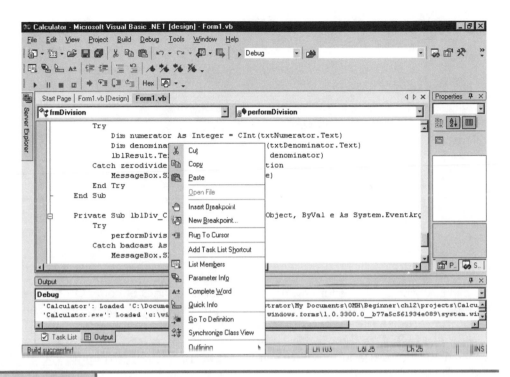

Figure 12-12 | The context menu for debugging

That execution automatically starts when you choose Run To Cursor differs from setting a breakpoint, where execution does not start until you affirmatively start execution, such as by the menu command Debug | Continue.

As with the breakpoint, you may not immediately reach the line of code where the cursor is set. When you do, as shown in Figure 12-13, a yellow arrow appears in the margin next to the line of code, and the line of code itself is highlighted in yellow.

The visual cue is the same as in Figure 12-5 except, with a breakpoint, the arrow in the margin appears inside of the dot, whereas with Run To Cursor, the arrow appears by itself.

12

Figure 12-13 Run to cursor reached

Tip

You can easily find a procedure even with thousands of lines of code. On the standard toolbar, type the procedure name in the Find box and press ENTER. This moves the cursor to the specified procedure or a call to that procedure. If the cursor is first moved to the specified procedure, and you want to move the cursor to the call to that procedure (or vice versa), just keep pressing ENTER until you are where you want to be. Once you are where you want to be, you can set a breakpoint or choose Run To Cursor from the context menu.

1-Minute Drill

● Must execution always stop when a breakpoint is encountered?

● Does setting a breakpoint put your application in break mode?

Controlling the Flow During Debugging

Once you have examined the line of code on which execution stopped, you need to decide where to go next. Your choices are essentially the same as when you started debugging. You can step through your program one line at a time

---

● Not necessarily. You can set a breakpoint's properties so execution only stops if an expression is true or has changed, or has been hit a certain number of times.

● No. Setting a breakpoint does not put your application in break mode. Only when the breakpoint is encountered does your application go into break mode.

Ask the Expert

Question: Setting a breakpoint or choosing Run To Cursor seem to do essentially the same thing. Why choose one over the other?

Answer: The breakpoint remains until you disable or remove it. By contrast, Run To Cursor in essence runs to a breakpoint that then is removed, so to repeat the action, you would have to choose Run To Cursor again. Thus, if you want the breakpoint to remain, set a breakpoint. However, if you only want a breakpoint for that particular debugging operation, choose Run To Cursor, which saves you the trouble of disabling or removing the breakpoint.

Question: Can I use code statements that stop execution similarly to setting a breakpoint?

Answer: Yes. You can use the Stop statement, including an If...Then control structure so a condition needs to be met for the program to Stop.

Question: Which is better to use, a breakpoint or a Stop statement?

Answer: I recommend using a breakpoint. A breakpoint can accomplish whatever a Stop statement can, and a breakpoint does not affect your program's source code, whereas the Stop statement does.

or run your code to a specified point and then stop. As when you started debugging, which alternative you choose often depends on how far along you are in debugging your application. If you have just started debugging your application, you may want to examine the next line of code. However, if you already have done significant debugging of your program, you may want to save time and bypass areas of the program that you believe are problem-free and go straight to the area of the problem that is your concern. Visual Basic .NET provides you with several ways of both stepping through your code and running to a particular location.

Breakpoints and Run to Cursor

You are not limited in your use of breakpoints and run to cursor when you start debugging.

You can have multiple breakpoints. If you are at one breakpoint and want to move to another, choose the menu command Debug | Continue. Execution will continue until the code reaches the next breakpoint. Similarly, you can run to a cursor, set the cursor further in your code, and run to that cursor.

You also can combine breakpoints and run to cursor. For example, you can go to a breakpoint, choose Run To Cursor, and execution will continue until the cursor point is reached. Conversely, you can first run to a cursor, and then go to a breakpoint using the menu command Debug | Continue.

In general, so long as you are in break mode, you can use breakpoints and run to cursor at any point in the debugging process.

Run to Function on a Call Stack

During the debugging process, you have an additional way of using Run To Cursor, by running to a function on the call stack. As discussed earlier in this module, if procedure A called procedure B which called procedure C, the call stack would consist, from top to bottom, of procedure C, procedure B, and finally procedure A.

In the Division project, the subroutine performDivision is called within the Click event procedure of lblDiv. Thus, once you are within performDivision, the call stack consists first of performDivision and then the Click event procedure of lblDiv. You can see the call stack from the Call Stack window, which is displayed by the menu command Debug | Windows | Call Stack. Figure 12-14 shows the Call Stack window when execution stopped in the subroutine performDivision.

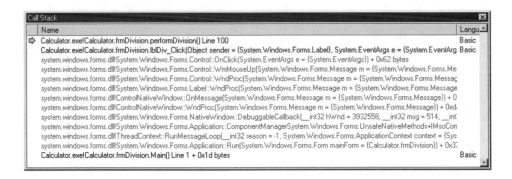

| **Figure 12-14** | The Call Stack window |

As Figure 12-14 shows, performDivision is on the first line of the Call Stack window and the Click event procedure of lblDiv is on the second line of that window. You can right-click the Click event procedure of lblDiv on the second line of the Call Stack window and choose Run To Cursor from the context menu.

Stepping

Stepping means executing code one line at a time. The Debug menu provides three commands for stepping through code:

- Step Into
- Step Over
- Step Out

Step Into and Step Over both instruct the debugger to execute the next line of code. They differ only when that next line of code is the call of a procedure. Step Into steps into the called procedure; execution next halts at the first line of the called procedure. By contrast, Step Over steps over the entire called procedure, executing the called procedure but not stopping within it, and then halts at the next line of the calling procedure.

For example, assume that in the Division project execution had halted in the Click event procedure of lblDiv at the call of the subroutine performDivision:

```
performDivision()
```

With Step Into, execution next would halt at the first line of code within performDivision. By contrast, with Step Over, performDivision would be executed, and execution next would halt at the next line of code in the Click event procedure of lblDiv. Notwithstanding the term *step over*, Step Over does not skip execution of the called procedure, it just does not break your application within the called procedure.

Whether you use Step Into or Step Over usually depends on how far along you are in debugging your project. If you have just started, you probably will use Step Into, as you may not know at that early point whether the problem is in the calling procedure or the called procedure. Additionally, Step Into gives you an excellent view of the actual flow of your code. However, if you have determined that the problem is not in the called procedure, then executing its code one line at a time would be a waste of time, and you would use Step Over instead.

12

You use Step Out when you are inside the called procedure and want to return to the calling procedure. Step Out resumes execution of your code until the called procedure ends, and then halts execution in the calling procedure.

Changing the Execution Point

You can move the execution point to set the next statement of code to be executed. A yellow arrow in the margin of the source window marks the current location of the execution point. By moving the execution point, you can skip over a portion of code or return to a line previously executed. This may be useful, such as if you want to skip a section of code that contains a known bug and continue debugging other sections.

You should exercise caution in changing the execution point. This causes the program counter to jump directly to the new location. If you move the execution point forward in your code, the code between the old and new execution points is not executed.

Note

You cannot change the execution point if your application is in break mode because an exception has occurred.

Stopping and Restarting Debugging

You stop debugging by the menu command Debug | Stop Debugging. Debugging also will stop automatically if you exit the application you are debugging.

Alternatively, you can restart debugging by the menu command Debug | Restart. This will stop the current debugging session, but then start a new debugging session.

1-Minute Drill

- Does Step Over skip a called procedure?
- What command do you use if you are stepping through a called procedure and want to return immediately to the calling procedure?

- No. Step Over executes the called procedure. It just does not break the application within the called procedure.
- Step Out.

Debugging Tools

The ability to step through or run to parts of your program, while useful, is only part of the debugging solution. Once you are at a specified location in your program, you need to be able to inspect the state of your program at that point. Visual Basic .NET provides you with debugging tools that you can use to view, and, in some instances, change the value of variables and expressions. These debugging tools include:

- DataTips pop-up
- Autos window
- Locals window
- The window
- Watch window
- QuickWatch dialog box
- Call Stack window

DataTips

If the debugger is in break mode, you can view the value of a variable within the current scope by placing the mouse pointer over the variable in the source window. A DataTips pop-up then appears. Figure 12-15 shows the pop-up *numerator = 5* when holding the mouse over the variable numerator in the Division project (the value is 5 because 5 was entered in the first text box).

DataTips are easy to use but somewhat limited. Unlike many other debugging tools that can be displayed both when the debugger is running and when it is in break mode, DataTips cannot be displayed unless the debugger is in break mode. Additionally, unlike some other debugging tools, DataTips cannot be used for expressions that involve function evaluation.

The Autos Window

The Autos window displays variables used in the current statement, which is the statement that will be executed next if execution continues. The Autos window also will display variables used in three statements on either side of the current

12

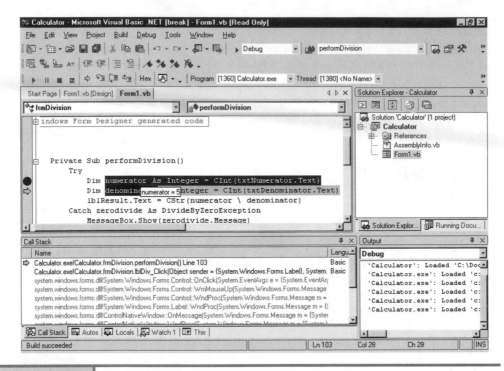

Figure 12-15 DataTips pop-up

statement. The Autos window gets its name from the debugger's ability to automatically identify these variables. Figure 12-16 shows the Autos window.

You may display the Autos window with the menu command Debug | Windows | Auto if the debugger is running or your program is in break mode. If the debugger is in break mode, you also can modify the value of a variable in the Autos window by double-clicking the value, typing a new value, and pressing ENTER.

Tip

As an alternative to double-clicking the value, you can single-click to select the line, and then press the TAB key.

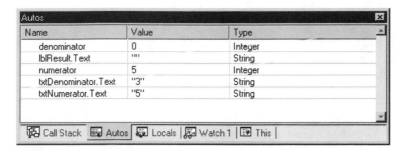

Figure 12-16   The Autos window

The Locals Window

The Locals window displays variables local to the current "context." The default context is the function containing the current execution location. You can choose an alternative context to display in the Locals window by using the Debug Location toolbar to select the other function, or by double-clicking an item in the Call Stack window. Figure 12-17 shows the Locals window.

You may display the Locals window with the menu command Debug | Windows | Locals if the debugger is running or your program is in break mode. However, the debugger must be in break mode to view or modify information in the Locals window.

Caution

Some information may appear in the Locals window while your program executes, but it will not be current until the next time your program goes into break mode, whether by hitting a breakpoint or by your choosing Break All from the Debug menu.

While the debugger is in break mode, you may modify the value of a variable in the Locals window by double-clicking the value (or single-clicking and using the TAB key), typing a new value, and pressing ENTER.

12

The This Window

The strangely named This window enables you to examine the data members of the object associated with the current method. "This" comes from other languages, such as C++, in which *this* is the name of a pointer to the current instance of a class, similar to the Me keyword in Visual Basic. Figure 12-18 shows the This window.

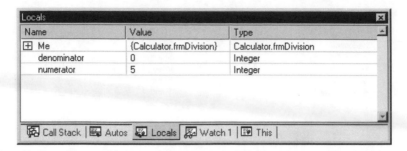

| **Figure 12-17** | Locals window |

You may display the This window with the menu command Debug | Windows | This if the debugger is running or your program is in break mode. If the debugger is in break mode, you also can modify the value of a variable in the This window by double-clicking the value (or single-clicking and using the TAB key), typing a new value, and pressing ENTER.

The Watch Window

You can use the Watch window to evaluate variables and expressions and view the results, and also to edit the value of a variable. Figure 12-19 shows a Watch window.

If the debugger is running or your program is in break mode, you may display the Watch window with the menu command Debug | Windows | Watch, and then click Watch1, Watch2, Watch3, or Watch4. However, the debugger must be in break mode to view or modify information in the Watch window.

| **Figure 12-18** | The This window |

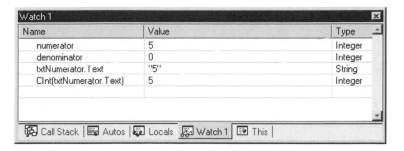

Figure 12-19   The Watch window

You use the Name column of the Watch window to evaluate a variable or expression by either:

- Double-clicking an empty row, typing or pasting the variable or expression in the Name column of the selected row, and pressing ENTER

- Dragging variable names and expressions from the code, the Locals window, or the Autos window to the Name column of an empty row

The result appears in the Value column. Figure 12-19 shows several variables and expressions already in the Watch window. If you type the name of an array or object variable, a tree control appears next to the name in the Name column. You then would click the plus (+) or minus (–) in the Name column to expand or collapse the variable.

Note

An expression remains in the Watch window until you remove it.

You use the Value column of the Watch window to edit a value. Double-click the Value column in the row corresponding to the variable or expression whose value you want to change. If you typed the name of an array or object variable in the Expression box, a tree control appears next to the name in the Current value box. Click the plus (+) or minus (–) in the Name column to expand or collapse the variable to find the element whose value you want to edit. Use the mouse and keyboard to edit the value, and press ENTER.

12

The QuickWatch Dialog Box

You use the QuickWatch dialog box to, as its name implies, quickly evaluate a variable or expression. Figure 12-20 shows a QuickWatch dialog box.

The QuickWatch dialog box is an alternative to the Watch window. The QuickWatch dialog box provides a quicker, simpler way of evaluating or editing a single variable or expression than does the Watch window. However, QuickWatch is a modal dialog box, so unlike the Watch window, you cannot leave the QuickWatch dialog box open to watch a variable or expression while you step through your program.

You can only open the QuickWatch dialog box if the debugger is in break mode. In a source window, right-click a variable or expression and choose QuickWatch from the context menu. This automatically places the variable into the QuickWatch dialog box. Click Recalculate. The value appears in the Current value box. If the variable is the name of an array or object variable, a tree control appears next to the name in the Current value box. Click the plus (+) or minus (–) in the Name column to expand or collapse the variable.

Note

You also can open the QuickWatch dialog box by the menu command Debug | QuickWatch.

| Figure 12-20 | The QuickWatch dialog box |

Tip

Previously chosen variables and expressions need not be retyped. They can be chosen from the Expression drop-down list box.

You use the Value column of the QuickWatch dialog box to edit a value. Double-click the Value column of the Current value box to select the value, use the mouse and keyboard to edit the value, and press ENTER.

The Call Stack Window

The Call Stack window was discussed and shown (in Figure 12-14) in the preceding section. As Figure 12-14 showed, the Call Stack window displays the name of each procedure and the programming language it is written in (the .NET Framework permits projects using more than one language).

The procedure name may be accompanied by optional information, such as module name, line number, byte offset, and parameter names, types, and values. The display of this optional information can be turned on or off. To change the optional information displayed, right-click the Call Stack window and set or clear by clicking items in the context menu such as Show Module Names, Show Parameter Types, Show Parameter Names, Show Parameter Values, and so on.

1-Minute Drill

- Which debugging tools may be displayed only when the debugger is in break mode, and not just when the debugger is running?
- What are the advantages and disadvantages of the Watch window and the QuickWatch dialog box?

Summary

There are three general categories of errors: syntax, runtime, and logic.

12

- The DataTips pop-up box and the QuickWatch dialog box.
- The QuickWatch dialog box provides a simpler and faster way of evaluating or editing a single variable or expression than does the Watch window. However, QuickWatch is a modal dialog box, so unlike the Watch window, you cannot leave the QuickWatch dialog box open to watch a variable or expression while you step through your program.

Syntax errors are the failure of your code to meet the requirements of the Visual Basic .NET programming language, such as not calling a procedure with the right number of parameters. While syntax errors are quite common, they also are the easiest to correct since the compiler will flag them.

Runtime errors are also called exceptions. Exceptions are problems that occur while your program is running that need to be resolved for your program to continue. The exception may be the result of faulty code, an error by the application user such as not putting a floppy disk in the floppy drive, or by circumstances beyond the programmer's control, such as the operating system running out of memory. Regardless of the cause, your program cannot continue unless the error is handled. Handling the exception may solve the error, or if solving the error is not possible, permit your application to end gracefully, such as by first saving any unsaved work.

You handle exceptions using structured exception handling, which involves the Try...Catch...Finally Statement. The Try block code contains code that might generate an exception, such as code used to open a file. The Catch block contains code that attempts to handle the exception. The code in the Finally section always executes, whether or not there was an error or if the error was successfully handled, and usually contains so-called "cleanup" code, such as that for closing files and releasing objects.

Logic errors do not cause your program not to compile or not to run. Instead, they may cause weird results, such as 2 + 2 equaling 22 instead of 4. You use the Visual Basic .NET debugger to fix logic errors, as well as to fix any programming errors that may be causing exceptions. This module explained break mode and how to place your application in it, showed you how to navigate your program during debugging using step and run commands, and described various debugging tools that permit you to inspect, and in some cases change, the values of variables and expressions while your program is being debugged.

☑Mastery Check

1. Which of the following types of errors is not handled by debugging?

   A. Logic

   B. Runtime

   C. Syntax

2. The CLR looks for Catch handlers only in the procedure in which the exception occurred.

   A. True

   B. False

3. The code in which section will execute only if an exception has occurred?

   A. Try

   B. Catch

   C. Finally

4. Exceptions are represented by or derived from a class with the name
   _____.

5. Which of the following statements is *not* true?

   A. You can set a breakpoint's properties so execution only stops if an expression is true.

   B. You can set a breakpoint's properties so execution only stops if an exception is thrown.

   C. You can set a breakpoint's properties so execution only stops if an expression has changed.

   D. You can set a breakpoint's properties so execution only stops if an expression has been hit a certain number of times.

12

☑ Mastery Check

6. Which of the following will *not* put your application in break mode?

    A. Encountering a breakpoint

    B. Run to cursor

    C. Setting a breakpoint

7. What command do you use if you are stepping through a called procedure and want to return immediately to the calling procedure?

    A. Step Into

    B. Step Out

    C. Step Over

8. Step Over skips a called procedure.

    A. True

    B. False

9. Which of the following debugging tools may be displayed only when the debugger is in break mode, and not just when the debugger is running?

    A. Autos

    B. Me

    C. QuickWatch

    D. Watch

10. Which of the following statements is *not* true?

    A. You can use the Call Stack window to run to a particular function on the call stack.

    B. The QuickWatch dialog box may be left open to watch a variable or expression while you step through your program.

    C. The Watch window may be left open to watch a variable or expression while you step through your program.

Appendix

Answers to
Mastery Checks

Module 1: What Is Visual Basic .NET?

1. What is the basic purpose of a programming language?

The basic purpose of a programming language is to give instructions to a computer, which then executes those instructions.

2. This type of application is event-driven:

B. A Windows application

3. GUI stands for _____.

Graphical user interface

4. A form's height is:

A. A property

5. The clicking of a form is:

C. An event

6. ShowDialog, used by a FileDialog object to display itself, is:

B. A method

7. You link the running of code with a user action by associating the code with:

C. An event

8. What is a class?

A class is a template that defines and describes an object and its properties, methods, and events.

9. Creating an object from a class is referred to as _____ the object.

Instantiating

10. .NET made Visual Basic more object-oriented as a programming language?

True

Module 2: Create A Visual Basic .NET Program Without Writing Code

1. Visual Studio.NET will not run under which of the following operating systems?

C. Windows 95

2. You can use *all* of the features of Visual Studio.NET only with the following operating system:

A. Windows 2000

3. The Visual Studio.NET installation program includes the .NET Framework.

True

4. Visual Studio.NET does not support console applications as an interface.

False

5. Which do you *need* to create a Visual Basic .NET application?

B. .NET Framework

6. In the statement System.Windows.Forms.Form, Form is a:

C. Class

7. The method in which values are assigned to a newly created object is:

B. InitializeComponent

8. In the statement Me.Text = "Godzilla" the equal sign (=) is called the _____ operator.

Assignment

9. In the statement Form1.Text = "Form1", "Form1" is the object Form1.

False. The double quotes indicate it is the literal string "Form1".

10. The value of a property given by Visual Studio.NET if you do not provide a value is the _____ value.

Default

Module 3: Event Procedures, Properties, and Controls

1. An event procedure connects an event to the code you want to run when the event occurs.

True

2. If you did not write an event procedure, nothing happens when an event occurs.

False. If you did not write an event procedure, the event is handled by default, which may or may not result in an action visible to you.

3. What are inside the parentheses of an event procedure?

C. Parameters

4. You can change the name of the event in an event procedure stub.

False

5. When you misspell code, such as Debug.Right instead of Debug.Write, it is a:

A. Syntax error

6. The Debug class is helpful to solve:

B. Logical errors

7. All properties:

C. Have a default value

8. You can use the Properties window to change the value of any property.

False. Some properties are read-only.

9. When you write to a property at runtime, you use the Properties window.

False. You use the Properties window at design time and code at runtime.

10. Properties whose values may change while the application is running are said to be:

B. Dynamic

11. The Toolbox is used to:

    C.   Add controls to your form

Module 4: Variables and Data Types

1. Which data type is the root type in Visual Basic .NET?

    C.   Object

2. Which type of number may be negative?

    A.   Signed

3. Which data type may hold the value 3.5?

    B.   Single

4. You have to declare variables before you use them when Option Explicit is off.

    True

5. You have to declare the data type of a variable when:

    C.   Option Strict is on

6. You have to initialize the value of a constant when you declare it.

    True

7. You can change the value of a constant:

    B.   In code view at design time

Module 5: Assignment and Arithmetic Operators

1. Which is a true statement of what can be on the left side of an assignment statement?

    C.   Any variable but only writable properties

2. Can an assignment statement be located at module level?

    C.   Only if combined with the declaration of a variable

3. Option Strict prohibits:

   D. Implicit narrowing conversions

4. Type conversion keywords permit the following when Option Strict is on:

   C. Explicit narrowing conversions

5. A type conversion that converts a value from a numeric data type to a string is:

   B. A narrowing conversion

6. Which of the following is a type conversion keyword?

   C. CInt

7. Which of the following operators is not overloaded?

   C. *

8. Concatenation means:

   B. Adding strings

9. Which arithmetic operator returns the remainder of division?

   C. Mod

10. What is the result of 3 + 4 * 5?

   B. 60

11. An algorithm is

   C. A logical procedure for solving a problem

Module 6: Comparison and Logical Operators

1. What data type do the comparison operators return?

   A. Boolean

2. Which data type does the Like comparison operator compare?

   D. String

3. Which comparison operator compares references to objects?

   C. Is

4. Which statement affects whether a string comparison is case sensitive?

   B. Option Compare

5. Which of the following is not used in pattern matching in string comparisons?

   B. ^

6. Comparison operations rank, in precedence:

   B. Lower than arithmetic operators but higher than logical operators

7. Which of the following logical operators works with only one operand rather than two?

   C. Not

8. Which of the following logical operators returns False if both operands are True?

   D. Xor

9. Which of the following logical operators has the highest priority?

   C. Not

10. Which of the following logical operators will not evaluate the second expression if the first one is True?

   D. OrElse

Module 7: Control Structures

1. The IIf function most closely resembles which of the If statements?

   B. If...Then...Else

2. Which of the If statements may concern the most alternatives?

   D. If...ElseIf

3. Which statement may be done with a single line of code?

   A. If...Then

4. Which can you have more than one of in an If statement?

    D. ElseIf

5. You would use the CheckBox instead of the RadioButton control for an If…ElseIf…Else statement.

    False

6. What control enables you to have more than one group of radio buttons on a form?

    B. GroupBox

7. What is the fundamental difference between a Select Case statement and an If…ElseIf…Else statement?

    If and ElseIf clauses each may evaluate completely different expressions. A Select Case statement may evaluate only one expression, which then must be used for every comparison.

8. In an expression list for a Select Case statement, which of the following is how you would express a number between 1 and 10 or 13?

    D. 1 To 10, 13

Module 8: Loops and Arrays

1. The condition in a loop is of which data type?

    A. Boolean

2. Which loop may test the condition at the bottom instead of at the top?

    A. Do

3. Which loop statement is designed to execute a fixed number of times?

    B. For…Next

4. Statements inside a For Each…Next loop must be executed at least once.

    True

5. You can use the _____ statement to change by code the upper bound of an existing array.

ReDim. Assignment statement also would be a correct answer.

6. You can change the lower bound of an array.

False

7. Which statement do you use to retain the values of the original array when you resize it?

B.   Preserve

8. Which of the following statements is true about a difference between a For Each...Next statement and a For...Next statement?

D.   You need to specify in a *For...Next* statement the number of elements in the array.

Module 9: Procedures

1. Which can only be called from a specific object, and cannot be called independently from an object?

B.   Method

2. Arguments have to be passed in the same order in which they are declared.

False (not if they are passed by name instead of by position).

3. The data type of an argument passed has to be identical to the data type of the argument declared.

D.   No, if the data type passed can be converted to the data type declared through a widening conversion.

4. What is the difference, if any, when returning the value of a function, between using the Return statement and assigning the return value to the function name?

B.   The Return statement immediately ends execution of the function, whereas assigning the return value to the function name does not.

5. Which way of calling a function will *not* enable you to use the function's return value?

    A. Using the Call keyword.

6. What is the effect, if any, that passing a scalar variable ByVal or ByRef as a procedure argument has on the called procedure's ability to modify the value of the variable passed as an argument in the calling code?

    A. The called procedure may modify the value of a scalar variable if it is passed ByRef, but not if it is passed ByVal.

7. What is the effect, if any, that passing an array variable ByVal or ByRef as a procedure argument has on the called procedure's ability to modify the value of the individual elements of the array passed as an argument in the calling code?

    C. There is no effect.

8. What is the effect, if any, that passing an array variable ByVal or ByRef as a procedure argument has on the called procedure's ability to change the array object pointed to by the array passed as an argument in the calling code?

    A. The called procedure may change the array object pointed to by the array if the array is passed ByRef, but not if it is passed ByVal.

9. Which of the following statements is true?

    C. Optional arguments may be declared only after mandatory arguments.

10. You have to specify a value for an optional argument.

    True

11. Which of the following statements is true?

    B. A procedure can have no more than one parameter array argument.

12. Overloaded procedures must differ from each other in respect to _____.

    B. Their argument list

Module 10: Helper Forms

1. Which of the following helper forms do you not have to create in the Windows Forms Designer?

    A. Message box

2. Which of the following helper forms is modeless?

    C. Owned form

3. In which of the following helper forms do you use the return value of the method used to show it to determine which button the user clicked?

    A. Message box

4. What is the difference between showing a form using its ShowDialog method or its Show method?

The ShowDialog method will show the form as modal, as with a dialog box. The Show method will show the form modeless, as with an owned form.

5. Which of the following helper forms does not automatically close when one of its buttons is clicked?

    C. Owned form

6. Which of the following helper forms cannot contain a TextBox control?

    A. Message box

7. The keyword Private means you cannot access the object, variable, or procedure in question.

False. The object, variable, or procedure in question still can be accessed from its own form, just not from *another* form.

8. You use a property procedure to access from one form the property of an object in another form.

True

9. Which part of a property procedure to do you use to retrieve the value of the property of an object?

    A. Get

10. Which of the following statements is correct?

    A. You can have an If without an Else.

Module 11: Menus and Toolbars

1. The Add method, which you use to add a menu item to a menu programmatically, is a method of a _____.

    D. MenuItems collection

2. Which of the following typically appears when you right-click a form or control?

    A. ContextMenu

3. You can use the Menu Designer to copy a menu item from a MainMenu component to a menu item in which of the following components?

    A. ContextMenu

4. Which of the following typically has a bitmap image on it?

    D. ToolBarButton

5. Hiding a menu disables it.

False. You can still access the menu using a shortcut key.

6. For which control will you use the ButtonClick event procedure when it is clicked?

    C. ToolBar

7. For which object will you use the event procedure of another object when it is clicked?

    D. ToolBarButton

8. Which of the following statements is *not* correct?

C. The Click event procedure of a menu item in a MainMenu also may handle the ButtonClick event of a ToolBar.

9. Which of the following statements is *not* correct?

B. A Click event may be raised for a menu item that has submenu items.

Module 12: Structured Exception Handling and Debugging

1. Which of the following types of errors is not handled by debugging?

C. Syntax

2. The CLR looks for Catch handlers only in the procedure in which the exception occurred.

False. The CLR will look for catch handlers in other procedures in the call stack.

3. The code in which section will execute only if an exception has occurred?

B. Catch

4. Exceptions are represented by or derived from a class with the name _____.

Exception

5. Which of the following statements is *not* true?

B. You can set a breakpoint's properties so execution only stops if an exception is thrown.

6. Which of the following will *not* put your application in break mode?

C. Setting a breakpoint

7. What command do you use if you are stepping through a called procedure and want to return immediately to the calling procedure?

B. Step Out

8. Step Over skips a called procedure.

False. Step Over executes the called procedure.

9. Which of the following debugging tools may be displayed only when the debugger is in break mode, and not just when the debugger is running?

C. QuickWatch

10. Which of the following statements is *not* true?

B. The QuickWatch dialog box may be left open to watch a variable or expression while you step through your program.

Index

INTERNATIONAL CONTACT INFORMATION

AUSTRALIA
McGraw-Hill Book Company Australia Pty. Ltd.
TEL +61-2-9417-9899
FAX +61-2-9417-5687
http://www.mcgraw-hill.com.au
books-it_sydney@mcgraw-hill.com

CANADA
McGraw-Hill Ryerson Ltd.
TEL +905-430-5000
FAX +905-430-5020
http://www.mcgrawhill.ca

GREECE, MIDDLE EAST, NORTHERN AFRICA
McGraw-Hill Hellas
TEL +30-1-656-0990-3-4
FAX +30-1-654-5525

MEXICO (Also serving Latin America)
McGraw-Hill Interamericana Editores S.A. de C.V.
TEL +525-117-1583
FAX +525-117-1589
http://www.mcgraw-hill.com.mx
fernando_castellanos@mcgraw-hill.com

SINGAPORE (Serving Asia)
McGraw-Hill Book Company
TEL +65-863-1580
FAX +65-862-3354
http://www.mcgraw-hill.com.sg
mghasia@mcgraw-hill.com

SOUTH AFRICA
McGraw-Hill South Africa
TEL +27-11-622-7512
FAX +27-11-622-9045
robyn_swanepoel@mcgraw-hill.com

UNITED KINGDOM & EUROPE (Excluding Southern Europe)
McGraw-Hill Education Europe
TEL +44-1-628-502500
FAX +44-1-628-770224
http://www.mcgraw-hill.co.uk
computing_neurope@mcgraw-hill.com

ALL OTHER INQUIRIES Contact:
Osborne/McGraw-Hill
TEL +1-510-549-6600
FAX +1-510-883-7600
http://www.osborne.com
omg_international@mcgraw-hill.com